Victoria Crosses on the Western Front
The Final Advance in Flanders and Artois

September–October 1918

Victoria Crosses on the Western Front
The Final Advance in Flanders and Artois

September – October 1918

Paul Oldfield

Pen & Sword
MILITARY

First published in Great Britain in 2024 by
Pen & Sword Military
An imprint of Pen & Sword Books Limited
Yorkshire – Philadelphia

ISBN 978 1 52678 815 3

A CIP catalogue record for this book is
available from the British Library

Typeset by Mac Style
Printed in the UK by CPI Group (UK) Ltd, Croydon, CR0 4YY.

MIX
Paper | Supporting responsible forestry
FSC® C013604
FSC www.fsc.org

Pen & Sword Books Limited incorporates the imprints of After the Battle,
Atlas, Archaeology, Aviation, Discovery, Family History, Fiction, History,
Maritime, Military, Military Classics, Politics, Select, Transport, True
Crime, Air World, Frontline Publishing, Leo Cooper, Remember When,
Seaforth Publishing, The Praetorian Press, Wharncliffe Local History,
Wharncliffe Transport, Wharncliffe True Crime and White Owl.

For a complete list of Pen & Sword titles please contact

PEN & SWORD BOOKS LIMITED
47 Church Street, Barnsley, South Yorkshire, S70 2AS, England
E-mail: enquiries@pen-and-sword.co.uk
Website: www.pen-and-sword.co.uk
or
PEN AND SWORD BOOKS
1950 Lawrence Rd, Havertown, PA 19083, USA
E-mail: uspen-and-sword@casematepublishers.com
Website: www.penandswordbooks.com

Contents

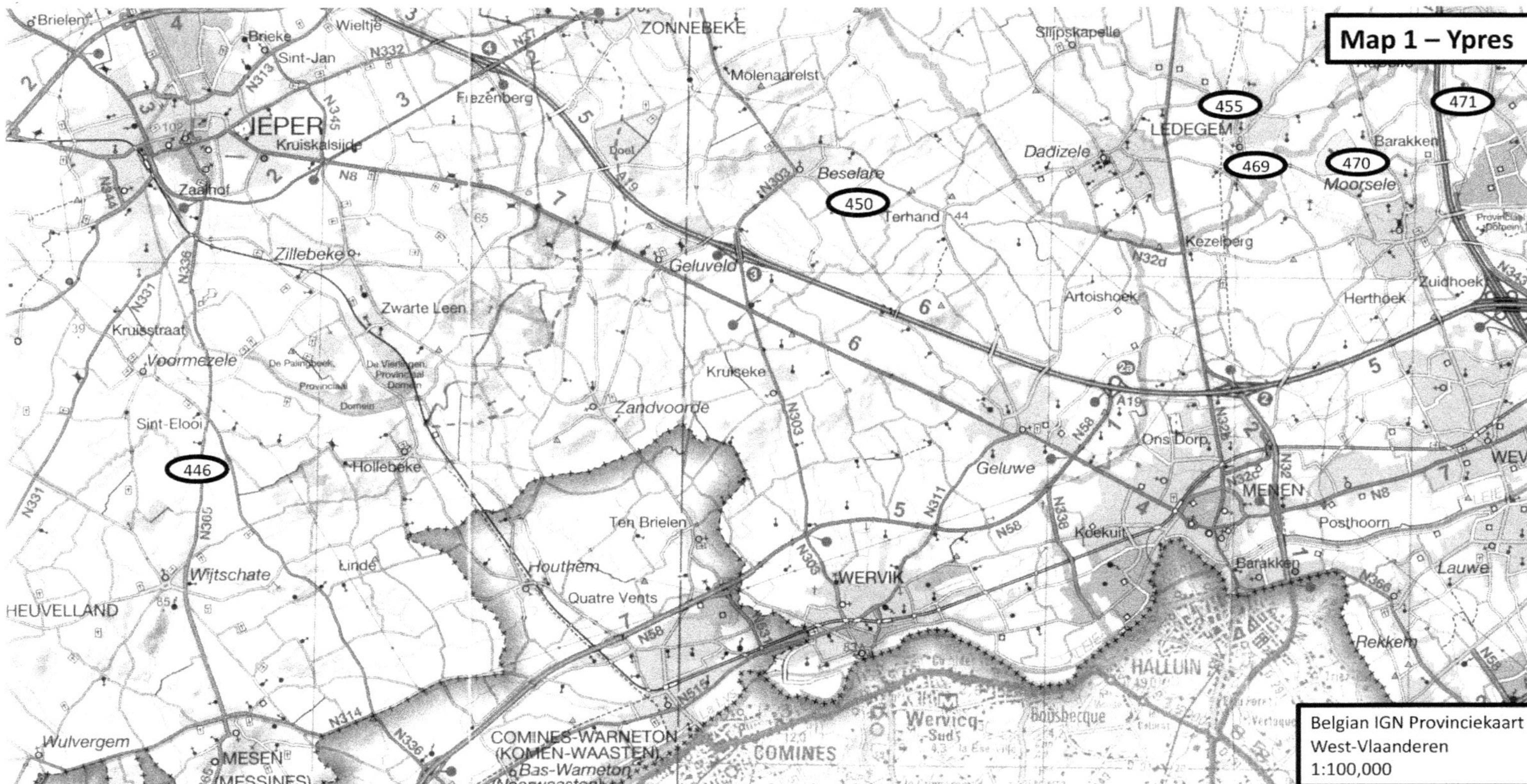
Map 1 – Ypres
Belgian IGN Provinciekaart
West-Vlaanderen
1:100,000
446
450
455
469
470
471
IEPER
ZONNEBEKE
LEDEGEM
MENEN
WERVIK
HALLUIN
COMINES
COMINES-WARNETON
(KOMEN-WAASTEN)
MESEN
(MESSINES)
HEUVELLAND
Geluveld
Beselare
Zandvoorde
Geluwe
Wijtschate
Zillebeke
Dadizele
Moorsele

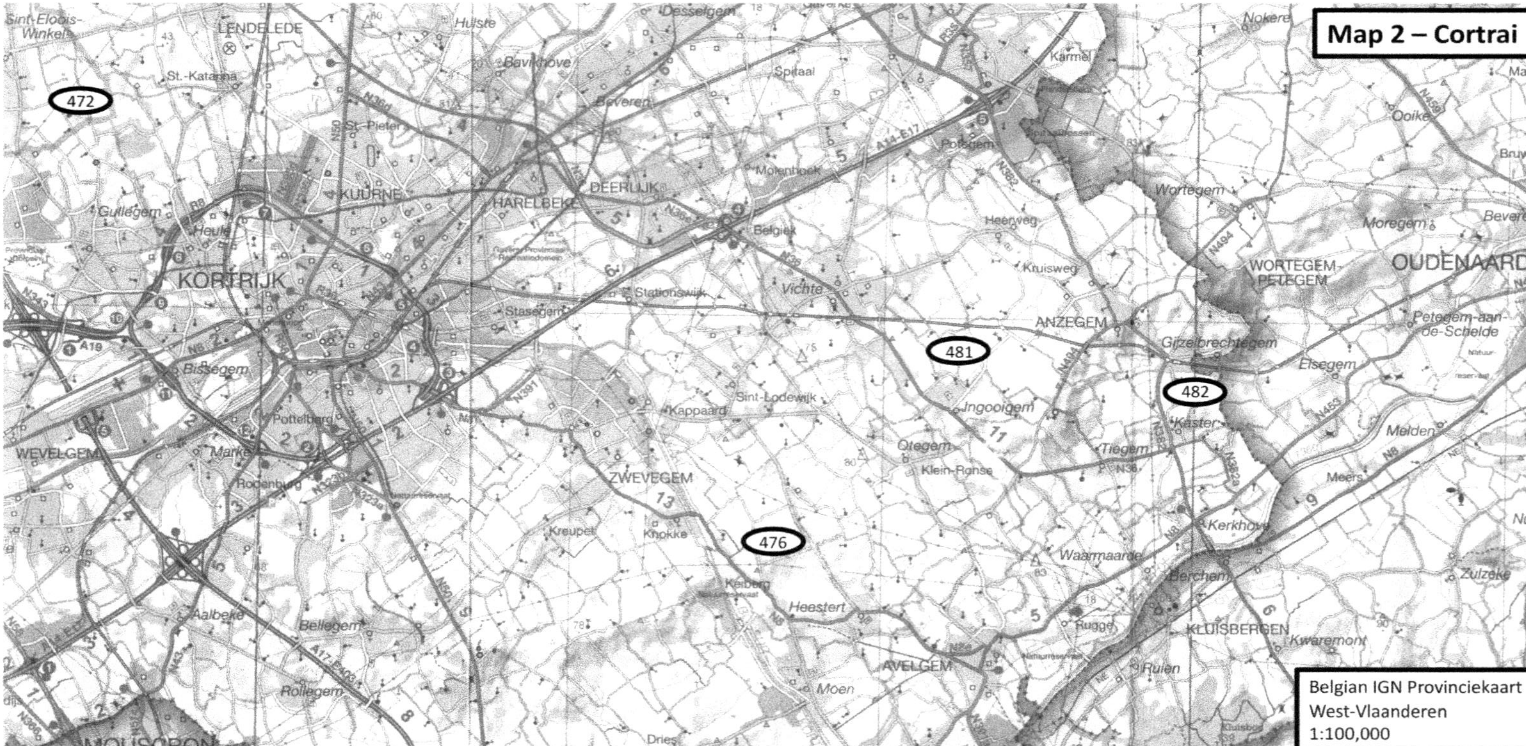

Map 2 – Cortrai
Belgian IGN Provinciekaart
West-Vlaanderen
1:100,000
472
476
481
482
KORTRIJK
LENDELEDE
KUURNE
HARELBEKE
DEERLIJK
ZWEVEGEM
ANZEGEM
AVELGEM
WEVELGEM
MOUSCRON
KLUISBERGEN
OUDENAARDE
WORTEGEM-PETEGEM
Vichte
Ingooigem
Tiegem
Kaster
Gijzelbrechtegem
Heestert
Sint-Lodewijk
Kappaard
Otegem
Bissegem
Heule
Gullegem
Marke
Aalbeke
Bellegem
Rollegem
Waarmaarde
Kerkhove
Berchem
Ruien
Elsegem
Petegem-aan-de-Schelde
Wortegem
Moregem
Ooike
Desselgem
Beveren
Bavikhove
Hulste
Spitaal
Potegem
Kruisweg
Heirweg
Moen
Kreupel
Knokke
Stasegem
Stationswijk
Belgiek
Molenhoek
Sint-Eloois-Winkel
St.-Katarina
Melden
Meers
Zulzeke
Kwaremont
Escanaffles
Karmel
Nokere

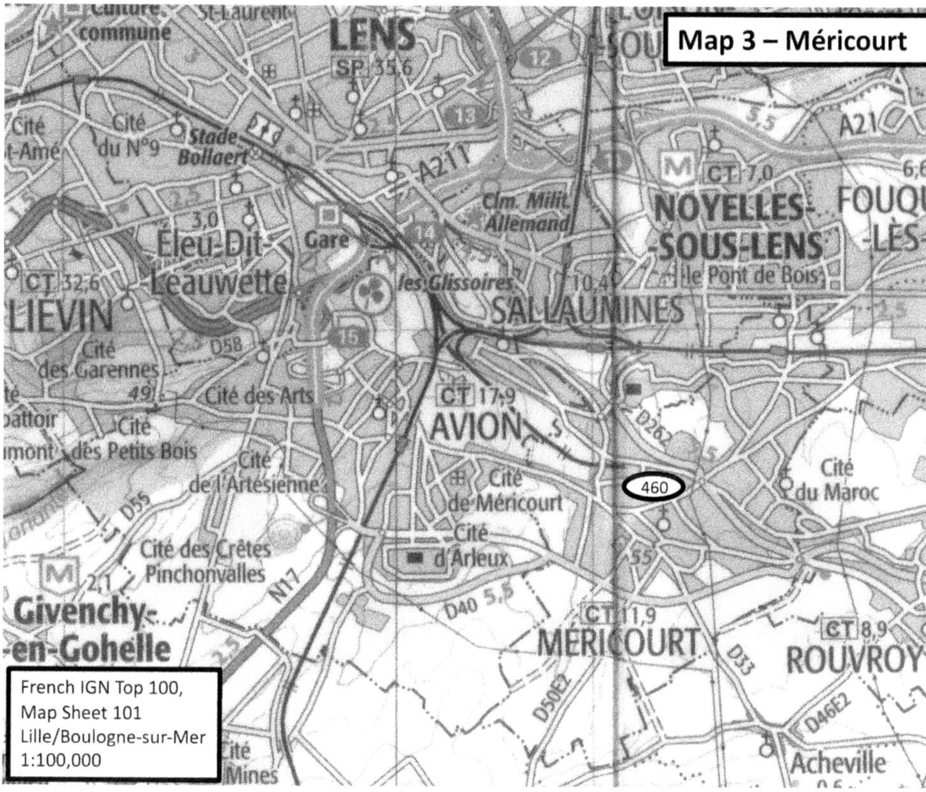

Map 3 – Méricourt

French IGN Top 100,
Map Sheet 101
Lille/Boulogne-sur-Mer
1:100,000

Abbreviations

ADS	Advanced Dressing Station
APM	Assistant Provost Marshal
ASC	Army Service Corps
AWOL	Absent without leave
Att'd	Attached
BAFTA	British Academy of Film and Television Arts
BEF	British Expeditionary Force
Capt	Captain
CCS	Casualty Clearing Station
C-in-C	Commander-in-Chief
CLB	Church Lads' Brigade
CO	Commanding Officer
Col	Colonel
Cpl	Corporal
CQMS	Company Quartermaster Sergeant
CSgt	Colour Sergeant
CSM	Company Sergeant Major
CWGC	Commonwealth War Graves Commission
DCM	Distinguished Conduct Medal
DL	Deputy Lieutenant
DSO	Distinguished Service Order
GAF	Group of Armies in Flanders
GC	George Cross
Gen	General
GHQ	General Headquarters
GOC	General Officer Commanding
GSO1, 2 or 3	General Staff Officer Grade 1 (Lt Col), 2 (Maj) or 3 (Capt)
HMHS	Her/His Majesty's Hospital Ship
HMNB	Her/His Majesty's Naval Base
HMS	Her/His Majesty's Ship
HMT	Her/His Majesty's Transport/Troopship/Hired Military Transport
IC	In Charge/Command
JP	Justice of the Peace
Kms	Kilometres

LCpl	Lance Corporal
LG	London Gazette
Lt	Lieutenant
Lt Col	Lieutenant Colonel
Lt Gen	Lieutenant General
Maj	Major
Maj Gen	Major General
MC	Military Cross
MID	Mentioned in Despatches
MM	Military Medal
MO	Medical Officer
MP	Member of Parliament
MT	Motor Transport
NZRB	New Zealand Rifle Brigade
OC	Officer Commanding
PoW	Prisoner of War
Pte	Private
RA	Royal Artillery
RAF	Royal Air Force
RAP	Regimental Aid Post
RDC	Royal Defence Corps
RE	Royal Engineers
RMMV	Royal Mail Motor Vessel
RMS	Royal Mail Ship/Steamer
RMV	Royal Mail Vessel
RSM	Regimental Sergeant Major
Sgt	Sergeant
SOE	Special Operations Executive
SS	Steam Ship
USAAF	United States Army Air Force
VC	Victoria Cross
WAAF	Women's Auxiliary Air Force
WO1 or 2	Warrant Officer Class 1 or 2

Introduction

The fifteenth book in this series covers the Final Advance in Flanders and Artois in September and October 1918. The book tells the story of eleven Victoria Crosses, including one to a Newfoundlander.

As with previous books in the series, it is written for the battlefield visitor as well as the armchair reader. Each account provides background information to explain the broad strategic and tactical situation, before focusing on the VC action in detail. Each is supported by a map to allow a visitor to stand on, or close to, the spot and at least one photograph of the site. Detailed biographies help to understand the man behind the Cross.

As far as possible chapters and sections within them follow the titles of battles, actions and affairs as decided by the post-war Battle Nomenclature Committee. VCs are numbered chronologically 469, 470, 471 etc and, as far as possible, they are described in the same order. However, when a number of actions were fought simultaneously, the VCs are covered out of sequence on a geographical basis in accordance with the official battle nomenclature. As a result, it may appear that 447–449, 451–454, 456–459, 461–468, 473–475 and 477–480 are missing. However, 447–449, 451–454, 456–459 and 461–468 appear in the previous two volume and 473–475 and 477–480 will be included in the next and final volume in the series.

Refer to the master maps to find the general area for each VC. If visiting the battlefields it is advisable to purchase maps from the respective French and Belgian 'Institut Géographique National'. The French IGN Top 100 and Belgian IGN Provinciekaart at 1:100,000 scale are ideal for motoring, but 1:50,000, 1:25,000 or 1:20,000 scale maps are necessary for more detailed work, e.g. French IGN Serie Bleue and Belgian IGN Topografische Kaart. They are obtainable from the respective IGN or through reputable map suppliers on-line.

Ranks are as used on the day. Grave references have been shortened, e.g. 'Plot II, Row A, Grave 10' will appear as 'II A 10'. There are some abbreviations, many in common usage, but if unsure refer to the list provided.

I endeavour to include memorials to each VC in their biographies. However, every VC is commemorated in the VC Diary and on memorial panels at the Union Jack Club, Sandell Street, Waterloo, London. To include this in every biography would be unnecessarily repetitive.

In any work of this scale, it is almost inevitable that some errors will be included unintentionally. Every effort is made to cross-check facts. If mistakes occur, I apologise for them and urge readers to let me know so that future revisions can be made.

Thanks are due to too many people and organisations to mention here. They are acknowledged in 'Sources' and any omissions are my fault and not intentional. However, I make no apology for mentioning again the contribution made by fellow members of the 'Victoria Cross Database Users Group', Doug and Richard Arman, and those no longer with us, without whom these books would never be completed. The work of Steve Lee and the Memorials to Valour website team is also invaluable.

Paul Oldfield
Wiltshire
December 2023

Battle of Ypres 1918

446 Sgt Louis McGuffie, 1/5th Battalion, The King's Own Scottish Borderers, 103rd Brigade, 34th Division near Wytschaete, Belgium

28th September 1918

The great Allied advance continued unabated on 28th September, with the French, Americans and British all pressing forward. In Flanders the British Second Army and the Belgians launched a new offensive, adding to the pressure. That evening the German High Command concluded that the war must be ended.

In the British First Army the main activity was in the Canadian Corps, where the emphasis was on the right wing catching up with the left. Orders were issued to push on through the night, with the intention of gaining crossings over the Schelde Canal. In Third Army, VI and XVII Corps were also ordered to seize crossings over the Schelde Canal, while IV Corps protected VI Corps' right flank.

The joint Belgian and British offensive in Flanders was launched between Dixmude, on the coast, and St Eloi, south of Ypres. The British Second Army's task was to protect the right flank of the Belgians by forming a line along the river Lys, from Armentières to Harlebeke (Harelbeke), northeast of Courtrai. Great secrecy was observed. Artillery brought up for the offensive was not allowed to fire before zero hour. On the day of the attack the potentially troublesome Wytschaete–Messines Ridge was to be masked with smoke, while to the south Fifth Army shelled the enemy opposite its front for two days as a diversion.

Second Army's main attack, in conjunction with the Belgians on the left, was led by XIX and II Corps, each with three divisions. On the right of Second Army, XV and X Corps, with two divisions each, were to seize opportunities to advance if the enemy showed signs of weakness. On the first day the British aimed to seize the crest of the ridge overlooking Ypres, between Wytschaete and Broodseinde. The German positions were not held in great strength, there being only five divisions on the twenty-six kilometres of front facing Second Army, but skilful use had been made of existing pillboxes and trenches to organise the defence in considerable depth. However, the Germans made a weak response to the attack and the many strongpoints were masked by smoke and overcome without difficulty.

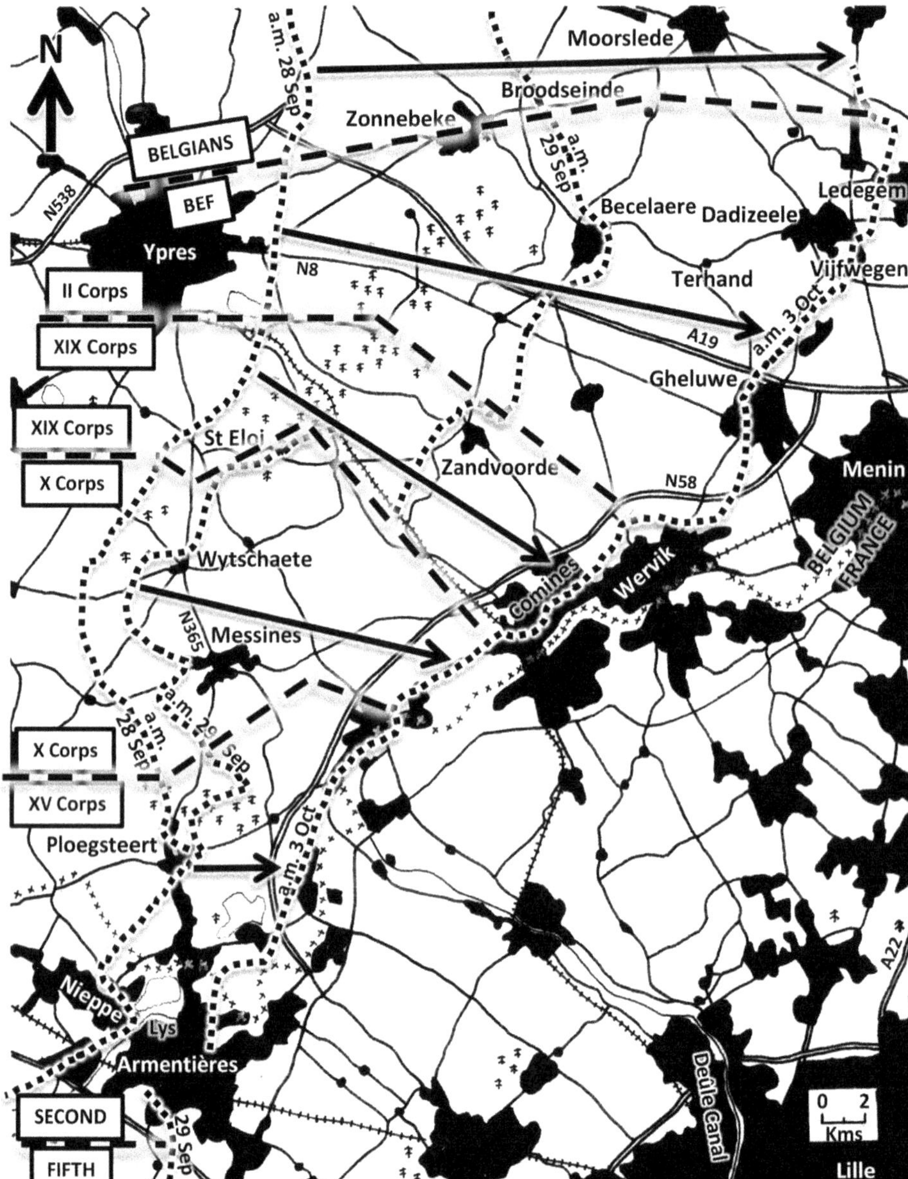

The advance of Second Army 29th September–3rd October 1918. From north of Armentières the border between France and Belgium follows the River Lys.

On the left, II Corps enjoyed success everywhere, with only isolated stiff resistance being encountered. The story was the same in XIX Corps, where all objectives were taken and in some places exceeded. Further north the Belgians also made significant advances.

The right (XV and X Corps) was given three objectives, but movement beyond the first could only be authorised at divisional level. The forward movement was staggered, with X Corps starting at zero hour (5.30 a.m.), in order to maintain contact with II and XIX Corps, while XV Corps to the south did not start until 3.00 p.m.

In 34th Division, (X Corps) patrols from 103rd Brigade were ordered to move forward at zero. The 1/5th King's Own Scottish Borderers was on the left, with 14th Division (XIX Corps) on its left, and 1/5th Argyll & Sutherland Highlanders on the right. The 1/5th King's Own Scottish Borderers' original line had been very exposed, so it had moved forward on the night of 23rd/24th September to more suitable positions. The most forward posts were withdrawn on the night before the offensive. The barrage opened five minutes before zero and included a smoke screen across the front of the ridge. This effectively masked the infantry as they set off towards the first objective on the line Piccadilly Farm–Zero House–Renty Farm–Northern Brickstacks.

D Company, on the left, advanced against Piccadilly Farm in conjunction with 14th Division. The leading platoon, commanded by Second Lieutenant Cairns,

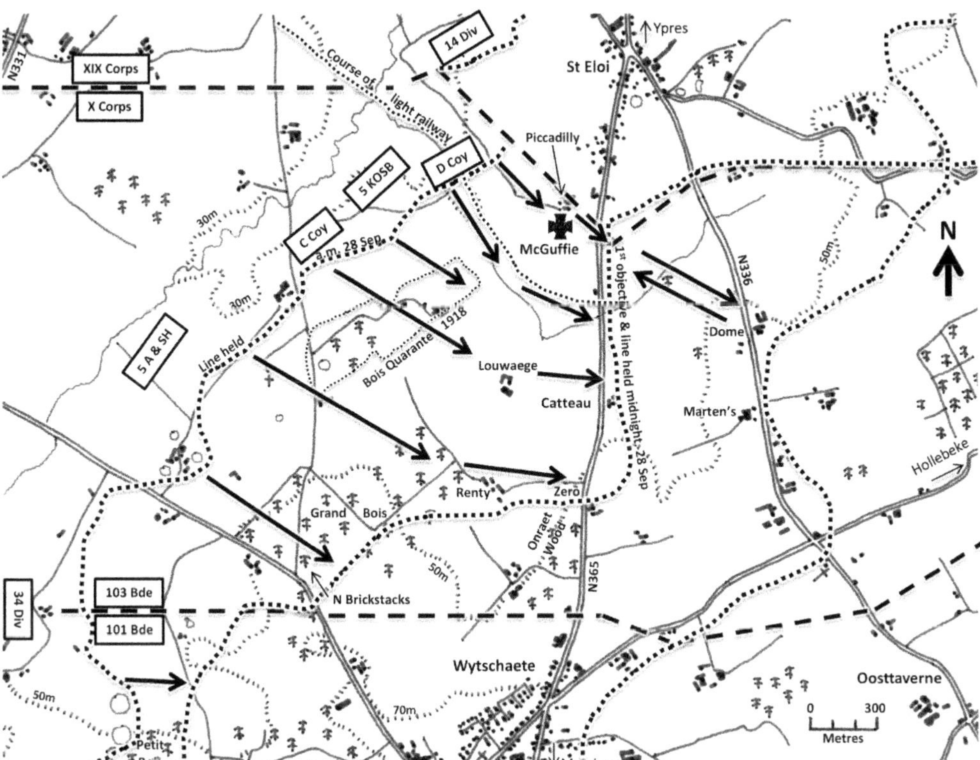

The area south of St Eloi over which 103rd Brigade advanced on 28th September.

Piccadilly Farm on the right, looking in the direction from which 1/5th King's Own Scottish Borderers attacked. The Farm is at the end of Oude Mesenseweg, south of the crossroads in St Eloi (Sint Elooi), just off the N365 road to Wytschaete, which is marked by the line of trees on the extreme left of picture. The farm is a private residence and the road is a dead end, with limited space in which to park and turn around without annoying the inhabitants.

supported by Second Lieutenant Hislop's platoon, followed closely behind the barrage. **Sergeant Louis McGuffie**'s platoon commander was killed and he took command, personally storming several dugouts. He took twelve of the total of thirty-nine prisoners himself. Two machine guns were also captured. The first objective, the enemy front line, which consisted mainly of machine gun posts, was reached by 6.00 a.m. About seventy prisoners were taken and casualties were light.

Accounts state that McGuffie took over his platoon after the death of his platoon commander but neither Cairns nor Hislop appear in CWGC records. In fact no King's Own Scottish Borderers' officers appear to have been killed in this action. The Battalion history states that the dead officer was Lieutenant J Alston. A Second Lieutenant James Alston, 1/5th Highland Light Infantry was killed on 28th September (Voormezeele Enclosure No.3 – XIII C 15). It is assumed that he was attached to 1/5th King's Own Scottish Borderers at the time, although the CWGC record of his death and burial makes no mention of this.

To the right of Cairns' platoon, Second Lieutenant Wallbank led his platoon along the light railway and captured nine prisoners, before taking up a position at the northeast end of Bois Quarante. At 5.40 a.m. a patrol of C Company, on the right of the Battalion, was sent to occupy the northeast corner of Bois Quarante. At 7.30 a.m. another patrol was sent through the Wood. However, the Company was held up at Lowaege Farm.

Having completed the capture of Piccadilly Farm, D Company took up positions along the Ypres–Messines road southeast of the Farm. From there McGuffie observed a party of British prisoners from another battalion being led away by a German guard. Regardless of the danger, he dashed out, disarmed the German escort and released the prisoners.

By 3.00 p.m. C Company had also reached the Ypres–Messines road. A line was then established by the Battalion east of the road, with C Company north of Catteau Farm, B Company at the railway crossing and D Company to the north. Heavy machine gun fire was received from Dome House and Marten's Farm.

On the right, 1/5th Argyll & Sutherland Highlanders was held up at Grand Bois, with its left flank exposed and under machine gun fire from Renty Farm. However, the objective at Northern Brickstacks on the right flank was reached. By 10.00 a.m., 1/5th Argyll & Sutherland Highlanders had reached a line across the centre of Grand Bois and was in contact with 1/5th King's Own Scottish Borderers on the left. However, the Battalion was under sniper and machine gun fire from Onraet Wood and from near Marten's Farm.

The advance by 103rd Brigade thus far had been successful but could not go on due to heavy long-range machine gun fire. Patrols also ran into the British barrage and fell back to the first objective. Later in the afternoon the enemy appeared to be withdrawing, as the volume of sniping reduced. Another barrage, followed by a resumption of the attack, was arranged for 4.45 p.m. Four machine guns were sent up and, while they subdued the enemy's fire, both battalions swept forward. Dome House was taken by D Company, 1/5th King's Own Scottish Borderers and 1/5th Argyll & Sutherland Highlanders captured Zero House. McGuffie again distinguished himself when he rushed a machine gun in a pillbox holding up the advance. He fired several rifle grenades through the loopholes and the garrison surrendered.

The request for artillery support for this attack did not get through in time and at 4.45 p.m. the British artillery fell amongst the attacking troops. At Dome House there were seven casualties from friendly fire and the position could not be held. The Brigade line withdrew and by midnight settled on the first objective of Piccadilly Farm–Zero House–Northern Brickstacks. During the night 1/5th King's Own Scottish Borderers retook Dome House. The day's fighting cost the Battalion 112 casualties according to the Battalion history (thirteen killed and ninety-nine wounded), although the CWGC only record five fatalities. Next day

From the east-west track just north of Zero House. On the right, between two prominent trees on the distant ridgeline, is Marten's Farm. Dome House is also on the ridgeline a little to the left surrounded by thick bushes and a few taller poplar trees. The N365 St Eloi–Wytschaete road runs across the middle of the picture, lined with tall poplars. Piccadilly Farm is on top of the ridge on the left. The 1/5th King's Own Scottish Borderers attacked it from the extreme right of picture.

8th Cameronians passed through the leading battalions and continued the advance to the Ypres–Comines Canal.

On the right flank of 34th Division, 101st Brigade opposite Wytschaete reached the first objective and remained there until evening. Following reports that the enemy was falling back off Messines Ridge, orders were issued to seize the third objective, but some troops did not receive the orders before zero hour. The Brigade set off on time, but the attempt to envelope Wytschaete from north and south failed.

To the south, 30th Division reached the first objective, and that evening a patrol entered Messines before the advance petered out. The XV Corps also made some progress, although opposition was heavier. The Belgians advanced five miles and took much of the high ground east of Ypres. Overall, the offensive on 28th September was a major success.

450 LCpl Ernest Seaman, 2nd Battalion, The Royal Inniskilling Fusiliers (109th Brigade, 36th Division), Terhand, Belgium

29th September 1918

On 29th September, Second Army continued the combined offensive with the Belgians east of Ypres. On the left, II Corps maintained contact with the Belgians while advancing on Terhand and Gheluwe. The XIX Corps, in the left centre, advanced south-eastwards to seize crossings over the Ypres–Comines Canal. The X Corps, in the right centre, cleared the Wytschaete–Messiness Ridge, while XV Corps on the right aimed to secure crossings over the Lys.

The II Corps had three divisions in line. On the right, 29th Division was to take Gheluwe, while 36th Division in the centre captured Terhand and 9th Division on the left kept in touch with the Belgians to the north. The 29th Division advanced about 1,600m before heavy fire forced a halt for the rest of the day. At 9 a.m., 9th Division advanced in cooperation with the Belgians and closed up to the German Flanders Position I. The 36th Division suffered a large number of casualties when it was held up at Terhand. The Belgians also had problems and 9th Division's reserve brigades were brought into the line. The new formation swept forward and broke through

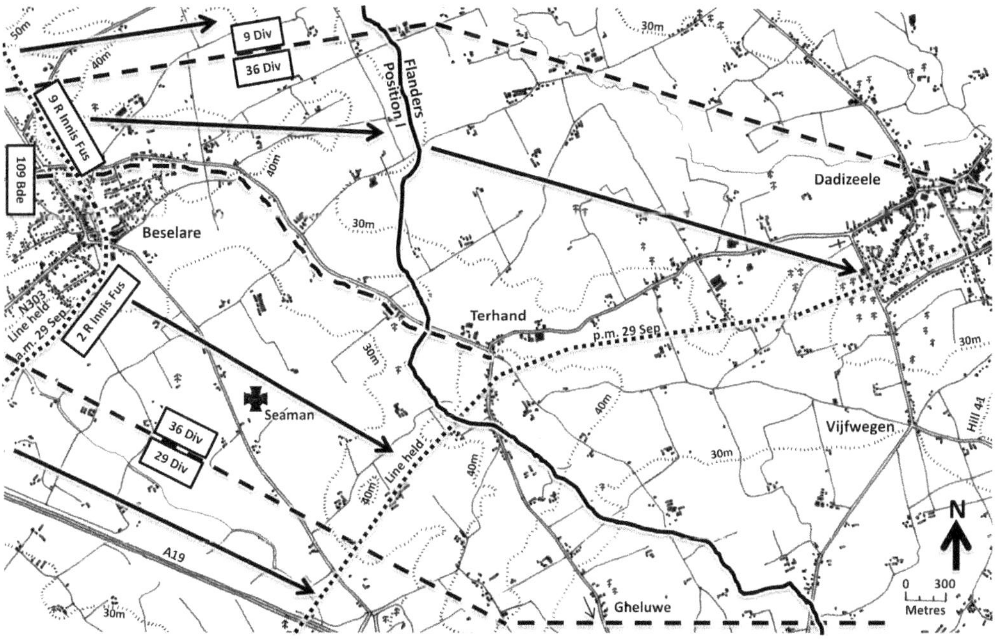

The location shown for Seaman's VC action is approximate. He was on the right of his company, one of two companies leading the attack. The advance started well but slowed later on the way to Terhand. The VC position shown is therefore about halfway to Terhand towards the right of the Battalion's frontage.

The area across which 2nd Royal Inniskilling Fusiliers advanced is best viewed from the Beselare – Gheluwe road just southwest of Beselare, from where this view was taken. As can be seen the country is wide open and dotted with small farmsteads. Seaman's VC action was somewhere to the left of the road.

the Flanders Position I on a frontage of 3,600m. By 4.00 p.m., 9th Division was in front of the Flanders Position II.

The 36th Division was led by 109th Brigade, which had been in reserve the previous day. It took time to struggle into the start positions and, as a result, the advance did not commence until 9.00 a.m. The 2nd and 9th Royal Inniskilling Fusiliers, right and left respectively, were supported by 1st Royal Inniskilling Fusiliers. Initially there was rapid progress, but this was slowed by defensive positions in hedgerows and farm buildings. The artillery had been unable to keep up due to the state of the roads and there was little fire support for the advancing troops. Fortunately German artillery fire consisted of spasmodic bursts of 77mm guns on roads and some hedgerows.

The 2nd Royal Inniskilling Fusiliers had the difficult task of taking numerous machine gun posts. The right flank of **Lance Corporal Ernest Seaman**'s company was held up by a post, which he rushed alone with a Lewis gun, killing three of the garrison, taking twelve prisoners and capturing two machine guns. Later Seaman captured another machine gun post under heavy fire; but he was killed almost immediately afterwards. However, his gallant acts enabled his company to reach its objectives and take many prisoners. By 4.00 p.m., Terhand had been reached, with the assistance of 1st Royal Inniskilling Fusiliers.

On the left of the Brigade, the Flanders Position I was overrun with relative ease, as a result of 9th Division breaking through on the left. The advance continued through Dadizeele and 9th Royal Inniskilling Fusiliers took Vijfwegen at 6.00 p.m. Outposts were pushed forward onto Hill 41. However, there was no contact on the right with the 2nd Battalion, despite the latter pushing forward its support company and half of the reserve company. The 1st Royal Inniskilling Fusiliers was ordered forward to fill the gap and formed a flank back to Terhand by 5.00 p.m. Unfortunately, the war diaries of 2nd and 9th Royal Inniskilling Fusiliers, 109th Brigade and 36th Division are incomplete for this period, with no operation orders

and no maps. As a result they are vague about precise locations. There is a map in HQ II Corps' war diary showing the start and finish lines for 29th September but not the divisional boundaries.

The XIX Corps was held up around Zandvoorde for much of the day and, although there was some progress to the south, resistance stiffened later. Southwest of the Ypres–Comines Canal, X and XV Corps captured all their objectives. However, despite the success enjoyed on the left, the overall results for Second Army were somewhat disappointing, due to lack of artillery support, poor weather and appalling ground conditions.

455 Lt Robert Gorle, A Battery, 50th Brigade Royal Field Artillery (9th Division), Ledeghem, Belgium

1 October 1918

On 30th September, while Second Army continued to act as flank guard for the Belgians, the Germans recovered from the previous day's onslaught and reinforced the front with six divisions. Apart from some small gains, the Allied advance was held up. Next day the Germans continued to fall back over the Lys and a general withdrawal was also underway south of Armentières in front of Fifth Army. However, further north it was clear that the Germans had no intention of relinquishing the Flanders Positions I and II easily.

On the left of Second Army, 9th Division was already well ahead of the Belgians, who were not prepared to move that day. Recent experience had shown that isolated attacks were unlikely to succeed. However, orders were issued by the British II Corps HQ for a further advance. Communications were difficult and the situation had not been resolved before zero hour at 6.15 a.m. The Division was ordered to seize Ledeghem and to press on to Cuerne and Harlebeke, north of Courtrai. Although the Belgians were not planning to attack, GOC 9th Division, Major General Henry Hugh Tudor, gained their agreement to safeguard the left flank.

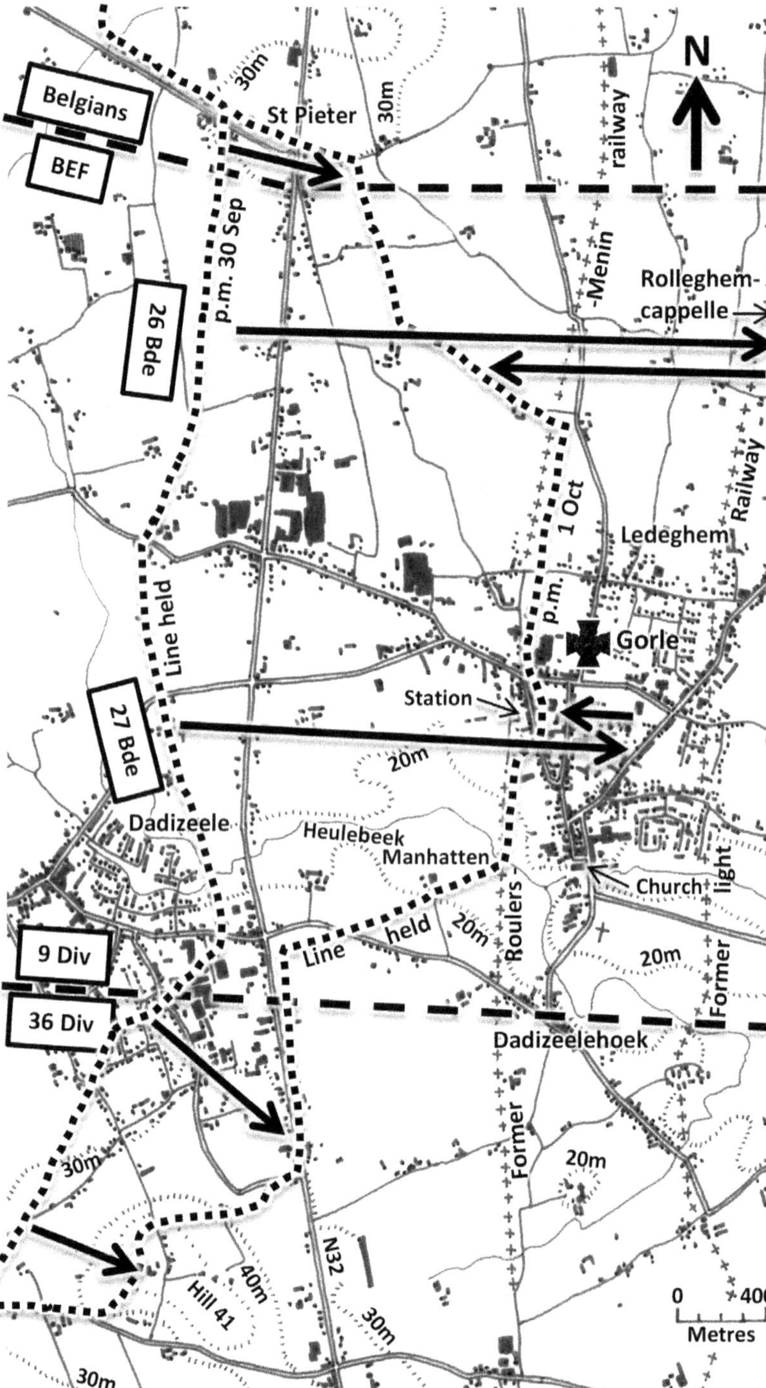

Boundaries and lines held are approximate. Ledeghem is much larger than it was in 1918.

The Belgian 17th Regiment (8th Division) was to advance at 11.00 a.m. However, 9th Division's left flank would be exposed early in the advance. As a result, that flank was to advance no further than the first objective on the Roulers–Menin railway, unless the Belgians came up in line.

In 9th Division there was also unease over the right flank, where Hill 41 presented a formidable threat. The 36th Division was ordered to take it at 5.45 a.m. The weather was very wet, as it had been the previous day, and traffic was held up on the Ypres–Zonnebeke road, resulting in artillery ammunition and rations being delayed. Despite the difficulties, the advance commenced on time. The 26th and 27th Brigades led 9th Division's attack under cover of a smoke screen.

Accounts disagree on the detailed dispositions of the various units involved. In addition, there are no maps showing accurately the boundaries and the various lines held. What follows is the most likely estimate of what happened. On the right, 27th Brigade led with 6th King's Own Scottish Borderers on the right and 12th Royal Scots on the left. On the left flank, A Company, 11th Royal Scots was to capture a fortified farm and pillboxes on high ground about 900m northwest of Ledeghem by outflanking it from the south. It was to be supported by a forward positioned field gun firing from the west. The rest of 11th Royal Scots was in brigade reserve.

Just before zero the enemy put down a heavy barrage on the right of 9th Division, which, due to the obscuration caused by the smoke screen and rain, fell to the rear of 27th Brigade. Field guns, deployed well forward to deal with strongpoints, greatly assisted the infantry in overcoming stiff opposition. On the right of 27th Brigade, 6th King's Own Scottish Borderers came under heavy machine gun fire from Hill 41 on the right in 36th Division's area as soon as it crossed the start line. There was also stiff resistance from farms west of Ledeghem. Heavy casualties were sustained on reaching the first objective and most of the Battalion had to be used to form a defensive right flank, due to the gap there. The 12th Royal Scots also encountered heavy machine gun and artillery fire in its advance. However, the line never wavered and the advance swept forward as planned. On the left A Company, 11th Royal Scots captured the fortified farm.

When the initial resistance had been broken, the advance swept on and it seemed that the enemy was collapsing. By 7.15 a.m. 27th Brigade had captured Ledeghem and went on another 450m to the light railway east of the village. The 26th Brigade came up on the left and took some of the last pillboxes encountered in Flanders, before also reaching the railway. By 8.00 a.m. 8th Black Watch had advanced as far as Rolleghem-Kapelle. A regiment of 3rd French Cavalry Brigade was asked to move forward and the Belgians were requested to fill the gap on the left. HQ II Corps was requested to move any available troops behind 9th Division, to either exploit success or protect its flanks. However, although the cavalry arrived later, it was too late to exploit any opportunities.

Although Ledeghem was taken and the opposition to the front was light, the Germans were quick to exploit 9th Division's overstretched and unsupported flanks.

There are no specific locations for Gorle's VC action. It was probably somewhere in the north of Ledeghem in support of the Royal Scots. A reasonable view of the area can be had from north of the village in Sint Pieterstraat, from where this view was taken, but that is about as good as it gets.

The right was under heavy fire from Hill 41, where the attack by 36th Division had been delayed. Heavy fire was also received from Dadizelehoek, south of Ledeghem, and 6th King's Own Scottish Borderers swung A and C Companies to the right to clear Hill 41 from the north. However, the volume of enemy fire foiled the attempt, and the Battalion formed a defensive flank, with a field gun brought up to fire at point blank range if the enemy counterattacked. Enemy pressure was maintained and 28th Brigade in reserve was stood by to move to the right flank.

Meanwhile on the left, where the Belgians had failed to advance, 26th Brigade's reserve battalion was used to cover the open flank. The Brigade was forced to pull back to the railway by 11.00 a.m., from where the line ran back to St Pieter. At about the same time the Belgians advanced and took St Pieter but could get no more than one hundred metres beyond it. This flank was therefore sloped back to join the Belgians and a machine gun company in divisional reserve was moved up to support 26th Brigade.

On the right, a counterattack against 27th Brigade from the southeast at 10.30 a.m., was driven back with heavy losses by four Lewis guns in Ledeghem cemetery (the current cemetery is south of the village on the Dadizeelehoek road, but there is nothing marked on contemporary maps and the cemetery in 1918 was probably a graveyard around the church). Two hours later the Germans attacked again, from the northeast and southeast simultaneously, and 9th Division was forced out of most of Ledeghem. By this time 12th Royal Scots was only about 300 strong. However, reinforced by 11th Royal Scots in reserve, another attempt was made to get forward. In the face of heavy enemy fire this proved impossible, but the northern end of the village was consolidated, including the station, and about 200m of the town was reoccupied. At 4.30 p.m. 11th Royal Scots took over the line and 12th Royal Scots was withdrawn 300m behind. The 6th King's Own Scottish

Borderers established a line on the railway, with the right flank thrown back through Manhattan Farm. Another counterattack threatened but, before it was delivered, 1st Royal Inniskilling Fusiliers (36th Division) made an attempt on Hill 41 from the north. Although the attack failed with heavy casualties, it threw the Germans back onto the defensive. After dark 28th Brigade took over the line and 27th Brigade withdrew to billets.

A tactic employed at this time was to deploy a section of 18 Pounder guns from each field battery forward with the infantry. They were to deal with machine guns immediately that they were encountered. During 9th Division's advance **Lieutenant Robert Gorle** commanded two field guns in support of the Royal Scots in the north of Ledeghem. Four times he calmly brought single guns into action at ranges between 275m and 725m and, with machine gun bullets clattering against the shield, knocked out the offending posts. He was not hit, although his uniform was holed. Later, when the infantry was pushed back by intense fire, he galloped a gun forward in front of them, came into action and knocked out two machine gun posts, thus stabilising the line and rallying the troops.

The advance on 1st October was disappointing when compared with previous days. However, 9th Division broke through the last line of concrete defences in Flanders and was only stopped because of lack of support on its flanks. The 27th Brigade post-action report praised 50th Brigade RFA, without whose efforts the infantry would have been unable to hold its gains. The action on 1st October marked the end of the first phase of the final Flanders offensive. Time was needed to bring forward stores and open supply routes through the devastated ground of the old Ypres battlefields before it could be resumed.

The Final Advance in Artois

460 Pte James Towers, 2nd Battalion The Cameronians (Scottish Rifles) (59th Brigade, 20th Division), Méricourt, France

6th October 1918

The left of First Army played a subsidiary role in the BEF's operations at the end of September and early October 1918. The 20th Division launched a successful diversionary attack on 27th September at Fresnoy, then stood by to follow up any German withdrawal. On 2nd October it was discovered that the Germans had slipped away during the night and the follow up mainly involved 58th Division. Lens was evacuated the next day and was occupied by 58th Division, while 20th Division returned to the line on the right. The 59th Brigade overcame stiff resistance and 2nd Cameronians reached the northern branch of the loop on the Méricourt–Lens railway (Bull Ring) and Sallaumines. Méricourt village was approached but no attempt was made to take it as it was held strongly.

Lieutenant Walter Brown Jack MC. He served with the Special Constabulary, was promoted to sergeant in Glasgow, Lanarkshire and was awarded the Special Constabulary Medal with clasp 'Long Service 1949'. His fulltime employment was as a representative for the Heinz Food Company.

On 4th October an attack was organised against the Triangle of railway lines at the south-eastern end of the Bull Ring. The aim was to improve the position held by D Company, 2nd Cameronians by clearing a number of machine guns that had held up the advance previously. B Company attacked the southern end of the Bull Ring and the Triangle, surprising the enemy. The objective in the Triangle and Menial Trench on the northern edge of Méricourt was gained. The Company established itself on the southern side of the railway Triangle. Touch was gained with D Company and next day with 6th King's Shropshire Light Infantry west of Méricourt, which continued to be held by the Germans.

Méricourt was to be cleared on 6th October. The village was on a low plateau with excellent all-round fields of fire for the enemy. Following a dawn barrage,

Méricourt is much larger than it was in 1918 and the area in which Towers' VC action took place is now completely built over. If you are feeling energetic an overview of the area can be gained from the spoil heap north of the D262. Park on Avenue de Flöha, south of the spoil heap. This road runs parallel with, and just south of, the D262. There are a few gaps in the bushes to access the main road. Cross with extreme care. On the north side there is a rough track running off to the northwest. Follow it for a few metres until there is a break in the vegetation on the right. Climb up the heap to obtain a view to the south. You should be able to pick out a prominent water tower and the spire of the church in Méricourt. Alternatively drive west along Avenue du 10 Mars to the junction on the right with Rue Ferrer. The best estimate is that Towers reached the patrol in the area to the northwest of this junction. Ave 10 Mars = Avenue du 10 Mars, Ch = church, Rue F – Rue Ferrer, WT = water tower.

From the lower slopes of the spoil heap looking southwest. The D262 is in the foreground with the parallel Avenue de Flöha just beyond. The prominent water tower is on the far right and the top of the church spire can just be seen over trees left of centre. In the centre of the picture is a large building with 'AD' on the front. Above this and beyond the trees is the approximate direction of Towers' VC action.

two strong patrols pushed into the village. C Company's patrol entered from the west but, when it ran into heavy machine gun and sniper fire, it was driven back. B Company's patrol, commanded by Second Lieutenant Walter Brown Jack, moved along the northern side of the village to the north-eastern corner, where it came under fire from three directions. Further advance was out of the question and the only way out was back over the 200m of open ground that they had just crossed. The patrol went to ground and found what cover it could. Jack was unaware that he no longer had the support of the C Company patrol. It was vital that a message got through to alert him.

Five runners attempted the hazardous mission: one was killed, another wounded and the other three were unable to reach the beleaguered patrol due to the intense fire. **Private James Towers**, who was on anti-aircraft gun duties at Company HQ, volunteered to make a sixth attempt, despite having seen the fate of the previous five. As soon as he broke cover, he came under heavy machine gun fire. Running from cover to cover he came upon the body of his comrade, 41917 Private Frank Dunlop, who had made an earlier attempt (Sucrerie Cemetery, Ablain-St Nazaire – VII A 7).

Towers leapt over an embankment and almost landed on a German gun team but escaped through his superb agility and speed. He eventually made it to Second Lieutenant Jack with the message. The platoon sergeant shook him by the hand in gratitude, while at the same time telling him he was a silly idiot for taking the risk. Towers remained with the patrol until darkness fell and guided it back to safety, reaching Company HQ at 6.45 p.m.

The action cost the patrol one man killed (11223 Private John Meir – Houchin British Cemetery – III C 32), one missing and five wounded, but it could have been much worse. The CWGC records another fatality on 6th October, possibly the missing man – 242784 Private John William Laycock (Lievin Communal Cemetery Extension – I A 15). In addition to Towers' VC, Jack received the MC, 43339 Private William McGinty a Bar to the MM and 51475 Lance Corporal Samuel Smith and 10257 Private John Allan the MM. The Battalion was relieved that night as part of the relief of the whole of 20th Division by 12th Division.

Battle of Courtrai and Subsequent Operations

469 Pte Martin Moffatt, 2nd Battalion, The Prince of Wales's Leinster Regiment (Royal Canadians) (88th Brigade, 29th Division), Ledeghem, Belgium
470 Sgt John O'Neill, 2nd Battalion, The Prince of Wales's Leinster Regiment (Royal Canadians) (88th Brigade, 29th Division), Moorsele, Belgium
471 Pte Thomas Ricketts, 1st Battalion, Royal Newfoundland Regiment (28th Brigade, 9th Division), Ledeghem, Belgium

14th October 1918

The main event on 14th October was the renewal of the offensive by the Group of Armies in Flanders (GAF), including the British Second Army. Elsewhere activity was confined to intensive local patrol actions to keep the Germans off balance.

The renewal of the offensive by GAF in Flanders had been delayed for a week, mainly due to disorganisation in the Belgian and French logistics. In the meantime, Second Army had maintained pressure on the enemy by constant bombardments, feint attacks and aggressive patrolling. It had already overrun the Flanders Position I (Terhand Line), except south of Gheluwe, and faced the Flanders Position II.

The main attack by the Belgians and French on 14th October met with considerable success. In support, the BEF's Second Army wheeled to the right, closed-up to the Lys as far east as Harlebeke, and formed a protective flank in the expectation that the Germans would soon evacuate Lille to the south. Second Army's corps were also instructed to establish bridgeheads over the Lys in preparation for, and to hasten, the enemy's abandonment of Lille.

Zero hour was at 5.35 a.m., with the creeping barrage commencing three minutes earlier. It was a fine day but thick mist lingered until 11.00 a.m. The German barrage fell at 4.15 a.m., a sure sign that the Allied attack was not a surprise to them. On the right, XV Corps was already on the Lys so its activities were confined to patrolling and establishing a small bridgehead near Comines. In the centre, X and XIX Corps secured almost all their objectives but not without difficulties in places.

On the left, II Corps advanced with 36th, 29th and 9th Divisions, the latter in contact with the Belgians to the north. In the centre, 29th Division's advance was led by 88th Brigade on the right and 86th Brigade on the left, each on a one battalion

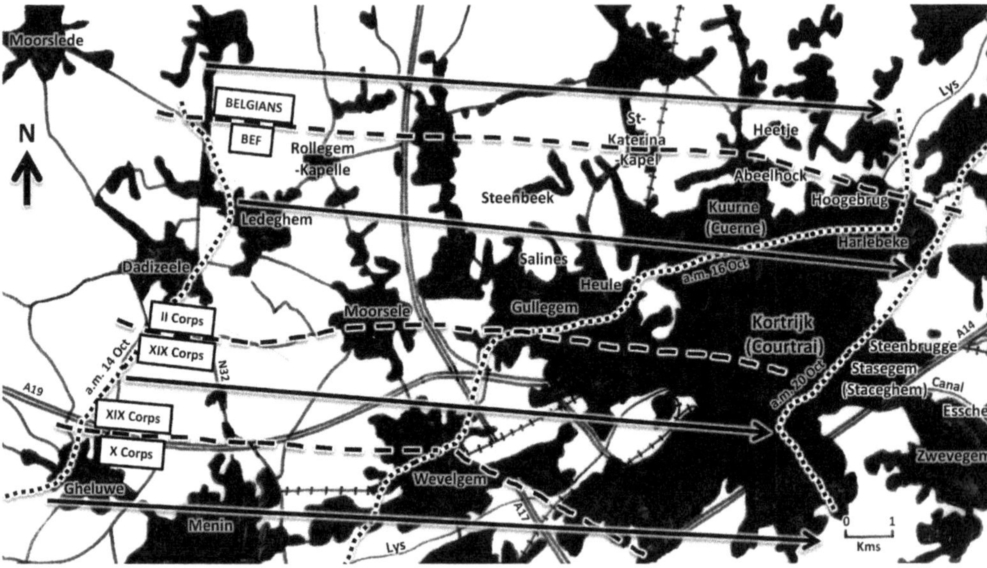

The advance of the centre and left of Second Army 14th–20th October.

frontage of about 725m. The previous night, while laying tapes on the start line, the CO of 2nd Leinster went to HQ 88th Brigade to complain about British shells falling short and causing casualties. He was greeted by the commander, Brigadier General Bernard Freyberg VC, covered in stinking black slime, having walked headfirst into the cesspool at Raymond Farm. The CO gave a very brief summary of the situation and beat a hasty retreat back to the shelling. Freyberg commented, *It was bad enough to fall into the mess, but worse to have everyone avoiding me.*

The attack started well in fog, which was thickened by smoke shells. Care had to be taken by the artillery as towns such as Ledeghem were still heavily occupied by civilians. Despite the constraints, the advance crossed the Menin–Roulers railway and 86th Brigade cleared Ledeghem before being held up. Many German gun batteries were overrun. Some Germans had packed their kit and were found waiting to be taken prisoner. In the afternoon resistance stiffened and the advance halted short of the final objective on the Courtrai–Roulers railway.

In 88th Brigade, 2nd Leinster led, with 4th Worcestershire following and 2nd Hampshire in reserve. B Company, 2nd Leinster deployed north of the Heulebeek and the remainder of the Battalion to the south of the stream. Nine metres long footbridges were carried forward from Raymond Farm by 2nd Hampshire and thirty-five pioneers from 1/2nd Monmouthshire, to assist in crossing the Heulebeek. All battalions were in position by 10.00 p.m. on the 13th. The day had been wet but the night was clear and starlit, followed by a foggy dawn.

The barrage came down on time at 5.32 a.m. and enemy retaliatory fire was generally slight. In the first wave of the attack A, B and C Companies, 2nd Leinster

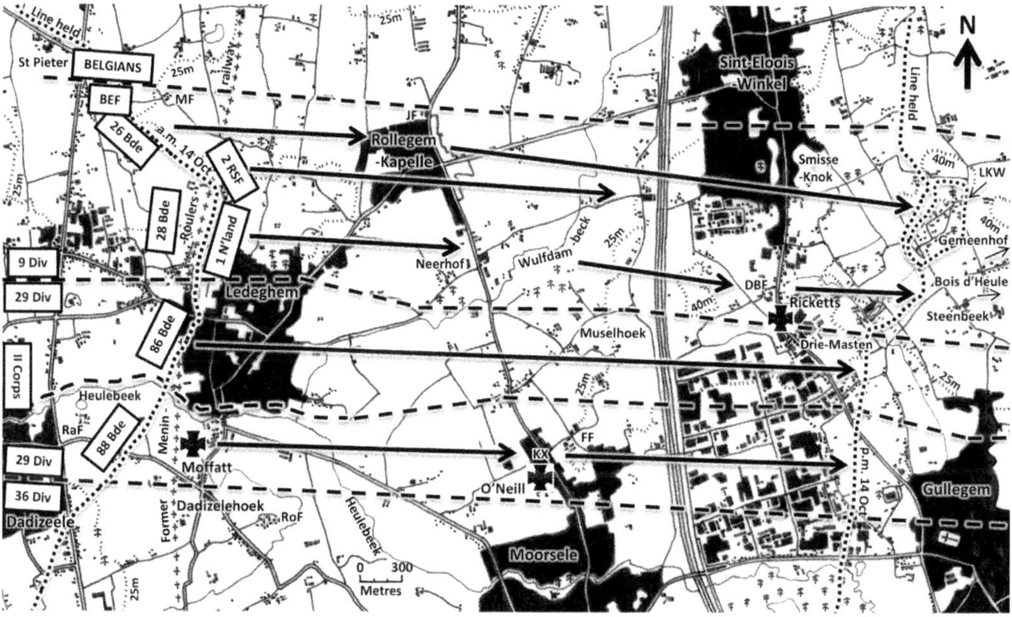

The precise locations of the VC actions by Moffat and O'Neill are not know and are marked on the map approximately.

DBF = De Beurt Farm, FF = Fatimar Farm, JF = Jerry Farm, KX = Kohinoor crossroads, LKW = former Laaga-Kapel Wood, MF = Mogg Farm, RaF = Raymond Farm, RoF = Rockstone Farm. The whole area has been heavily developed since the Great War. In places the ground bears no resemblance to what the soldiers would have seen in 1918. A reasonable view of 2nd Leinster's area in the early stages of the advance, and about where Moffatt's VC action took place, can be had from the south side of the cemetery south of Ledeghem and north of Dadizelehoek. This is roughly in the centre of the Battalion's area. The cemetery is on a fast road (Kasteelstraat) that can be busy but there is space to park there. The best view of the area of the O'Neill VC action is from the Moorsele–Ledeghem road (Ledegemstraat) just northeast of Moorsele from where you can look eastwards from the roadside. The Ricketts VC action site is also difficult to see. The depression has been covered with large industrial buildings. To the west the high ground around which Ricketts skirted to the south is covered in fruit trees and there are very limited views. About the best option is from De Beurt Farm on Driemastenstraat.

swept forward three minutes later. Many enemy positions were missed in the fog and elements of the Battalion and 4th Worcestershire became mixed up. They were over the Menin–Roulers railway by 6.15 a.m. but, by 9.15 a.m., were held up south of Kohinoor crossroads. At 10.00 a.m. HQ 88th Brigade received a report that 2nd Leinster and some of 4th Worcestershire had reached Fatimar Farm. About the same time, it was reported that 86th Brigade on the left had reached the Muselhoek road. However, 36th Division to the south was behind at Rockstone Farm southeast of Ledeghem.

When the mist cleared the advance was held up by field guns and machine guns, firing from high ground around De Beurt Farm northeast of Muselhoek. They were engaged by a field battery and at 11.15 a.m. 9th Division assisted by clearing other

From 2nd Leinster's start line on the Dadizeele – Dadizelehoek road, seen on the right, looking eastwards. Ledeghem is left of centre. Just right of centre is a concrete bunker. Moffatt's VC action was probably in that area.

guns firing into the flank from the north (see below for an account of this action). Despite these hold ups, the Battalion advanced 3,750m and was on its objective almost on time.

In the advance near Ledeghem, **Private Martin Moffatt** and five other soldiers in his section came under heavy close-range fire from a defended house. Moffatt charged the house alone, tossed grenades in through the front and raced to the rear, where he kicked in the door and stormed inside. He killed two of the enemy who came at him and took thirty prisoners. His action allowed the advance to resume in that area. Shortly afterwards he marched 120 prisoners to the rear and obtained a signature for them from the APM.

Sergeant John O'Neill's company was halted by two machine guns and a gun battery firing over open sights close to Moorsele. O'Neill led his eleven-man section into the attack and captured four guns, two machine guns and sixteen prisoners. Some of the guns were then turned on their former owners to great effect.

Reverse of the previous view, with the hedge around the cemetery on the far left. Dadizelehoek is in the centre and the road to Ledeghem is in the right foreground. In the right distance is the church in Dadizeele. Left of the church spire is a lone bushy tree, to the left of which is the same bunker seen in the previous view.

By 1.30 p.m., 2nd Hampshire had taken the lead, with 4th Worcestershire in support. The 2nd Leinster was in reserve having taken 263 prisoners, sixty machine guns and eleven field guns, for the cost of ninety-one casualties, including eleven killed. The regimental history says the casualties totalled 136 (eleven killed, seventy-five wounded and fifty missing).

North of 86th Brigade, 9th Division was held up west of Bois d'Heule and, on the right, 36th Division was held up in front of Gulleghem. At last light it was decided to dig in on the line reached. The night passed quietly except for German harassing fire on roads etc. Next morning 87th Brigade passed through 88th and 86th Brigades to continue the advance. Over the next few days the advance continued steadily and arrangements had to be made to evacuate and feed large numbers of civilians.

North of 29th Division, the 9th Division advanced alongside the Belgians. The attack was made by 28th Brigade on the right, with the support of 26th Brigade on the left. The latter was to maintain contact with the Belgian 9th Regiment (3rd Belgian Division). It was also to capture a pillbox at Mogg Farm and to secure Jerry Farm. The 28th Brigade was to halt on reaching the high ground around De Beurt Farm and the Drie-Masten–Smisse-Knok road. It was only to continue towards the second objective (railway) if GOC 28th Brigade believed it was practicable to do so without adequate artillery support.

From the Moorsele – Ledeghem road just northeast of Moorsele. The line of houses in the right distance are along the Moorsele (right) – Rolleghem-Kapelle road. O'Neill's VC action was probably somewhere in this area.

The 28th Brigade's advance was led by 1st Newfoundland on the right and 2nd Royal Scots Fusiliers on the left, with 9th Cameronians in support. One light trench mortar and a section of machine guns was attached to each assault battalion, in addition to a section of 18 Pounder field guns. The Brigade had two 6″ Mortars and additional machine guns attached to fire a supporting barrage. Some of the machine guns were allocated to cover the left flank when the advance ended.

The Brigade began moving forward at 5.30 p.m. on 13th October. 1st Newfoundland set off from Keiberg, east of Zonnebeke, towards the front line on the railway north of Ledeghem. Considerable hostile shelling was encountered on the way, resulting in fifteen casualties. The 2nd Royal Scots Fusiliers suffered another fifty casualties but, by 12.30 a.m., both battalions were in position.

When the advance commenced at 5.30 a.m. the combination of fog and smoke reduced visibility to just two metres. The left of 28th Brigade was checked temporarily but, in general, the advance progressed well. In 1st Newfoundland B Company was on the right, with D Company on the left and A and C Companies in support. Prior to the fog lifting contact was only maintained by shouting and direction was kept by compass alone. However, despite causing some confusion, the fog denied the enemy effective use of his machine guns. A large number of prisoners were taken in cellars and pillboxes, without them offering much resistance. One platoon alone captured thirty-four machine guns. 3606 Private Edward O'Brien (Duhallow ADS Cemetery – IV H 29) and 3156 Private Heber Trask (Beaumont Hamel (Newfoundland) Memorial) dodged bombs thrown at them from one pillbox, bayoneted three Germans outside it and then tossed in a grenade. On entering the pillbox they took the surrender of an officer, thirty-four men and two machine guns. Both were awarded the MM but neither survived long enough to receive it.

The number of prisoners was a problem and could have drained a large number of assault troops as guards. However, one company commander solved the issue by

herding sixty-six Germans into a cellar. He left them in the charge of an NCO and a private, with instructions to march them back to the PoW cage when the fog lifted, thus avoiding the need to leave behind a large number of escorts. The NCO was later wounded but, before the day ended, Private Pelley returned with a receipt for sixty-six prisoners delivered to the advanced PoW cage.

The Battalion reached Neerhof about 10.30 a.m. and, to the north, Rolleghem-Kapelle had been taken by 26th Brigade. A slight breeze sprang up, dispersing the fog and smoke. D Company was close to a battery of field guns, which opened fire at point blank range, causing numerous casualties. The Brigade halted on a north-south line in front of Neerhof.

Having reorganised, the advance continued but came under machine gun fire while crossing the Wulfdambeck, which was up to two metres deep and too wide to jump over. Many sections were wiped out attempting to get over the stream. Eventually, by wading or swimming, some troops got across and this opposition was overcome. The advance pressed on to De Beurt Farm until being hit by fire from a battery of four guns, supported by four machine guns, located between two farmhouses just north of the crossroads at Drie-Masten. The intention was to bombard the enemy position with field guns and trench mortars but signal rockets failed to bring down any supporting fire. The advance had outrun the range of the guns. Attempts to get forward on both flanks failed with more casualties.

A platoon of B Company, under Lieutenant Albert Stanley Newman (MC for this action), moved south of the ridge to outflank the German gun position. He took with him the only unwounded members of the platoon that had been on his right, a Lewis gun section consisting of 1368 Lance Corporal Matthew Brazil MM (DCM for this action) and **Private Thomas Ricketts**. The Lewis gun section advanced in short rushes and reached a depression south of the ridge. Brazil and Ricketts volunteered to go forward with their Lewis gun. They continued to advance by short rushes under very heavy fire until their ammunition was exhausted. They were still about 275m from the battery when the enemy decided to move their field guns and began to bring up their gun teams. Ricketts doubled back one hundred metres

The 2nd Leinster advance crossed this road (Driemastenstraat) from the right. De Beurt Farm is on the left, where there is a memorial to Ricketts. The road continues to join the main Drie-Masten – Smisse-Knok road just north of the Drie-Masten crossroads. Note the thick orchards on the right.

under heavy fire and gathered two ammunition carriers that they had dropped, together weighing over thirty-four kilograms, before dashing back to the Lewis gun and Lance Corporal Brazil. They opened fire, driving the enemy gun teams into a farm, where they took cover. Covered by Brazil, Ricketts charged, firing the Lewis gun from the hip and captured eight prisoners. It is not known how many

The junction of Driemastenstraat with the Drie-Masten – Smisse-Knok road. The Drie-Masten crossroads are just off to the right of picture. The German strongpoint was in this area. The depression is now covered in industrial buildings, the pitched roofs of which can be seen on the far side of the road.

Germans were killed in this action but it must have been a significant number. The platoon then advanced without casualties and captured the enemy, including four field guns, four machine guns and an ammunition wagon. One of the gunners was bayonetted, possibly by Brazil. A fifth field gun was subsequently intercepted by fire from Ricketts' Lewis gun. The crew was forced into another farmhouse, where they were captured with the gun and an ammunition wagon. The captured machine guns were turned on the enemy as they tried to escape. As a result of this action, 28th Brigade was on its first objective just after midday.

The brigade commander decided that the advance was to resume towards Laaga-Kapel, where considerable resistance was encountered from Laaga-Kapel Wood and Steenbeek. As the advance progressed 2nd Royal Scots Fusiliers was squeezed out of the line by 26th Brigade on the left and fell back into reserve. The advance was then continued by 1st Newfoundland, supported by 9th Cameronians.

By 4.00 p.m. 1st Newfoundland had two companies in line about Drie Masten, in touch with 87th Brigade on the right and 26th Brigade on the left. The latter held most of 9th Division's front by this time, with the Belgians on the left. Fighting continued until dusk but no further progress was made. At 6.30 p.m. 28th Brigade was ordered to consolidate the line held and to keep touch with the enemy by active patrolling. The 27th Brigade was to continue the advance at 9.00 a.m. on 15th October.

At 7.00 p.m. 28th Brigade's front was reorganised, with 1st Newfoundland on the right, 9th Cameronians on the left and 2nd Royal Scots Fusiliers in support. The forward battalions were urged to gain the high ground around Steenbeek and Gemeenhof. However, a 27th Brigade patrol found that the enemy was holding a strong position east of Laaga Kapel Wood that would not be shifted by patrols alone. The Germans shelled the line heavily from 4.00 a.m. until 6.00 a.m. but there were few casualties.

The advance by 1st Newfoundland resulted in about 500 prisoners being taken, plus eight guns and ninety-four machine guns. Lieutenant Frank M Burke, commanding A Company, was killed just after advancing over the heights at De Beurt Farm (Cement House Cemetery, Belgium – XVII D 12). Second Lieutenant Albert E Taylor MC & Bar DCM of B Company was fatally wounded shortly afterwards (Duhallow ADS Cemetery, Belgium – IV G 18). The Battalion suffered another twenty-six fatalities up to 16th October, including 4020 Private Thomas Ricketts, Tommy Ricketts VC's cousin. In addition to the awards already mentioned there were another three DCMs (Private Arthur Whalen, Private Thomas Corbin and Private Samuel Greenslade) and four MMs (Corporal Richard Power DCM, Private Andrew Smith, Private William King and Private Hamer Gardner).

On 17th October, 88th Brigade (29th Division) extended its front to the left to take over from 27th Brigade (9th Division) as far north as Hoogebrug on the Lys. The next night 26th Brigade (9th Division) took over the line from Hoogebrug northwards. Troops that had gained the east bank of the Lys were brought back using pontoons south of Cuerne. This operation was supervised personally by Brigadier General Freyberg. The plan for 19th October was to pass two companies of 2nd Hampshire over the Lys to secure the line of the Harlebeke–Courtrai road. The rest of the Battalion was to follow then, as soon as bridges had been constructed by the engineers, 2nd Leinster would cross and pass through 2nd Hampshire. It was to secure the line of the Harlebeke–Courtrai railway and then advance beyond. Four ferries were to operate south of Cuerne and there were infantry bridges at two of the ferry sites.

By 11.00 p.m. on 19th October two companies of 2nd Hampshire had secured a crossing over the Lys south of Cuerne. Enemy reaction was confined to some artillery and machine gun fire but was limited overall. The line of the Harlebeke–Courtrai road was secured. Then 2nd Leinster crossed by a temporary foot bridge and took up assembly positions along the railway embankment. However, A Company did not get into its start position until 4.00 a.m. as the enemy was still occupying it. Accounts of what happened that day are confusing. HQ 88th Brigade's war diary states that 2nd Hampshire led the advance with 2nd Leinster passing through, later succeeded by 4th Worcestershire. The 29th Division war diary has 2nd Leinster attacking on the right and 2nd Hampshire on the left, with 4th Worcestershire in support. The latter's war diary agrees. However, 2nd Leinster's war diary mentions attacking in conjunction with 4th Worcestershire and does not mention 2nd Hampshire, whose war dairy varies from all the other versions and does not even have the same date. Such is the fog of war!

Relying mainly on 2nd Leinster's war diary, at 6.00 a.m. on 20th October the Battalion attacked in conjunction with 4th Worcestershire. Staceghem was seized by 8.30 a.m. and Steenbrugge was also captured. More resistance was met east of Staceghem but, despite heavy machine gun fire, the objective on the Esscher road was consolidated by 9.20 a.m. following an advance of 4,575m. Forty prisoners, a field gun and six machine guns were taken for seventy-nine casualties, including six killed. At 10.30 a.m., 2nd Hampshire passed through, supported by part of B Company.

Later in the morning 86th Brigade passed through and established a line from Pont Levis on the Courtrai–Bossuyt Canal north-eastwards through Krote and St Louis. That evening 88th Brigade moved into billets around Staceghem. It had suffered 137 casualties (fourteen killed, ninety-eight wounded and twenty-five missing).

Before the attack John O'Neill had heard that his brother, who was serving in 36th Division, had been killed the previous day. He 'saw red' and was always up with the barrage, sometimes ahead of it, and was the first into every farm and village encountered in the advance. At Staceghem he joined forces with a 4th Worcestershire sergeant who had 'liberated' and drunk at least one bottle of wine. The two of them cleared a number of houses. In one instance they captured a machine gun and routed one hundred enemy, causing them many casualties. O'Neill was also in the lead in clearing Esscher, another strongly held village. Throughout the day he exhibited the greatest bravery and determination to close with and destroy the enemy. He later discovered that his brother had been wounded.

472 Cpl Roland Elcock, 11th Battalion, The Royal Scots (27th Brigade, 9th Division), Capelle St Catherine, Belgium

15th October 1918

All elements of the GAF continued the advance on 15th October. Because three of Second Army's Corps (XV, X and XIX) were already on their objectives, they were ordered to maintain contact with the enemy through extensive and aggressive patrolling. They were also to establish bridgeheads over the Lys, but without becoming embroiled in a major battle.

Resistance was heavy early in the day but slackened later. That evening the Germans began to retire. This allowed XV Corps to make a number of crossings over the Lys around Comines. To the south Fifth Army also forced the Germans back, which removed any threat to Second Army's right flank. The X Corps found Menin had been abandoned but all the bridges over the Lys had been blown. It was late in the night before the sappers constructed a bridge.

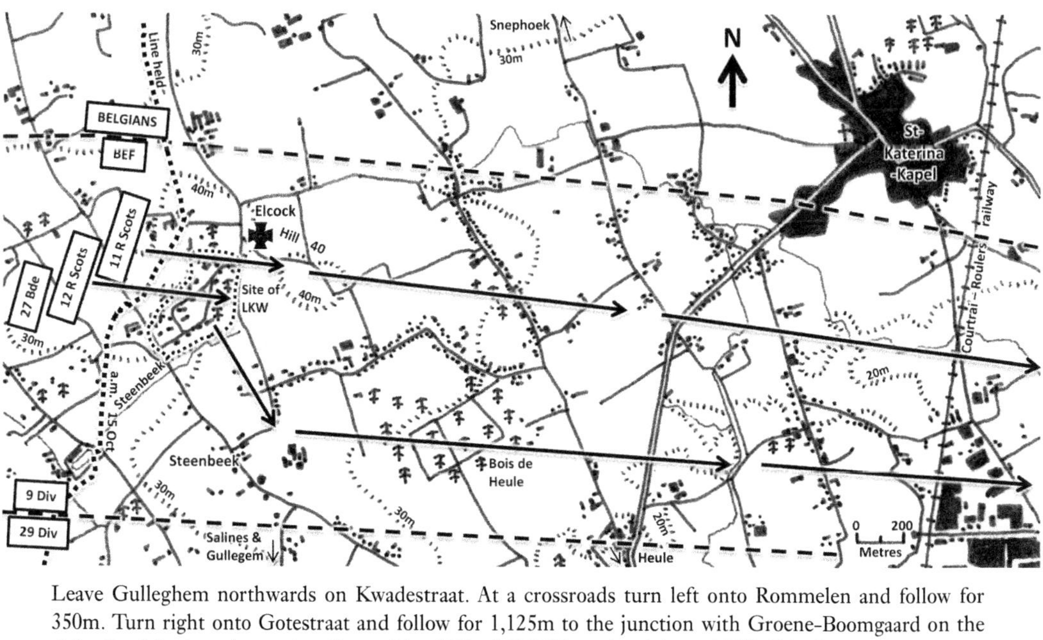

Leave Gulleghem northwards on Kwadestraat. At a crossroads turn left onto Rommelen and follow for 350m. Turn right onto Gotestraat and follow for 1,125m to the junction with Groene-Boomgaard on the right. Look back to the south to Laage Kapel Wood (LKW) on the right and Hill 40 in front of it.

On the left of Second Army, II Corps advanced with the Belgians at 9.00 a.m. The first objective was the Courtrai–Roulers railway, the previous day's final objective. Thereafter crossings over the Lys were to be seized. On the right 36th Division reached its objective on the railway line, seizing Gulleghem and Heule, but there was hard fighting on the way. In the centre 29th Division took Salines under heavy fire and the railway was reached at 12.45 p.m.

In 9th Division, which formed the link with the Belgians, 27th Brigade led with 11th Royal Scots. Initially it was to advance north of Laage Kapel Wood to seize Hill 40. The Battalion advanced at the double, covered by a barrage on selected targets, a machine gun barrage and a smoke screen. Direction was kept by a Brigade HQ staff officer with a compass in the centre of the line. He fired three green flares when the battalions signalled their intention to advance with a single green flare. Laage Kapel Wood was thought to be unoccupied, but this notion was immediately dispelled by a torrent of machine gun fire from the northern end. The attackers surged on and cleared the Wood. Emerging on the eastern side, they encountered thick wire and two machine guns on Hill 40, which forced them into cover.

Corporal Roland Elcock, a Lewis gun team leader, dashed forward into the hail of fire. When only ten metres from one of the guns he opened fire with a Lewis gun and killed the two-man crew with the first burst. He then jumped into their shelter, engaged the second gun, put it out of action and took five prisoners. His audacious action allowed the whole advance to be resumed and the northern end of Hill 40 was taken.

The 12th Royal Scots followed the 11th Battalion through the Wood and swung south to clear the southern end of Hill 40 and Steenbeek. After a half hour long bombardment, the advance continued and Bois d'Heule fell to 12th Royal Scots. The 11th Royal Scots came up on the left and both battalions advanced again. There was a pause on the Snephoek–Heule road, where touch was gained with the Belgians and 29th Division on the flanks. The Courtrai–Roulers railway was

Laage Kapel Wood on the right and in the centre from the northeast on Groene-Boomgaard. Hill 40 is the slightly higher ground left of the prominent white building left of centre. Laage Kapel Wood is much smaller than it was in 1918 and much of it has been covered in housing.

reached by midday. From there forward deployed field guns destroyed a number of German guns and machine guns. From here onwards the left flank was protected by 1/1st Yorkshire Cyclist Battalion (II Corps) and 11th Motor Machine Gun Battery (1st Motor Machine Gun Brigade).

The advance continued for another 1,800m in the afternoon to reach the Courtrai–Bruges road. However, the Belgians did not keep up on the left, due to concern about a counterattack on their left flank. On the right the 29th Division units had no immediate orders to continue. Despite being isolated, 9th Division's advance continued for another 1,600m to between Cuerne and Abeelhoek. Stiff resistance was encountered by 11th Royal Scots from Heetje on the left in the Belgian area, which caused some delay. Heavy opposition was also encountered at the windmill at Abeelhoek and from a farm 550m to the northeast. The cyclists and 11th Royal Scots failed to take the windmill but the pressure on the enemy eventually forced them to pull back over the Lys.

The Belgians advanced and began to flood into 27th Brigade's area. Some of them were persuaded to go north to Heetje, where they relieved the British by 10.00 p.m. The Belgians also secured Bavichove and Hulste. However, the Belgian line was much extended and there was the danger of a counterattack from the northeast. As a result 28th Brigade, in reserve to 9th Division, was moved up to near Capelle St Catherine (St Katerina-Kapel) to be prepared to cover the Division's left flank. Patrols from 29th Division to the south were contacted just west of Cuerne by last light.

In the fighting later in the day near the Lys, Elcock attacked and captured the crew of another machine gun. Resistance increased as the Lys was approached at Harlebeke. The cyclists and motor machine guns were held up at Leyhoek but succeeded in taking it. From there the four motor machine gun teams engaged targets on the crowded Courtrai–Harlebeke road. Forward deployed field guns with the infantry joined in and searched other communications arteries. With the situation in the flanks still uncertain, HQ 9th Division halted the advance in order to prepare for a deliberate assault across the Lys next day.

During the night the Germans gassed Cuerne, where there were many civilians who did not have respirators. The windmill was taken just after dawn on 16th October and crossing points over the Lys were covered by patrols from the west. However, heavy fire was encountered by a patrol as it approached a bridge that was blown at 8.20 a.m.

476 Lieutenant David McGregor 6th Battalion, The Royal Scots attached 29th Battalion Machine Gun Corps (29th Division) Near Hoogmolen, Belgium

22nd October 1918

There was a pause on the Fourth and Third Army fronts on 21st and 22nd October to prepare for the next stage. First Army carried on the advance but under instructions to make ground only if there was light resistance. The centre and left made good progress and in places advanced thirteen kilometres. Fifth Army continued to make gains in its advance towards the Schelde, which was reached on the left, as was the Scarpe on the right.

In Flanders, Second Army opened the next phase of its campaign. Having crossed the Lys, the next objective was the Schelde. Between the two waterways was an area of higher ground on which stood numerous farmsteads, which were ideal for defence, with excellent fields of fire over the open country.

The direction of advance south of Courtrai was eastwards towards the Courtrai–Bossuyt Canal, but northeast of the town the advance was generally south-easterly, parallel with the Canal. The operation began on 20th October. The II Corps on the left, in contact with the French, had all three divisions in the line. At first good progress was made over the boggy ground but resistance stiffened later. The 29th Division, on the Corps' right, advanced at 6.00 a.m., with 88th Brigade leading, commanded by Brigadier General Bernard Freyberg VC. Staceghem was taken by 7.30 a.m. and later Esscher on the Canal. The 86th Brigade passed through and made more headway before being halted on the line Pont Levis No.2 – Wolfsberg–St Louis.

Next day little progress was made. Both corps on the right were on the west bank of the Schelde, but the two on the left, including II Corps, had more limited success. The 29th Division was ordered to maintain contact with 41st Division (XIX Corps) on the right and conform to its movements. In the afternoon it was believed that 41st Division had taken Hoogmolen Ridge and at 12.30 p.m. 86th Brigade was ordered to move forward to capture the high ground about Banhout Bosch. This was achieved by 5.00 p.m. On the left 9th and 36th Divisions made almost no headway.

The 22nd saw no change on the right, west of the Courtrai–Bossuyt Canal. On the left XIX and II Corps ran into strong resistance. The enemy in these areas

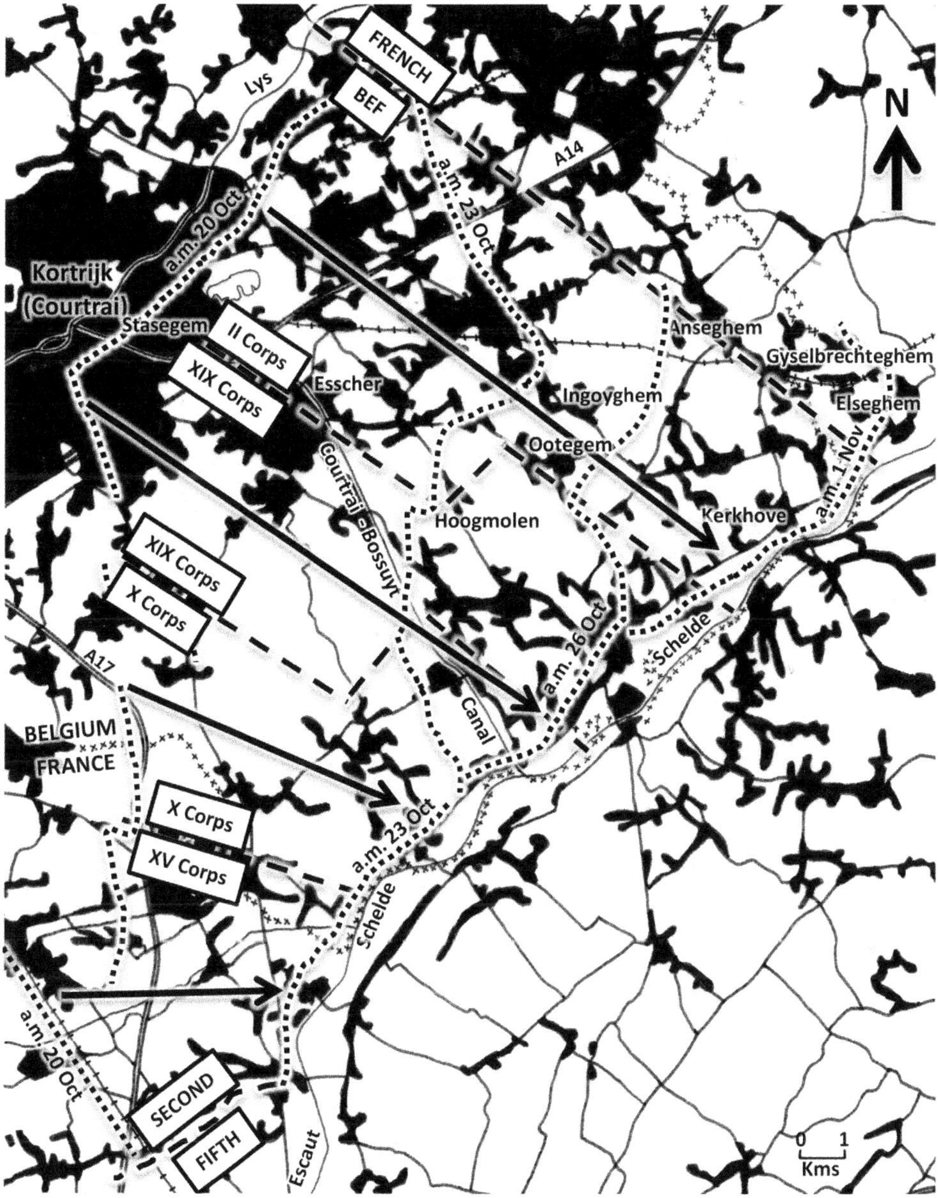

The progress of Second Army 20th October–1st November.

needed to delay the advance, while their troops opposite the French to the north fell back in line. There was also a problem bringing the artillery across the Lys, which meant that the Germans enjoyed superior firepower. As a result, counterattacks regained some of the ground lost in the previous days.

The II Corps' objective was the ridge between Ooteghem and Ingoyghem. In 29th Division, 87th Brigade was to lead the attack, having passed through 86th

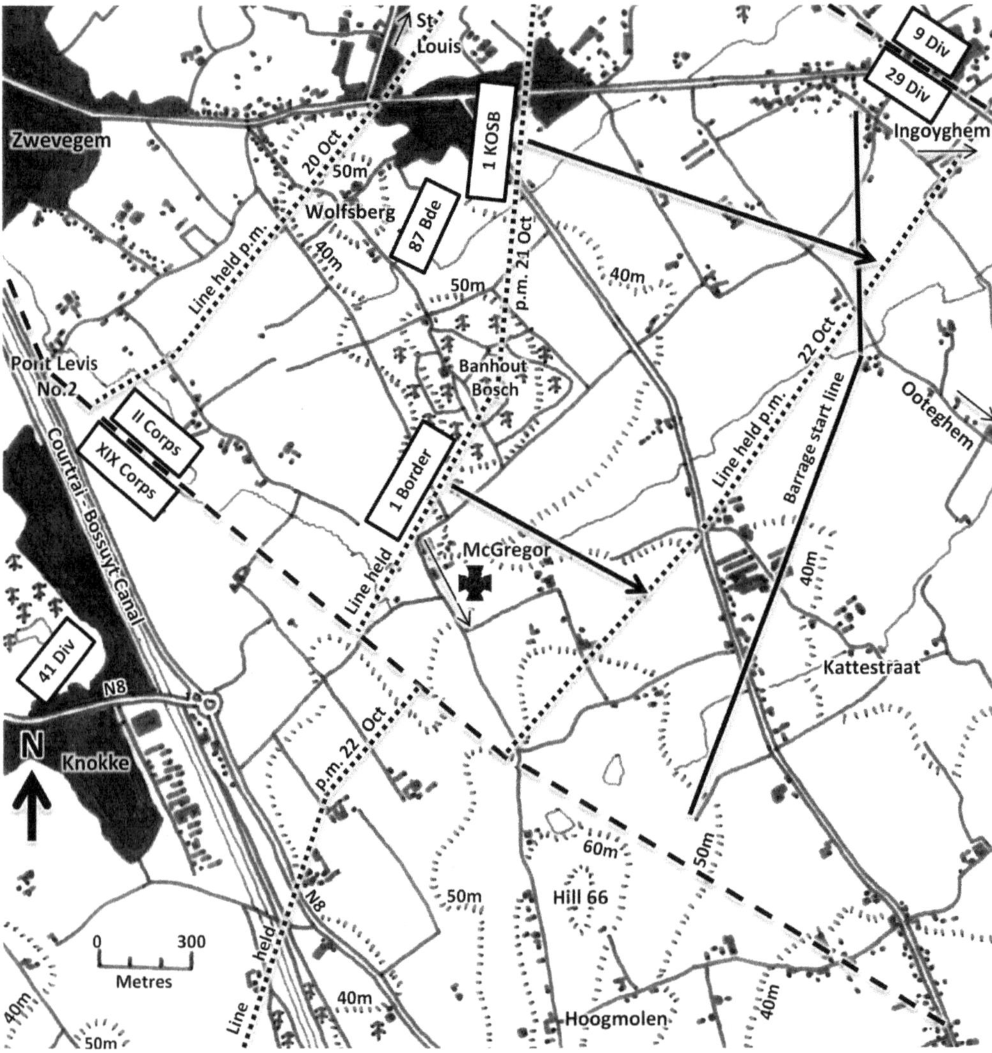

Cross the Courtrai–Bossuyt Canal on the N8 eastwards to the large roundabout and continue along the N8 (Keiberg) southwards for 200m. Turn left onto Kwadestraat and follow north-eastwards for 900m to a t-junction. There is a large farm on the left. Turn right, remaining on Kwadestraat, and continue southwards for 550m. Park at a small brick building at the junction with Dokkestraat.

Brigade, with 1st Border on the right and 1st King's Own Scottish Borderers on the left. There was insufficient time to arrange a proper artillery barrage. In addition, the precise locations of 86th Brigade's forward troops were not known until midnight. As a result, orders to the battalions were not sent out until 2.00 a.m. and the brigadier rode around the units to brief the COs personally. Early in the morning the Germans shelled the troops with gas and high explosive.

The two assault battalions set off for their assembly positions behind the wooded high ground of Banhout Bosch. Unusually there was no early morning mist and, having observed the battalions forming up, the Germans opened heavy fire upon them. When the advance commenced at 9.00 a.m. the battalions again came under the fire of these machine guns. The barrage fell 1,450m ahead of the start line and provided no protection to the assault troops as they struggled forward over the sodden ground.

On the left 1st King's Own Scottish Borderers encountered stiff opposition from farms scattered throughout its area. Progress was made by using drainage ditches to approach them. One farm attacked on the right was seized, together with forty-nine prisoners and six machine guns, three of which were soon in use against their former owners. This allowed the left of the Battalion to make progress and heavy casualties were inflicted on the enemy retreating towards Ooteghem. Another farm, 200m ahead of the line reached by the Battalion, was seized adding another fifty prisoners and four machine guns to the bag.

At 6.30 a.m. 1st Border set off with B Company on the right and C Company on the left. A and D Companies were in support on the right and left respectively. During the move into the assembly area, which was completed by 8.25 a.m., the Battalion came under heavy machine gun fire from Hill 66, north of Hoogmolen, and suffered several casualties in covering the last 775m. The Battalion was troubled by fire from this high ground all day, which 41st Division (XIX Corps) failed to take. A platoon of A Company, under Second Lieutenant A Smith, was detailed to protect this flank, with a section of machine guns attached, under Second Lieutenant K Thompson MGC.

The wooded high ground of Banhout Bosch from the south. McGregor hid his machine guns behind the farm on the left, prior to rushing them along the road that runs across the centre of the picture. He got them into the cover of a low bank just out of sight to the right of the small brick building at the road junction on the extreme right of picture. Hill 66 is behind the camera position.

The reverse of the previous view. McGregor and Harris galloped along the exposed road in the centre to the shelter of the low bank to the left of the small brick building. Hill 66 is in the background.

By 9.45 a.m., A Company had formed a defensive right flank facing towards Hill 66. However, all the advantages were with the enemy. The sodden ground made movement difficult and the Germans had an unusually large number of machine guns. There was no cover in front of the Hill and Lewis guns were only partly successful in neutralising the enemy machine gun posts. The barrage was lost and forward movement by short rushes, covered by the Lewis guns, was only made with extreme difficulty. Eventually the advanced troops were close enough to Kattestraat to engage houses with trench mortars and rifle grenades. On the left D Company had to reinforce C Company due to heavy casualties.

Two machine guns, commanded by **Lieutenant David McGregor,** were attached to 1st Border for the operation from D Company, 29th Battalion MGC. The guns were on a limber on the right flank. Prior to the attack McGregor had concealed them under the bank of a sunken road. As the advance commenced McGregor was aware of the enfilade fire from Hill 66 and went forward over the open to locate suitable locations for the machine guns. He realised that to pack or manhandle the guns into position would take too long and was unlikely to succeed over the open bullet swept ground.

Instructing his team to make their way forward using a more covered route, he jumped onto the limber, lay on top and ordered the driver, 19069 Private William George Harris (DCM for this action), to move forward. They galloped along the road in full view of the enemy and were engaged by every weapon that could be brought to bear. In the mad 350m dash the horses and limber were hit, but remarkably they made it to the cover of a bank, where McGregor immediately brought the guns into action. They gave invaluable support to the beleaguered infantry and were so successful in suppressing the enemy fire that the Battalion managed to advance a little further. McGregor continued to direct fire from a most exposed position but an hour later he was killed while observing fire for the Trench Mortar Battery.

Patrols from 4th French Cavalry Brigade, attached to 29th Division for this operation, were sent out at 11.00 a.m. However, in the face of the enemy machine gun fire no progress was made. The enemy launched a counterattack at about

2.00 p.m., which was repulsed by B Company, 1st Border. A Company reported a similar action. Another attempt to advance was made in the afternoon by B Company, in conjunction with 41st Division on the right. The left of B Company quickly ran out of steam but 5 and 6 Platoons on the right penetrated 1,375m beyond the general line reached by the Battalion. However, with no support on either flank, and under heavy fire, the nineteen survivors were forced to retire. It was then decided to consolidate the ground held for the night. In 87th Brigade, 2nd South Wales Borderers took over the front from the two assault battalions by 11.00 p.m. The 1st Border suffered 104 casualties (six killed, ninety-three wounded and five missing).

In the centre of II Corps, 9th Division made the longest advance. On the left, 36th Division had a similar experience to 29th Division. McGregor's VC was the last of twenty-seven awarded to the 29th Division during the Great War. It was earned on the Division's last day of active combat operations in the war.

Action of Ooteghem

481 Pte Norman Harvey, 1st Battalion, The Royal Inniskilling Fusiliers (109th Brigade, 36th Division), Ingoyghem, Belgium

25th October 1918

There was a pause in the relentless British advance following the conclusion of the Battle of the Selle on 24th October. The troops were thoroughly exhausted and a rest was welcomed. However, Haig did not want to give the Germans time to prepare defensive positions for the winter and thereby prolong the war. He believed, contrary to many others, that continuing pressure would bring about a collapse of the once proud and powerful German Army before the end of the year and avoid the war dragging on into 1919.

Fourth Army spent the 25th reconnoitring possible crossings points along the Sambre Canal and in general patrolling. Third Army tidied up a few loose-ends from the previous day and, in places where the enemy slipped away, followed up and established outpost lines. Opposition was generally light and that night an attack seized Englefontaine in V Corps' area.

Fifth Army remained static all day and to Second Army fell the main operation on 25th October, the Action of Ooteghem. The three corps on the left were involved, together with a French division. The objective was to complete closing up to the Schelde (Escaut). During the night of 23rd/24th October, XIX Corps extended to the north, taking over the front on the right of II Corps, thus relieving 29th Division, which withdrew for rest.

Orders were issued on 23rd October for a resumption of the attack on the 25th. With 9th Division on the right and 36th Division on the left, II Corps' ultimate objective was to secure crossings over the Schelde. All available heavy artillery was to be moved over the Lys to support the attack. There were two intermediate objectives. The first was over the crest of the ridge beyond Ooteghem and Ingoyghem. At the second there was to be a two-hour halt to allow the artillery to move forward, in order to cover the later stages of the attack. Zero hour was at 9.00 a.m.

On the right of Second Army only 34th Division attacked in X Corps. A subsidiary operation to seize crossings over the Courtrai–Bossuyt Canal was checked until the main force closed-up, but thereafter better progress was made and the Schelde was

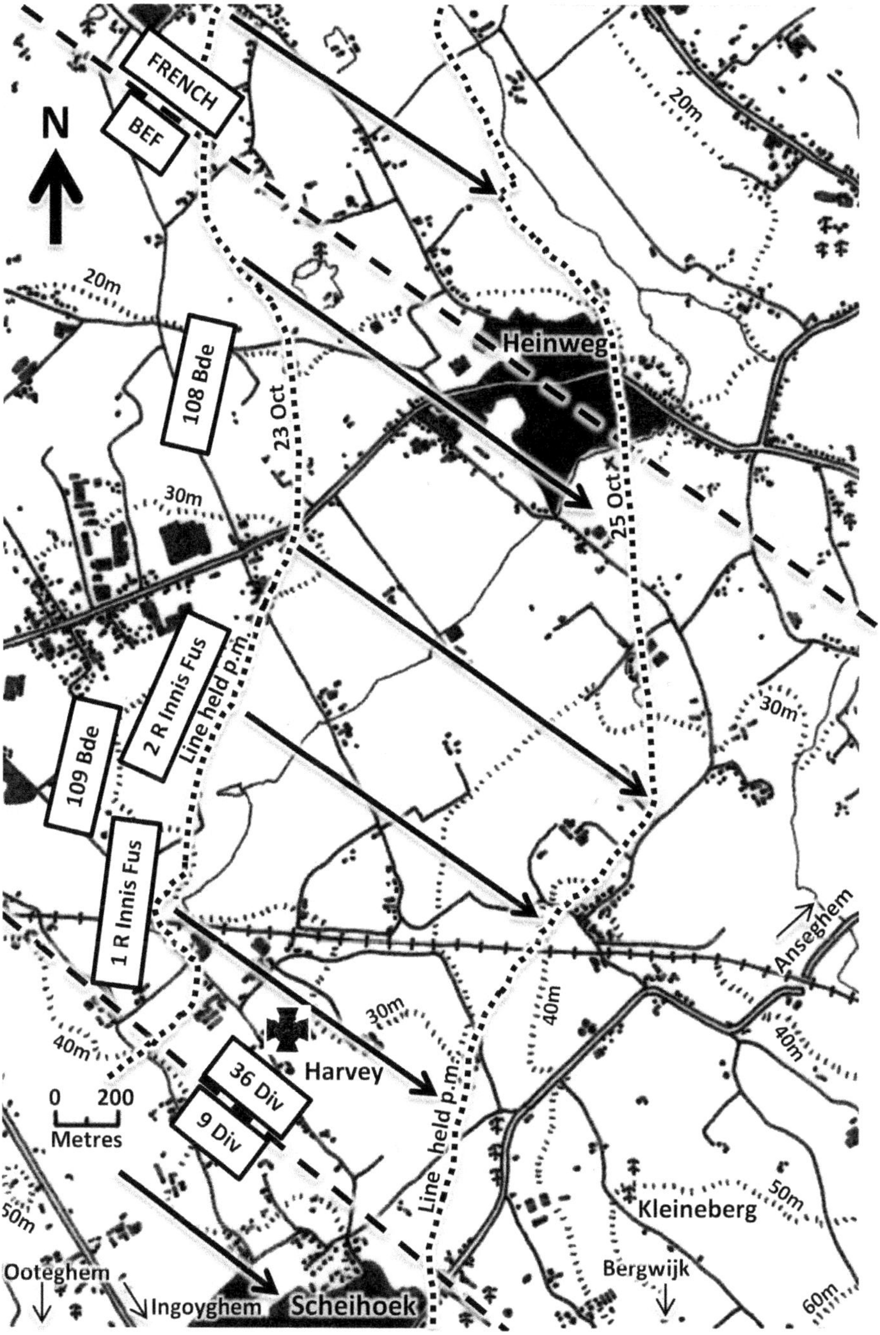

Leave Ingoyghem (Ingooigem) northwards along Sint-Antoniusstraat and follow for 800m to the junction on the right with Hulstweg. There is space to park here for a short period. The Battalion's start line was about 400m northwest of Hulstweg. Look to the southeast, the direction in which 1st Royal Inniskilling Fusiliers advanced.

From the road junction with Hulstweg on the left and Sint-Antoniusstraat on the right. The railway line can be seen in the left distance. 1st Royal Inniskilling Fusiliers advanced across Hulstweg from left to right. Harvey's VC action was probably in the buildings towards the right of the picture.

gained just before nightfall. In XIX Corps, the attack by 41st Division had mixed results. Heavy fire and resistance were met throughout the day, with the longest advances being made on the right.

On the left in II Corps there was stiff resistance from the outset. By mid-afternoon 9th Division was still short of the crest line. Later Ingoyghem was taken, but Ooteghem held out.

On the right of 36th Division was 109th Brigade, with 1st Royal Inniskilling Fusiliers on its right flank, in contact with 9th Division, and 2nd Royal Inniskilling Fusiliers on the left. The barrage came down as planned 225m in front of the start line and the two battalions set off at a quick pace. The 2nd Battalion ran into the British barrage just before crossing the railway and suffered some casualties. Enemy machine gun fire was heavy from the outset and the Battalion was held up by fire from the left, where 108th Brigade had been unable to keep up.

The 1st Battalion advanced with B and C Companies leading, A Company in support and D Company in reserve. At zero numerous machine guns opened fire from hedges and farms. **Private Norman Harvey**'s platoon was pinned down by machine guns in a farm forty metres in front. Everyone dived for cover, but not before five men were wounded. On his own initiative Harvey rushed forward single-handed and engaged the enemy. He killed two Germans and badly wounded a third before the remaining fifteen gave up. Two machine guns were taken.

At 9.40 a.m. the right company reported that it was still advancing, but a little later the forward troops came under heavy machine gun fire from the ridge on the left flank. As a result the advance lost direction and slipped to the right. However, at 12.00 p.m. the forward companies were still in contact with 9th Division on the right and with 2nd Royal Inniskilling Fusiliers on the left. Overall 36th Division was short of the crest of the Ooteghem–Ingoyghem–Anseghem ridge. Fire from the left made further movement impossible, although the leading companies tried to get on towards Bergwijk.

The French on the left were well behind 108th Brigade's left flank and it had to swing this flank back to Heinweg. On the right, 109th Brigade was ordered to make another attack to keep up with 9th Division. Orders were not received until minutes before zero hour at 5.00 p.m. and only two companies of 1st Battalion and one of 2nd Battalion moved forward. Despite this some progress was made initially. Heavy enfilade fire halted the advance and eventually most were forced back to the 5.00 p.m. start positions. The 1st Battalion enjoyed some early success in this attack but, when it came under fire from the Kleineberg ridge, it also had to retire to the start position. At 10.10 p.m. HQ 109th Brigade ordered the line held to be consolidated.

In the 5.00 p.m. attack Harvey's company was held up by a strongpoint in a farmhouse. Without any support he again rushed forward. His platoon sergeant later recalled that Harvey returned fifteen minutes later laughing out loud because the Germans had beat it as he approached. Harvey's achievement is more remarkable as he had badly sprained an ankle early in the attack but continued to run around for the rest of the day. After last light he conducted a daring personal reconnaissance and gained valuable information. Only then did he have his ankle attended to.

Action of Tieghem

482 Sgt Thomas Caldwell, 12th Battalion, The Royal Scots Fusiliers (94th Brigade, 31st Division), Tieghem, near Audenarde, Belgium

31st October 1918

The period 26–31st October was comparatively calm as the BEF made preparations for what was to be the final offensive of the war. A number of small actions were fought with the aim of finishing elements of previous operations, follow up enemy retirements and improve start positions for the next stage. However, in the main, the troops rested and prepared for the next battle.

The Germans were almost at the end of their tether. They had fought bravely and skilfully, but four long years of war had taken their toll. Ludendorff resigned on 27th October, Bulgaria signed an armistice on the 29th, Turkey capitulated on the 31st and Austria followed on 3rd November. The end was in sight.

In Second Army, the period 26th and 27th October was spent closing up to the Schelde, where it had not yet been reached. In some places there was hard

From the road running east from St Arnoldspark car park looking west, the direction from which 12th Royal Scots Fusiliers advanced. The church in Tieghem is in the extreme left distance. It is believed that Caldwell's VC action was somewhere in this area.

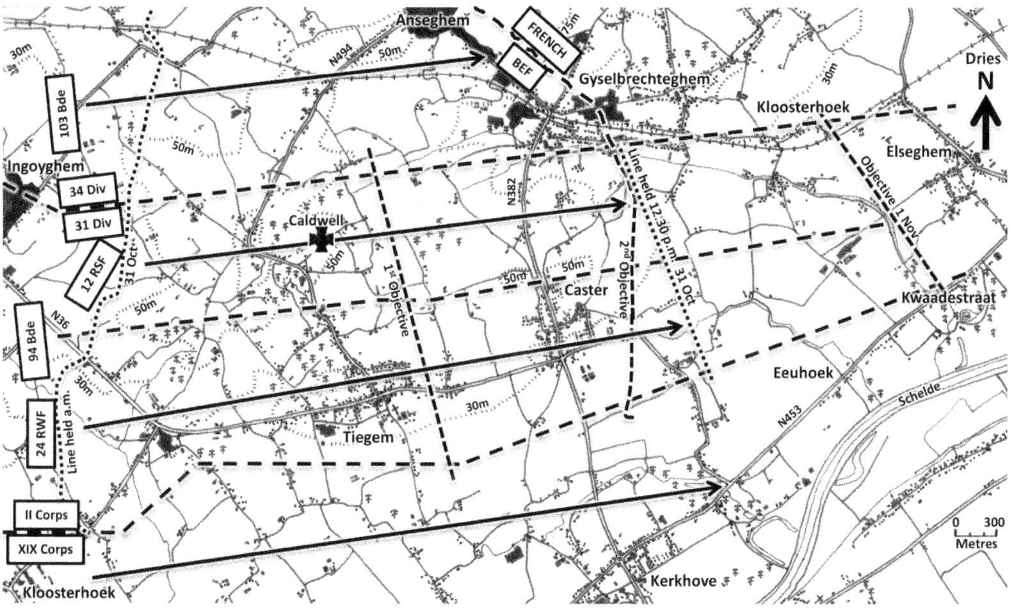

Drive north out of Tiegem on the N494 towards Anseghem. After a kilometre park in the St Arnoldspark car park on the right. The buildings to the north of here seem to be likely candidates for Caldwell's VC action. However, this is not certain as the information given in the various accounts lacks sufficient accuracy.

fighting, but elsewhere the enemy retired voluntarily. By the end of the 27th the left of the Army was still some distance from the Schelde. The next two days were spent preparing for a deliberate operation on 31st October to complete this move. The attack was launched by XIX Corps on the right and II Corps on the left, in conjunction with the French VII Corps to the north. An Anglo-French liaison team was to move along the boundary on the left to ensure coordination throughout the operation.

The XIX Corps attacked on a one division frontage with 35th Division. The II Corps employed 31st Division on the right and 34th Division on the left in its attack, each led by one brigade. These were 94th Brigade and 103rd Brigade respectively. The 94th Brigade had two battalions forward: 24th Royal Welsh Fusiliers on the right and 12th Royal Scots Fusiliers on the left. The leading battalions were to combine their flank platoons with those of their flanking units.

To guarantee success the artillery had to neutralise the still powerful German artillery and mask off their observers on the high ground with smoke. Four brigades of field artillery were allocated to support 94th Brigade, two brigades of heavy artillery and three machine gun companies were allocated for the creeping barrage. The Brigade was also allocated three 6″ Newton mortars. Each assault battalion was allocated a section of field guns, a section of machine guns and two light trench mortars.

Zero hour was set for 5.25 a.m. In the event the enemy artillery was not a major problem after zero, although it was heavy on the left. The Germans used a large proportion of gas shell and a build-up of gas west of Ingoyghem did cause difficulties. Enemy machine gun posts proved as obstinate as ever. The intensity of resistance increased noticeably in the north of the attack frontage, but French tanks lent a hand in this area. The 94th Brigade encountered stiff resistance between the outpost line and the first objective, but this was overcome after severe hand to hand fighting, particularly on the left in 12th Royal Scots Fusiliers' area. Apart from a portion of Anseghem in 34th Division's area, the first objective was taken by 8.50 a.m.

Sergeant Thomas Caldwell was in command of a Lewis gun section in the van of 12th Royal Scots Fusiliers' advance. His platoon was attacking a strongly held farmhouse when it came under intense close-range fire from another farm. Despite the terrific fusillade directed at him, Caldwell rushed the second farm and captured it single-handed, taking eighteen prisoners. By removing this important position in the German defences he allowed the rest of his platoon, led by Second Lieutenant Andrew Giffin Shearer, to overcome the first farmhouse. In all they captured seventy prisoners, eight machine guns and a trench mortar.

A planned pause of two hours followed the capture of the first objective before the advance was resumed by the two support companies. Less opposition was encountered in this phase, although a number of machine gun posts on the left had to be captured or destroyed on the way. The 24th Royal Welsh Fusiliers was on the final objective by 10.15 a.m. and 12th Royal Scots Fusiliers at 10.45 a.m.

In XIX Corps the success was exploited and the Schelde was reached at Eeuhoek, northeast of Kerkhove. The II Corps ordered its divisions to support the further advance of XIX Corps on the right and also to assist the French on the left, who were behind. The 34th Division formed a defensive flank. The further advance of II Corps after dark was into the French area as they were unable to organise another attack that day. Opportunities to get forward as the enemy retired were exploited, including the occupation of Gyselbrechteghem. Touch with the international liaison team was gained and the gap between the British left and French right flanks was filled.

The 31st Division gave orders to advance after dark and to be ready for a major resumption of the attack next morning at 6.30 a.m. Early on 1st November, 94th Brigade sent patrols into the French area and found the Germans had already withdrawn over the Schelde. The line Kloesterhoek–Kwaadestraat, one kilometre south of Elseghem, was reached without further loss and patrols were pushed through Elseghem towards Driesch (Dries). Later the French came forward and passed in front of the British to take up posts along the Schelde, prior to taking over the area taken by the British the previous night. The II Corps was then withdrawn into reserve.

The 94th Brigade alone took 713 prisoners, thirteen field guns and seventy-three machine guns. The 12th Royal Scots Fusiliers war diary records taking sixty prisoners and three field guns. However, this ignores Caldwell's platoon alone taking seventy prisoners, eight machine guns and a trench mortar. It is likely that the figures given by the Brigade HQ are more accurate than those of the Battalion. The 94th Brigade suffered 209 casualties in this operation (twenty-seven killed and 182 wounded).

Biographies

295536 SERGEANT THOMAS CALDWELL
12th (Ayr & Lanark Yeomanry) Battalion, The Royal Scots Fusiliers

Thomas Caldwell was born on 6th February 1894 at Kirkton Street, Carluke, Lanarkshire, Scotland. His father, George Caldwell (7th August 1867–5th January 1945), also born at Carluke, was an ostler in 1891, living with his parents. By 1893 he was a carter, living on Orchard Street, Carluke. He married Margaret 'Maggie' née Craig (10th November 1866–10th September 1925), born at Eastfield, Bothwell, Lanarkshire, on 22nd December 1893 at 6 Taylor Row, Lochtannochside, Bothwell. She was a domestic servant living with and working for the Porteous family at Hill Farm House, Bothwell in 1881. They were living at Orchard Street in 1901. Maggie died at 52 Chapel Street, Carluke. George was living at

Kirkton Street in Carluke, where Thomas Caldwell was born. Carluke, which lies on a plateau overlooking the River Clyde, is mentioned in a charter by King Robert I in 1315 and has had many spellings since. The town was chartered to Captain Walter Lockhart of Kirkton and spouse as a Burgh of Barony in 1662. It expanded during the Industrial Revolution, with corn mills, cotton weaving, coal mining and various manufacturing processes, including bricks, glass, confectionery and jam. Carluke is now Clydesdale's largest town with a population of 13,300. Its largest employer is the jam company of Renshaw Scott, which has been making preserves from locally grown fruit since the 1880s. Ramsay of Carluke have been curing bacon in the town since 1857. The town was home to two other VCs – William Angus (1888–1959) and Donald Cameron (1916–61). It is also the birthplace of Major General William Roy (1726–90), founder of the Ordnance Survey.

Hallcraig, Carluke when he died at the County Hospital, Cleland, Lanarkshire. Thomas had eight siblings, all born at Carluke, including:

Chapel Street, Carluke.

- Janet Caldwell (19th October 1895–1984), a domestic servant, married George Kerr (born 1887), a coalminer, on 28th December 1917 at Chapel Street, Carluke. They possibly had four children – Agnes Loudon Kerr 1916, Margaret Craig Kerr 1919, Andrew Loudon Kerr 1923 and Morrison Loudon Kerr 1930.
- Joseph Caldwell (born 16th September 1897). He may be 2814 Private Joseph Caldwell, 6th Highland Light Infantry, who was killed in action on 14th August 1915 (Helles Memorial, Turkey).
- Helen Clarkson Caldwell (31st August 1899–15th July 1972), a tailoress, married Andrew Forrest Pringle (5th March 1898–16th October 1980), a ploughman, on 29th June 1923 at Chapel Street, Carluke. They emigrated to Québec, Canada, arriving on 13th May 1928. They both died at Fergus, Wellington Co, Ontario. They had five children including:
    - Samuel Pringle (1927–1st July 1928), born at Carluke and died at Harriston, Ontario.
    - Robert Forrest Pringle (4th March 1932–7th January 2001), born at Harriston, Ontario, married L Anne Sparry (born 1935) on 11th June 1955 at St Andrew's Presbyterian Church, Fergus, Ontario. They had six children – Lynne Pringle, Bryan Pringle, Barbara Pringle, Rhonda Pringle, Darrell Pringle and Tammy Pringle.
- Robert Caldwell (born 9th August 1902).
- David Caldwell (born 13th February 1904).
- Agnes Caldwell (7th April 1906–27th October 1989), a domestic servant living at 12 Hamilton Street, Carluke, married Robert Bennett Sloan (1893–1950), a coalminer, on 16th July 1932 at the Congregational Church Manse, Carluke. He died at Forth, Lanarkshire. Agnes emigrated to Canada after his death, where she died at Kingston, Ontario. Her ashes were taken back to Scotland by her son, Robert, and interred with her husband. They had two children:
    - Margaret Caldwell Craig Sloan (19th May 1933–14th April 2005), born at Forth, Lanarkshire, married Robert 'Bob or 'Scotty' Johnston (2nd August 1929–22nd February 2017), born at Bellshill, Lanarkshire, on 20th March 1954. They emigrated to Canada and lived at Kingston, Ontario. They had four children – Craig Johnston, David Johnston, Ian Johnston and Anne Johnston.

  - Robert Sloan (24th May 1937–9th January 1993) is believed to have married Helen Ann Grieve (born 1942) in 1963 and they had a son and a daughter.
- Jane Craig Caldwell (24th August 1908–1989), a domestic servant, married John Watson (1907–81), a coalminer and later a jointer's mate, on 16th December 1938 at 33 Cassel's Row, Carluke. She was living at 56 Glenfeoch Road, Carluke when she died at St John's Hospital, Livingston, West Lothian. They had two children:
  - Margaret Watson (born 3rd September 1940).
  - James Watson (born 25th January 1945).

Thomas' paternal grandfather, also Thomas Caldwell (c.1825–2nd May 1901), a carting contractor born at Inchinnan, Renfrew, Renfrewshire, married Helen 'Ellen' née Clarkson (4th September 1825–27th May 1896), born at Wandel and Lamington, Lanarkshire, on 25th June 1847 at Carnwath, Lanarkshire. They lived at Orchard Street, Carluke, where they both subsequently died. In addition to George they had eight other children:

- Agnes Caldwell (15th April 1848–1878), born at Carnwath, was a tilemaker in 1871, living with her parents.
- Elizabeth Caldwell (c.1850–13th October 1921), born at Cambusnethan, Lanarkshire, married John Smellie (c.1846–21st August 1929), a limestone miner, on 30th December 1870 at Carluke, where he was born. By 1881 he was a carrier and they were living at Kirkton Street, Carluke. They had seven children

Inchinnan, where Thomas Caldwell was born c.1825. The village is situated near a ford at the confluence of the Black and White Cart Rivers. Later there was a ferry, then a stone bridge over the Black Cart and, more recently, a bascule bridge over the White Cart. St Conval's Chariot, the stone that legend says brought St Conval to Inchinnan from Ireland c.590, is located near the ford. With it is Argyll's Stone, where the 9th Earl is said to have rested when captured in 1685, before being executed in Edinburgh. A 12th century church to Saint Conval was given to the Knights Templar by King David I. It was replaced by Hallows Church, seen here, in 1900, which in turn was replaced by part of Abbotsinch airfield. The latest parish church is in the village centre and contains burial stones dating back to the 9th century. A palace was built by Matthew, Lord Darnley, 2nd Earl of Lennox c.1506 but nothing of it remains today. There were quarries in the village in the 1700s and they produced high quality freestone until the 1900s. The former India of Inchinnan office block of the India Tyres factory was occupied by the company from 1927 until the early 1980s. It is now Category A listed. The site was used to build airships during the Great War, including R24, R27, R34 (first aircraft to make an east–west transatlantic flight in July 1919 and the first return flight) and R36 (not completed until after the Great War, converted into an airliner and became the first airship to carry a civil registration, *G-FAAF*). There were many other industries locally, including coal mining. Wilhelmina Alexander (1756–1843), made famous by Robert Burns as 'The Bonnie Lass of Ballochmyle', is buried in Old Inchinnan Cemetery.

– Alexander Smellie (28th February 1872–1888), Thomas Smellie (1874–1905), Helen Smellie (17th November 1878–1950), John Smellie (19th November 1880–1966), Margaret Smellie (13th April 1886–1979), Elizabeth Smellie (27th December 1887–21st December 1983) and Archibald Smellie (27th March 1892–1955).

- Helen Caldwell (c.1853–1912) was a domestic servant in 1871, living with her parents. She married James Hastie (c.1852–1928) on 31st December 1872, a railway engine driver, at Carluke, where he was born. At the time of the 1881 Census, James was living at 48 Polmadie Road, Hutchesontown, Glasgow, while Helen and their daughter were staying with her parents. They were living at 128 Cathcart Road, Glasgow in 1891 and at 621 Dumbarton Road, Partick, Lanarkshire in 1901. They had a daughter, Helen Hastie (1879–1916).
- Alexander Caldwell (c.1855–77).
- Ann 'Annie' Caldwell (21st October 1856–1879).
- Thomas Caldwell (14th March 1859–1925) was a carter living with his parents at Orchard Street, Carluke in 1881. He married Margaret Gilchrist (1856–85), a domestic servant, on 24th August 1883 at Carstairs, Lanarkshire. Margaret probably died due to complications with the birth of her son. She had two children:
    - Betsy 'Bessie' Jane Wotherspoon Caldwell (born 14th June 1883) married Peter Fleming (born 1878), a coalminer of Graystonelea Road, Shotts, Lanarkshire, at Anderston, Glasgow on 6th December 1907.
    - Thomas Caldwell (born 26th September 1885).

  Thomas is understood to have married Agnes Thornton née Wylie (c.1858–1944), born at Wilshaw, Lanarkshire, on 2nd September 1890 at Carluke. Agnes had at least two sons from her first marriage – Peter Thornton 1882 and John Thornton 1884. Thomas and Agnes had four children:
    - Annie Caldwell (born 1891).
    - Helen 'Nellie' Caldwell (5th August 1892–1966) never married.
    - George Caldwell (1898–1926).
    - Alexander Caldwell (1900–84).
- Jean Caldwell (27th March 1861–1870). Her death was registered as Jane..
- Janet Caldwell (1863–70).

His maternal grandfather, Joseph Craig (c.1837–5th June 1895), a coalminer born at Lesmahagow, Lanarkshire, married Janet Dick née Mair (c.1834–24th September 1899), born at Bothwell, Lanarkshire, on 21st March 1862 at Eastfield, Holytown, Lanarkshire. They were living at Turnpike Road, Bothwell in 1871 and at 49 Tannochside, Bothwell in 1881 and 1891. Joseph died at 6 Double Row, Tannochside, Bothwell and Janet at Police Station House, Drumpark, Coatbridge, Lanarkshire. In addition to Margaret they had eight other children:

Thomas' maternal grandfather, Joseph Craig, was born at Lesmahagow c.1837. The town is also known as Abbey Green or the Gow. The name means 'Enclosure of St Machutus', born in Wales and later emigrating to Brittany, where he was known as St Malo. The Benedictine Lesmahagow Priory was founded in 1144. It no longer stands but its foundations were excavated in 1978 next to the Old Parish Church. Sir Alexander Kirkland Cairncross (1911–98) was born at Lesmahagow. He was a leading economist, Professor of Applied Economics at Glasgow, Economic Adviser to the Government, Head of the Government Economic Service, Master of St Peter's College, Oxford and Chancellor of the University of Glasgow. By contrast his brother, John Cairncross (1913–95), also born at Lesmahgow, became a civil servant, intelligence officer and spy for the Soviet Union. He was the 'fifth man' of the Cambridge Five with Guy Burgess, Donald Maclean, Kim Philby and Anthony Blunt.

Bothwell was primarily a mining village but more recently has developed into an affluent commuter town for Glasgow. Bothwell Castle, on a bluff above a bend in the River Clyde, belonged to Sir William Moray, who died in 1300. It eventually passed by marriage to the Douglas family. The lordship of Bothwell was bestowed on Patrick Hepburn, 3rd Lord Hailes and 1st Earl of Bothwell, in 1487. In 1491 the title passed to Archibald Douglas, 5th Earl of Angus and later to the Earls of Home. The parish church contains the choir of the old Gothic church of 1398. The church was restored at the end of the 19th century. The Battle of Bothwell Bridge on 22nd June 1679, fought between government troops and Presbyterian Covenanters, marked the end of the brief rebellion. Marion Gilchrist (1864–1952), the first female graduate of the University of Glasgow and one of the first two women to qualify in medicine from a Scottish university, was born at Bothwell. She was also a leading activist in the women's suffrage movement.

- Grace Purdie Craig (26th May 1862–20th October 1893), a twin with Janet, born at Bothwell, married Thomas McIntyre (4th July 1853–23rd March 1926), born at Kilmore and Kilbride, Argyllshire, on 5th June 1885 at Bothwell. She died at Inverkip, Renfrewshire. They had five children – Duncan McIntyre (1886–1912), Joseph McIntyre 1887, Janet McIntyre 1889, Catherine McIntyre 1891 and Thomas McIntyre 1893. Thomas married Mary Burns (born 1873) on 31st October 1894 at Inverkip. He died at Busby, Renfrewshire. Thomas and Mary had a daughter – Mary McIntyre (born 2nd February 1897).
- Janet Craig (26th May 1862–26th August 1915), a twin with Grace, married William Brown (1860–11th January 1898), born at Buchanan, Stirlingshire, on

16th January 1885 at Bothwell. He was a carter in 1891, when they were living at 3 Glebe Street, Glasgow. William died at St Rollox, Glasgow. Janet was a charwoman in 1901, when she was living at 26 Glebe Street, Glasgow and subsequently died there. They had six children – Janet Brown (1887), William Brown (1889), Joseph Craig Brown (22nd September 1890), Alexander Brown (13th April 1893), Catherine Brown (1896) and Marion Brown (1898).

- John Mair Craig (28th February 1865–3rd July 1941), born at Eastfield, Bothwell, was a coalminer. By 1897 he was living at 6 Double Row, Tannochside, Lanarkshire. He married Janet 'Jessie' Robb née Clow (21st September 1868–2nd October 1948), a worker in a jelly preserve factory born at Bothwell, on 4th June 1897 at Waddell's Land, Uddingston, Lanarkshire. She had married Samuel Robb (c.1862–94) at Bothwell in 1889 and had two children – Joseph Robb (c.1891) and Agnes Robb (c.1894), who later changed their surname to Craig. John and Jessie lived at Waddell's Land, Uddingston and emigrated to the United States in 1910. He worked as a coalminer and they lived at Ridge Street, Universal, Clinton Township, Vermillion Co, Indiana. Jessie was living at 611 Kingsport Lane, La Porte, Indiana at the time of her death there. John and Jessie had six children – Susan Clow Craig (6th June 1898–29th April 1998) married as Aitken, James Clow Craig (26th March 1903–14th December 1981), Janet Dick Mair Craig (13th March 1905–7th December 1989), John Clow Craig (15th August 1906), Marion Mair Craig (14th March 1908) and Jane Clow Craig (12th April 1910).
- Jane Craig (5th June 1868–3rd January 1928) was a general servant in 1881. She was a dairy maid when she married Andrew Brown (born 1865), a ploughman born at Walston, Lanarkshire, on 2nd December 1887. They were living at Carnwath, Lanarkshire in 1891 and at Dunsyre, Lanarkshire in 1901. Jane died at Shotts, Lanarkshire. They had four children – Andrew Brown 1890, Joseph Brown 1893, William Brown 1895 and John Brown 1898.
- Catherine Craig (25th December 1869–2nd March 1905) was an agricultural servant. She married Adam Blackley (26th August 1867–25th June 1952), a cab driver and later a steelworks labourer born at High Blantyre, on 23rd June 1891 at Double Row, Tannochside. They lived at 295 Gartsherrie Road (also known as Cornish Row), Coatbridge, Lanarkshire and Catherine subsequently died there. Adam was living with his children, William, Adam and Agnes, at 73d Burnbank Street, Coatbridge in 1930. He died at 40 Dudley Drive, Coatbridge. They had six children:
    - Janet 'Jessie' Blackley (born 28th September 1891), a domestic servant, married Robert Johnston (born c.1891), a colliery engineman, on 4th June 1915 at 93B Burnbank Street, Coatbridge.
    - Marion Brown Blackley (29th November 1892–1932), married Alexander T Tennant (1892–1958), a locomotive fireman born at New Monkland, on 26th December 1919 at 93B Burnbank Street, Coatbridge.

  - William Blackley (6th March 1896–1977), a colliery joiner, married Margaret Gray (born c.1905) on 11th July 1930 at Free Church Manse, Coatbridge. They had two children – William Craig Waterston Blackley 1930 and Susannah Waterston Blackley 1934.
  - Joseph Craig Blackley (born 31st October 1897), a blast furnace keeper, married Margaret McKendrick (born c.1906), a domestic servant, on 30th April 1926 at The Manse of New Monklands.
  - Adam Blackley (15th October 1899–1988), a blast furnace keeper with William Baird & Co, married Annie Ewart (c.1899–1927), a carpet finisher, on 2nd July 1926 at the United Free Church, Coatbridge. He enlisted at Motherwell on 15th November 1917 and was called up for service in 5th (Reserve) Battalion, The Cameronians (Scottish Rifles) on 2nd July 1918 (55853), joining at St Andrews the following day. He was described as 5′6″ tall, weighing 117 lbs and was living at 93R Waverley Terrace, Burnbank Road, Coatbridge. He transferred to the Class W Reserve on 14th November 1918 and was discharged surplus to requirements on 10th March 1919.
  - Agnes Craig Blackley (30th July 1902–1932) married William Hunter (born c.1904), a locomotive fireman, on 17th July 1930 at 73D Burnbank Street, Coatbridge.
- James Mair Craig (1st March 1871–24th October 1948) married Janet 'Jessie' Love Birrell (19th April 1869–17th January 1948), born at Bridgeton, Glasgow, on 1st September 1893. They both died at Glasgow. They had four children including – Joseph Craig (14th March 1895), James Craig (1897) and William Birrell Craig (28th September 1899).
- Agnes Crawford Craig (26th August 1873–9th November 1944) was a domestic servant when she married William Stott (1873–3rd July 1944), born at Brechin, Angus, on 23rd April 1897 at 6 Double Row, Tannochside near Bothwell. He was a police constable in 1901, when they were living at 6 Drumpark, Old Monkland, Coatbridge. They both died at 2 Reid Street, Forth and Haywood, Lanarkshire. They had five children:
  - Janet Dick Mair Stott (23rd July 1897–1st July 1982), was a nurse living at 2 Reid Street, Forth, Lanarkshire, when she married James Wilson (1891–1975), a miller and later a maintenance engineer of Hill of Cruick, Brechin, Angus, on 5th April 1939 at The Royal Oak Hotel, Lanark. She died at Woodside Cottage, Balbeggie, Perthshire.
  - John Stott (3rd November–1st December 1898).
  - Joseph Craig Stott (6th February 1900–22nd March 1976), a railway platelayer of County Buildings, Forth, Lanarkshire, married Mary Ballantine Park (2nd June 1899–10th February 1973), a domestic servant of 15 Alexander Street, Tranent, East Lothian and born at Blackridge, West Lothian, on 18th August 1923 at The Wishart Manse, Tranent. They had a

son, William Stott (5th February 1924 -2000) at New Row, Forth. Mary and Joseph both died at Law Hospital, Carluke.

- ◦ William Stott (born and died 2nd January 1902) at Drumpark Cottage, Coatbridge.
- ◦ James Mair Craig Stott (9th July 1905–20th September 1965), a railway surfaceman born at the Police Station, Drumpark, Coatbridge, married Margaret Caldwell (19th October 1901–16th July 1980), born at 41 Gartlea Road, Airdrie, on 14th September 1945 at 58 Wilton Road, Carluke. Margaret was living at 70 Station Road, Law when she died at Law Hospital, Carluke.

- Russell Craig (6th February 1876–17th October 1890), born at Tannochside, Bothwell, was a coalminer when he died of scarlet fever at 13 Double Row, Tannochside.

Carluke Primary School was demolished in the 1970s and replaced with a modern building.

Thomas was educated at Carluke Primary and Secondary Schools. He was employed as a farm servant near Dolphinton and later as a carter in Carluke. He enlisted in the Lanarkshire Yeomanry (569) and served with 1/1st Lanarkshire Yeomanry, Lowland Mounted Brigade at Gallipoli from 11th October 1915. The unit served in Egypt in 1st and later 2nd Dismounted Brigade from February 1916. On 4th January 1917, 1/1st Lanarkshire Yeomanry and 1/1st Ayrshire Yeomanry amalgamated to form 12th Royal Scots Fusiliers (295536) in 229th Brigade, 74th Division. The Battalion landed in France in May 1918 and on 21st June joined 94th Brigade, 31st Division.

Awarded the VC for his actions near Tieghem, near Audenarde, Belgium, on 31st October 1918, LG 6th January 1919. Thomas was later appointed company sergeant major. He

The Rankin Memorial Town Hall & Library, which opened on 18th July 1884, was named after Dr Daniel Rankin, who died in March 1882. At its centre was a large public hall that could seat up to 700 people. There was also a library and a savings bank office. In 1900 the clock tower was heightened by seventeen feet. The bell that hung in the tower was used to alert the fire brigade. The Hall was demolished with many other buildings in 1979 as part of a road improvement scheme.

The Good Templars Lodge in Carluke in 1907. The International Order (Organisation from 1970) of Good Templars is an international body, part of the temperance movement, founded in America in 1851. It promotes the avoidance of alcohol and other drugs by supporting communities and societies around the world. Its structure was modelled on Freemasonry but it admitted men and women equally and made no distinction by race. A lodge was established in Britain at Birmingham in 1868 and the movement spread across Europe and the rest of the world. In an attempt to modernise its image some titles and ritualistic features were changed in the 1970s. The Carluke lodge was later used as a drill hall, a doctor's surgery and, rather ironically, a bar and disco.

Jeanie Kerr was born at Law Junction. It was a railway station on the Caledonian main line from 1879 until 1965.

was presented with a clock and £1,000 at a public reception at Carluke Town Hall on 1st February 1919 by Lord Newlands, Lord Lieutenant of Lanarkshire. William Angus VC was in attendance. The same day he was presented with an illuminated address by Charles Douglas CB DL, Chairman of the Lanarkshire Territorial Force Association. Thomas was demobilised on 25th February 1919. The VC was presented by the King in the quadrangle at Buckingham Palace on 8th May 1919.

Thomas returned to farming. He married Jane 'Jeanie' McLaren Kerr (8th July 1897–19th June 1982), born at Law Junction, Carluke, on 14th January 1921 at the Templar Institute, Carluke. They emigrated to Australia, arriving on 5th December 1927, when he was described as a railway brakeman. William Angus VC travelled out with them. They set up home at 57 Tiparra Avenue, Park Holme, South Australia. They were living at 32 Penzance Street, Glenelg, SA in 1947 and at Seaton Park, Adelaide, SA in 1962. Thomas worked as a linesman for the Electricity Trust of South Australia from 1930 and retired as a line foreman in 1959. They had three children:

32 Penzance Street, Glenelg, where Thomas lived with his family.

- Sheena 'Jeanie' Armstrong Caldwell (13th October 1922–2013), born at 24 Commonwealth Road, Carluke, married John Richard Wylie (born 14th July 1921), born at Perth, Western Australia, in 1945 at Adelaide, SA. He was living at Narembeen, WA when he enlisted in the Royal Australian Air Force on 12th September 1940 at Perth (406228). He was discharged as a flying officer on 20th November 1945 from No.2 Aircraft Depot, Richmond, New South Wales. They had a daughter, Ann Wylie (born 25th July 1946), born at Adelaide, SA, who married as Hedge and had two children – Tamara Hedge and Steven Hedge. Sheena married William Easton Dempsey (25th August 1922–15th January 1994), born at Patna, Ayrshire, Scotland, on 15th November 1952 at Bath Street Methodist Church, Glenelg, SA. He died at Adelaide. They had three children:
    - Jane Easton Dempsey (born 8th April 1954), born at Rose Park, Adelaide, was a schoolteacher. She married Melvin John Charlton (born 15th August 1951), a farmer born at Tumby Bay, SA, on 14th April 1979. They had a daughter, Elizabeth Hayley Charlton, in 1986.
    - Craig Easton Dempsey (born 11th December 1955) graduated in Geophysics from Flinders University in 1978. He married Helen Therese Kitch (born 28th November 1959), a primary schoolteacher, on 21st July 1979. They had three children – Alasdair Robert Dempsey 1982, Benjamin Mark Dempsey 1984 and Miranda Jane Dempsey 1985.
    - Robert Easton Dempsey (born 11th August 1962) married Katherine Hobson and they had three children – Joshua Dempsey, Thomas Dempsey and Rebecca Dempsey.
- Margaret 'Greta' Craig Caldwell (born 17th June 1924–19th February 1995), born at Carluke, was living at Glenelg, SA when she enlisted in the Women's Royal Australian Air Force on 26th October 1942 at Adelaide, SA (107285). She was discharged on 15th March 1946 from the Telecommunications Unit, Air Force Headquarters. Greta married Stanley Jack Shotbolt (30th July 1926–11th March 2012), born at Belmore, NSW, on 16th August 1947 at Adelaide. Stanley was living at Marrickville, NSW when he enlisted in the Royal Australian Air Force on 15th August 1944 at Sydney, NSW (165330). He was discharged as a leading aircraftman on 21st November 1945 from RAAF Command Headquarters. He was a clerk in 1949, when they were living at 33 Moore Park Road, East Sydney, NSW and at 135 Boundary Road, Epping, NSW by 1958. They had three children:
    - Geoffrey Thomas Shotbolt (born 16th July 1955), an aircraft engineer, married Caryn Lynette Slater (born 27th August 1958), born at Brisbane, Queensland, on 26th November 1977 at Sydney. They had a daughter, Natalie Kathleen Shotbolt, in 1987.
    - Margaret Lyn Shotbolt (born 15th November 1958), a twin with Karen, was a clerical assistant in 1980.
    - Karen Jean Shotbolt (born 15th November 1958), a twin with Margaret, married Stephen Charles Ross (formally Peddell) (born 14th February

1956). They had four children – Deacon Thomas Ross 1985, Caitlin Jean Ross 1987, Lachlan Charles Ross 1989 and Helen Margaret Ross 1994.
- Heather McLaren Caldwell (born 19th May 1940) married Andrew Cardwell Duncan (19th May 1936–31st October 2011), born at Jamestown, SA, on 8th April 1961 at Adelaide. He was a bank clerk in 1963, when they were living at 21 Ipima Street, Braddon, Australian Capital Territory. They had three children – Alison Duncan (born 21st September 1962), Christopher Duncan (born 22nd September 1963) and Ian Duncan (born 3rd February 1968).

Jeanie's father, Thomas Kerr (born 17th April 1872), a coalminer born at Cambusnethan Street, Stonehouse, Lanarkshire, was living with his parents at Wilson's Row, Law Hill, Carluke, Lanarkshire in 1881 and 1891. He married Jane née Armstrong (born 17th October 1878), born at Wellgate Street, Larkhall, Lanarkshire, on 31st December 1895 at Mount Stewart, Carluke. They were living at Wildman Road, Carluke in 1901.

Thomas Caldwell towards the end of his life.

Thomas attended three VC reunions – the VC Garden Party at Buckingham Palace on 26th June 1920, the VC Centenary Celebrations at Hyde Park, London on 26th June 1956 and the 6th VC & GC Association Reunion at the Café Royal, London on 19th July 1968. For the VC Centenary Celebrations in June 1956, he travelled aboard SS *Arcadia* with other Australian VCs.

Thomas Caldwell died at Adelaide on 6th June 1969. He was cremated at Centennial Park Crematorium, Adelaide on 12th June 1969 and his ashes were interred in Wall 104, Row E, Niche 12. He is commemorated in a number of other places:

- Carluke, Lanarkshire, Scotland
  - Caldwell Road.
  - Caldwell House, Crawforddyke Primary School, Eastfield Road, opened in 1957.

Centennial Park Crematorium, Adelaide. Sir Donald George Bradman (1908–2001) was also cremated there. Bradman was the greatest cricket batsman of all time with a test batting average of 99.94.

- Four Famous Military Men of Carluke Memorial unveiled by the Rotary Club to commemorate the Millennium in 2000 – William Angus VC, Thomas Caldwell VC, Donald Cameron VC and Major General William Roy.
- The Lifestyle Centre on Carnwath Road, opened in October 2009, included a stained glass window dedicated to Major General Roy and Carluke's three VCs.
- A Department for Communities and Local Government commemorative paving stone was dedicated at Market Place on 31st October 2018.

The Famous Military Men of Carluke Memorial (Memorials to Valour).

- Memorial arch in Hamilton, Lanarkshire to the fifteen Lanarkshire VCs. The other VCs commemorated are – Frederick Aikman, William Angus, Donald Cameron, John Carmichael William Clamp, William Gardner, John Hamilton, David Lauder, Graham Lyall, David MacKay, William Milne, John O'Neill, William Reid and James Richardson.

William Angus VC. His story is told in the second book in this series, *Victoria Crosses on the Western Front, Second Ypres to the Eve of the Somme April 1915–June 1916.*

Donald Cameron was awarded the VC for an attack on the German battleship *Tirpitz*, when he was commanding the midget submarine X-6 in September 1943.

The plaque in the South Australian Garden of Remembrance, Centennial Park Cemetery.

- Memorial unveiled at Glasgow Central Station on 8th May 2022 honouring fifty-five VCs from Glasgow and the West of Scotland.
- Office of Australian War Graves plaque at South Australian Garden of Remembrance, Centennial Park Cemetery, Pasadena, Adelaide, South Australia (Wall 002, Row N).

In addition to the VC he was awarded the 1914–15 Star, British War Medal 1914–20, Victory Medal 1914–19, George VI Coronation Medal 1937 and Elizabeth II Coronation Medal 1953. The VC was presented to the Regiment by his widow on 4th February 1971 and was received by Major General Charles Dunbar CBE, Colonel of The Royal Highland Fusiliers. She was presented with a framed copy of the citation and a diamond regimental brooch. The VC is held by the Royal Highland Fusiliers Museum, 518 Sauchiehall Street, Glasgow, Lanarkshire.

The Royal Highland Fusiliers Museum on Sauchiehall Street, Glasgow. The building was purpose-designed for the leading Glasgow photographic firm of T & R Annan & Sons, by John Kepple of Honeyman, Keppie & Mackintosh. This Mackintosh was Charles Rennie Mackintosh (1868–1928), although he is not believed to have been involved with this building. Annan's was established in the 1850s and is first listed at 518 Sauchichall Street in the 1904–05 *Glasgow Post Office Directory*. In 1959 Annan's moved to West Campbell Street and the building was taken over as an Army recruiting office. In 1992–93 it was converted into a regimental museum.

271410 CORPORAL ROLAND EDWARD ELCOCK
11th Battalion, The Royal Scots (Lothian Regiment)

Roland Elcock was born on 5th June 1899 at 52 Alma Street, Wolverhampton, Staffordshire. His father, George Henry Elcock (1856–1906), born at Stourbridge, Worcestershire, was an iron bundler in 1871 and a general labourer in 1881, living with his mother. He married Fanny Johnstone née Jones (22nd November 1857–1945) in 1888 at Wolverhampton, where she was born. George was later a carpenter's machinist. They were living at 10 New Sun Street, Wolverhampton, Staffordshire in 1891 and at 52 Alma Street, Wolverhampton by 1899. Fanny was living there with her children in 1911. By 1939 she was incapacitated and was living with her daughter, Sarah Riley and family, at 52 Skidmore Avenue, Wolverhampton. Roland had five siblings:

- Florence Elizabeth Elcock (20th March 1889–3rd December 1962) was a domestic servant in 1911 at Park Hall, Sedgley, Staffordshire. She was a cook at Bedford Hotel, Llandudno, Caernarvonshire in 1939. She never married and was living at St Kilda Promenade, Llandudno, Caernarvonshire at the time of her death at The General Hospital, Llandudno.
- George Henry 'Harry' Elcock (23rd March 1890–8th May 1956) was an elementary schoolteacher in 1911, living with his mother. He served during the Great War as a sergeant in the Royal Warwickshire Regiment (306378) and was awarded the MM (LG 26th May 1917). He married Eliza Dale (3rd July 1889–10th January 1967), a printing machinist, in 1919. She was living with her parents at 3 Tremont Street, Wolverhampton in 1911. He was a schoolmaster in 1939, when they were living at 14 Naunton Park Road, Cheltenham, Gloucestershire. They were living at 518 Walsall Road, Great Barr, Birmingham, Warwickshire at the time of his death at Queen Elizabeth Hospital, Birmingham. Eliza was still living there at the time of her death at 18 Highcroft Road, Erdington, Birmingham. They had a son:
    - George Roland Elcock (born 28th February 1921) was a transport manager in 1939, living at 518 Walsall Road, Great Barr and was also an Air Raid Precautions Warden.
- Joseph Henry Elcock (9th May 1892–1971) was living with his paternal grandmother at the time of the 1901 Census. He was a Corporation destructor engine driver in 1911, living with his mother. He married Lucy Annie Langley (14th April 1890–1975) in 1926. By 1939 he was an electrical engineer and they

By tradition Wolverhampton is named after King Wulfhere of Mercia, who founded the Abbey of St Mary there in 659. Wolverhampton is the site of a battle between the victorious Mercian Angles and West Saxons against the raiding Danes in 910. In 985 King Ethelred the Unready granted lands to Lady Wulfrun by royal charter, which founded the settlement. In 994 a monastery was consecrated, which became the site for the current St Peter's Church. Wolverhampton is recorded in the Domesday Book in 1086 as a settlement of fifty households. Although a market was recorded in 1179, it was not granted a Royal Charter until 4th February 1258 by King Henry III. In the 14th and 15th centuries Wolverhampton was a staple town of the woollen trade. In 1512, Sir Stephen Jenyns, former Lord Mayor of London, who was born in Wolverhampton, founded Wolverhampton Grammar School. From the 16th century onwards, Wolverhampton became increasingly known for metal industries. The town suffered two Great Fires in April 1590 and September 1696, both of which started in today's Salop Street. On 27th January 1606, farmers Thomas Smart and John Holyhead were executed on High Green (now Queen Square) for sheltering two of the Gunpowder plotters. There is evidence that Wolverhampton was the location of the first working Newcomen Steam Engine in 1712. In the Industrial Revolution the town was a major centre for coal mining, steel production, lock making and the manufacture of cars and motorcycles. There were more than 200 bicycle manufacturers at the peak of the industry, which lasted from 1868 until 1975. None exist today. The modern economy is still based on engineering, including aerospace. The first railway reached Wolverhampton in 1837 on the Grand Junction Railway. As a result of the Reform Act 1832, Wolverhampton and twenty-one other towns were allocated two members of parliament. In 1866 Queen Victoria made her first public appearance after the funeral of her husband to unveil a statue in his memory in Queen Square. In 1918, Prime Minister David Lloyd George announced a General Election at The Mount, Tettenhall Wood. He also made his 'homes fit for heroes' speech at Wolverhampton Grand Theatre the same year. Mass council house building followed the Great War. England's first automatic traffic lights were installed in Princes Square in 1927. Historically part of Staffordshire, the town was incorporated as a municipal borough in 1848, a county borough in 1889 and in 1974 it became a metropolitan borough, transferring from Staffordshire into the newly formed West Midlands. Wolverhampton was granted city status on 31st January 2001. Amongst the famous people born or associated with the city are:

- Sir Edward Elgar (1857–1934), the composer, was an ardent Wolverhampton Wanderers fan.
- Baroness Rachael Heyhoe Flint OBE DL (1939–2017) was Captain of the English Cricket Team 1966–78 and was unbeaten in six Test series. She was captain when the team won the inaugural 1973 Women's Cricket World Cup. She was also the first female cricketer to hit a six in a test match and one of the first ten women to become a member of the MCC.
- Eric Idle (born 1943), actor, comedian, singer, musician, writer and former member of the Monty Python comedy group, attended the Royal Wolverhampton School as a boarder.
- Baron Mervyn Allister King of Lothbury KG GBE DL FBA (born 1948), Governor of the Bank of England 2003–13, attended Wolverhampton Grammar School.
- Denise Lewis OBE (born 1972) won gold in the heptathlon at the 2000 Sydney Olympic Games. She was also twice Commonwealth Games champion and the 1998 European champion.
- Ernest Thomas 'Bob' Lilley MM BEM (1914–81) was a founding member of the Special Air Service.
- John Enoch Powell MBE (1912–98) served in staff and intelligence posts during the Second World War and was promoted to brigadier. He represented Wolverhampton as its Conservative MP 1950–74 and was Minister of Health 1960–63. Powell is mainly remembered for his 'Rivers of Blood' speech in April 1968.
- William 'Billy' Ambrose Wright CBE (1924–94) spent his entire football club career with Wolverhampton Wanderers. He was the first footballer in the world to earn one hundred international caps. He made a total of 105 appearances for England and captained the national team ninety times, including in the 1950, 1954 and 1958 World Cup finals. His ashes were scattered on the pitch at Molineux.

were living at 2 Eagle Villas, Trench Road, Oakengates, Shropshire. Both their deaths were registered at Shrewsbury, Shropshire. They had two children:

- ◦ Norman Victor Elcock (12th June 1927–4th September 1978) married Patricia June Wadsworth (1926–7th October 2019) in 1949 at Fylde, Lancashire. She was living with her parents at The Croft, Mains Lane, Fylde in 1939 and later at Ridgeway House, Greenham, Newbury, Berkshire. Norman was a farm manager at Farm Gate, East Ilsley, Berkshire at the time of his death there. She was living at 19 Marshalls Court, Speen, Newbury in 2010. They had triplets – John S, Michael D and Richard L Elcock in 1951.
- ◦ Douglas John Elcock (5th January 1931–10th August 2009) married Sylvia Prior (31st December 1935–30th May 2011), born at Port Talbot, Glamorgan, in 1957 at Neath, Glamorganshire. She was living with her parents at 39 Prosser's Terrace, Cymmer, Port Talbot in 1939. They both died at Port Elizabeth, Eastern Cape, South Africa. They had two children – Elaine C Elcock 1961 and David J Elcock 1964.

- John William Elcock (4th January 1894–22nd May 1969) married Gertrude Rosecleer Atkins (20th January 1894–31st January 1988), born at Baldwell, Hertfordshire, on 8th November 1924 at Oakengates, Shropshire. He was an electrical maintenance engineer in 1939, when they were living at 65 Third Avenue, Wolverhampton. He was living at The Clive, Mossey Green, Telford, Shropshire at the time of his death. She was living at Palins Farmhouse, Adbaston, Staffordshire at the time of her death. They had two children:
  - ◦ Iris May Elcock (20th March 1926–1st January 2017) married John Thomas Wyeld Amos (19th February 1922–1st October 2001), born at Basford, Nottinghamshire, at Wellington, Shropshire in 1953, where she was born. John was living with his parents at 92 Kimberley Road, Basford in 1939. John died at Nottingham and Iris at Oldbury, West Midlands. They are believed to have had a son, Bryan R Amos, in 1962.
  - ◦ Claude 'Clive' Rutland Elcock (9th April 1931–5th January 2006) married Elizabeth Y Perkins (born 13th December 1924) in 1958 at Wellington, where they were both born. She was living with her parents at 21 Sunningdale, Hadley, Telford, Shropshire in 1939, when she was an assistant in a chemist's shop. The marriage ended in divorce. Elizabeth was living in Hereford, Herefordshire in the early 2000s. They had two children – Mark R Elcock 1960 and Edith C Elcock 1963. Claude emigrated to Ontario, Canada. He married Christine Dorothy Berry (21st February 1944–24th January 1998), born at Chester, Cheshire. She died at Toronto, Ontario and he at Markham, Ontario.
- Sarah Annie Elcock (19th September 1895–4th September 1976) was working in a lamp manufacturer's warehouse in 1911, living with her mother. She married Harold Claude Riley (7th July 1894–May 1979) in 1925. He was an errand boy in a shop in 1911, living with his parents at Bradmore, Wolverhampton. He

worked for Richard Shelton & Sons, Timber and Slate Merchants, Broad Street, Wolverhampton and qualified as a circular sawyer in 1914. Harold enlisted in the Royal Engineers on 9th December 1915 at Wolverhampton (213072), described as 5′ 8½″ tall, weighing 143 lbs and his religious denomination was Roman Catholic. He transferred to the Army Reserve next day and was mobilised on 9th November 1916. He was appointed a sapper skilled sawyer on 11th November and joined 1st Reserve Battalion RE, Chatham, Kent on 6th December. On 6th August 1917 he was posted to 6th Reinforcement Company and went to France. Harold joined 234th Field Company RE in 39th Division on 12th August. He was treated at 14th Convalescent Depot, Trouville 5th November–30th December and joined the RE Base Depot, Rouen next day. On 10th January 1918 he was posted to 29th Advanced Park Company and joined the RE Base Depot, Rouen on 2nd June. On 21st June he was posted to 80th Field Company RE in 18th Division. He was granted fourteen days' leave from 7th April 1919 and was posted to 32nd Lancashire Division in Germany on 28th April. On 30th April he transferred to 218th Field Company RE in 32nd Division. Harold was confined to barracks for two days for neglect of duty on 7th July and attended a course at the Cookery School, Cologne, Germany 13th August–2nd September. He was demobilised to the Class Z Reserve on 14th November 1919 at Chatham. He was a heavy wood machinist in 1939, when they were living at 52 Skidmore Avenue, Birches Barn Estate, Wolverhampton. Sarah was living at 34 Fountain Street, Leek, Staffordshire at the time of her death there. Harold emigrated to Australia and was living at 26 Wilding Street, Marsfield, New South Wales in 1977. He died at Ryde, NSW. They had a daughter:

- Kathleen M Riley (born 1927) married William Ronald Turner (1925–68) in 1947. William and Kathleen sailed to Sydney, NSW aboard SS *Esperance Bay*, departing Southampton, Hampshire on 2nd November 1951. Their last address in Britain was Kathleen's parents' home at 52 Skidmore Avenue, Wolverhampton. William died at Ryde, NSW. They had two sons – Timothy Turner 1948 and Anthony S Turner 1949.

Roland's paternal grandfather, Joseph Elcock (c.1825–70), born at Kingswinford, Staffordshire, married Eliza Elizabeth née Jones (c.1827–1901) in 1846 at Wellington, where she was born. He was a glass cutter in 1861, when they were living at 21 Chapel Street, Kingswinford. His death was registered at Stourbridge, Worcestershire. She was living with her children at The Green, Kingswinford in 1871 and at 60 Inkerman Street, Wolverhampton, Staffordshire in 1881. Also living with the family in 1881 was Eliza's granddaughter, Florence 'Florry' Anne Elcock (born 1872), born at Stourbridge. By 1891 Eliza had moved to 83 Inkerman Street and was still there in 1901. In addition to George they had six other children, all born at Kingswinford:

- Sarah Elcock (1847–79) was a domestic servant in 1871 living with her mother. She never married.
- Anne Elcock (born 1851) was a domestic servant in 1871 living with her mother. She may have died in 1878.
- Joseph Elcock (1853–84) was a glass cutter in 1871 and 1881 living with his mother.
- John William Elcock (1858–5th September 1939) married Emma Rebecca Peplow (1866–May 1948), born at Wellington, Shropshire, on 6th October 1889 at Holy Cross, Shrewsbury, Shropshire. He was a timekeeper for the Midland Carriage Works in 1901, when they were living at Midland Yard, Shrewsbury. By 1911 John was the landlord of the Omnibus Inn, Wombridge, Shropshire. They emigrated to Victoria, Australia and were living at Lake Street, Reservoir, Victoria when their son, Wilfred, enlisted in 1915. In August 1918 they moved to 12 Stanley Avenue, Auburn, Victoria. He died at Pascoe Vale, Victoria and she at East Brunswick, Victoria. They had seven children:
  - Joseph Harry/Harris Elcock (born and died 1890).
  - John William Elcock (born and died 1892).
  - John Robert Elcock (born and died 1893).
  - Winifred Lily Elcock (born 1895) is believed to have married Llewellyn Bawden in Victoria in 1917.
  - Harold Victor Elcock (1st November 1897–1977), a twin with Wilfred, married Dorothy Ivy Blankley (c.1907–40) in Victoria in 1936.
  - Wilfred Trevor Elcock (1st November 1897–1960), a twin with Harold, enlisted in the AIF (2028) at Melbourne, Victoria on 27th December 1915. He was described as a joiner's improver, 5′4½″ tall, weighing 115 lbs, with medium complexion, blue eyes, brown hair and his religious denomination was Church of England. He had served for two years in the Senior cadets and six months in the Citizens' Forces. He joined 24th (Depot) Battalion, Royal Park on 17th January 1916, transferred to 2nd (Depot) Battalion, Royal Park on 7th February, to the AIF Signal School on 6th March and to 3rd Reinforcements, 57th Battalion on 10th May. Wilfred embarked at Melbourne aboard HMAT A31 *Ajana* on 8th July and disembarked at Devonport on 31st August, joining 15th Training Battalion at Camp 26, Larkhill later the same day. On 31st December he embarked aboard SS *Princess Henrietta* at Folkestone and joined 5th Australian Division Base Depot, Étaples on 1st January 1917. He was taken on the strength of 57th Battalion on 4th January and was severely wounded by a gunshot to the right hand/arm on 13th February. He was treated at No.15 Casualty Clearing Station on 15th February and was moved by ambulance train next day to 1st Australian General Hospital, Rouen, arriving on 17th February. He was evacuated to England aboard HMHS *Grantully Castle* from Le Havre on 23rd February and was admitted to Reading War Hospital next day. He was discharged on leave on 11th June and reported to No.3 Command Depot, Hurdcott,

Wiltshire on 25th June. Medically he was upgraded to B1 on 26th June, to A3 on 4th July and transferred to the Overseas Training Depot, Perham Down on 6th July. Wilfred embarked at Southampton on 26th July and joined 5th Australian Division Base Depot, Le Havre next day. He rejoined the Battalion on 14th August but reported sick on 21st October. Having been treated at 8th Australian Field Ambulance and No.3 Canadian Casualty Clearing Station next day, he was transferred to 55th General Hospital, Boulogne on 23rd October. On 27th October he was evacuated to England aboard HMHS *Stad Antwerpen* and admitted to Norfolk War Hospital, Norwich with the old arm wound the same day. He was discharged on leave on 26th November and was ordered to report to No.1 Command Depot, Sutton Veny on 10th December. He was confined to barracks for four days and forfeited two days' pay for being absent without leave at Sutton Veny from 3.30 p.m. on 10th December until 5.00 p.m. on 11th December. He transferred to the Overseas Training Depot, Longbridge Deverill on 7th January 1918, to 3rd Training Brigade, Codford on 1st February, to 15th Training Battalion, Codford on 2nd February and joined 5th Division Signal School the same day. He transferred to 14th Training Battalion, Codford on 13th March and to No.2 Command Depot, Weymouth on 20th November. Wilfred embarked aboard SS *Takada* on 22nd December and returned to Australia on 11th February 1919. He was discharged from 3rd Military District on 21st March 1919. Wilfred married Ethel Mary Spence (1894–1986) at Ballarat, Victoria on 26th October 1933. They had a daughter, Marjorie Mary Elcock (3rd November 1937–14th July 2011). Wilfred enlisted in the Citizen Military Forces at Melbourne and served again during the Second World War (V81977).
    - Eileen Victoria Elcock (c.August 1913–5th February 1914), born and died in Victoria.
- Rebecca Elcock (1863–71).
- Albert Elcock (1867–1911) was described as an imbecile in the 1881 Census. He was a school cleaner in 1891 and a general porter in 1901.

His maternal grandfather, John Jones (22nd September 1801–1877), born at Broseley, Shropshire, was a widower in 1851 but his wife in not known. He married Fanny née Johnstone (c.1819–1912), born at Wellington, Shropshire, on 10th August 1851 at St Peter and St Paul's Church, Aston, Warwickshire. He was an engine tender in 1861, when they were living on Cleveland Road, Wolverhampton. By 1871 they had moved to 22 Chapel Place, Wednesfield, Staffordshire. Fanny was a charwoman living on her own at 27 East Terrace, Wolverhampton, Staffordshire in 1891 and was still there in 1901. By 1911 she had moved in with her daughter, Fanny. In addition to Fanny they had two other children:

- James Johnstone Jones (born 1854).
- Elizabeth Johnstone Jones (born 1856).

Broseley, Shropshire was linked to Coalbrookdale and Madeley over the River Severn by the world's first iron bridge in 1779. The Ironbridge Gorge is now part of a World Heritage Site. A settlement existed at Broseley at the time of the 1086 Domesday Book. In 1600 there were only twenty-seven houses but the area was increasing in importance. Evidence suggests that wooden wagonways existed as early as 1605, possibly the oldest railways in Britain. The wagonways were used to transport coal and clay and led to the huge expansion of the town during the Industrial Revolution. Broseley became a centre for iron making and pottery. The earliest known pipe-maker was working there in 1590. John Wilkinson constructed the world's first iron boat whilst living in the town and the plans for the Iron Bridge were drawn up there. However, the area suffered significant economic decline towards the end of the 19th century as industries moved elsewhere. In the latter part of the 20th century Broseley underwent a revival, but it still has fewer inhabitants than 200 years ago. Abraham Darby (1677–1717) developed a method of producing pig iron in a blast furnace burning coke rather than charcoal, which increased the temperature considerably. It was a major step forward in the Industrial Revolution. He is buried in the Quaker burial-ground at Broseley.

The origins of the Parish Church of St Peter and St Paul, Witton Lane, Aston are uncertain. There was a British Roman settlement there and the 1086 Doomsday Book valued Aston five times more than Birmingham. Aston Hall was constructed in 1618 and at that time the wealth came from agriculture. It was overtaken by Birmingham in the Industrial Revolution but, in the 19th century, it was also a centre of industry. It prospered until British industry collapsed at the end of the 20th century. The church probably dates from the 9th century but nothing of the original wooden building survives. It served a huge parish, with chapels of ease in Yardley, Water Orton and Castle Bromwich. The first masonry structure was completed in 1120 and it was reordered in 1480. The tower and spire remain from this church. The spire was renovated in 1776–77. The Church was reordered again in 1879 and there have been some gentle changes since. There are many notable monuments within the church including three chest tombs of the Arden family, ancestors of William Shakespeare. Two other tombs are associated with the Wars of the Roses (Oosoom).

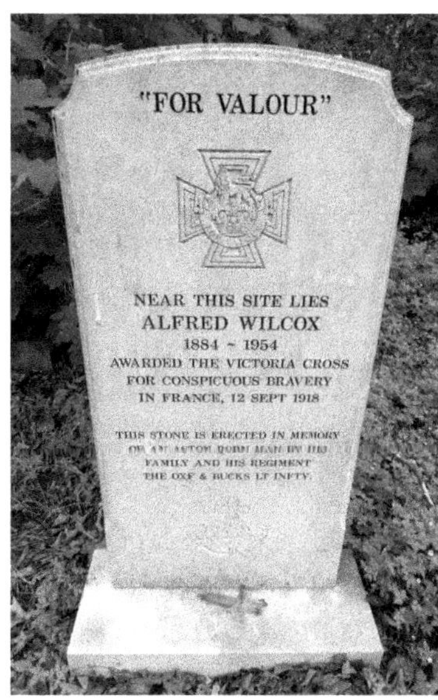

The churchyard is closed to burials and it was partly cleared in the 1950s. Within it are thirty-one CWGC headstones and the Aston War Memorial. To the north of the church is a gravestone dedicated to Alfred Wilcox VC on 12th September 2006, close to where he is buried. His story is told in the eleventh book in this series, *Victoria Crosses on the Western Front, Second Battle of Bapaume, August–September 1918* (Memorials to Valour).

Roland was educated at Causeway Lake School, Wolverhampton. He was employed as a clerk in the office of Alderman J Whitaker at the Labour Assembly Rooms, Queen Square, Wolverhampton. He enlisted in 6th South Staffordshire in October 1914 (3239) and went to France on 28th June 1915. When it was discovered that he was underage, he was sent home and discharged. Roland worked for the Corporation Electricity Works, Wolverhampton until he re-enlisted.

Roland enlisted in 11th Royal Scots in June 1917 (271410) and served in France and Belgium. **Awarded the MM for his actions prior to 5th June 1918, LG 13th November 1918. Awarded the VC for his actions at Capelle St Catherine, Belgium on 15th October 1918, LG 26th December 1918.** He was demobilised in 1919. The VC was presented by the King in the ballroom at Buckingham Palace on 13th February 1919. On 9th February he was presented with a gold pocket watch by the Mayor of Wolverhampton, Alfred George Jeffs.

Roland returned to work for the Wolverhampton Corporation Electricity Department. He attended the VC Garden Party at Buckingham Palace on 26th June 1920 and was one of the Honour Guard at the burial of the Unknown Warrior at Westminster Abbey on 11th November 1920. He moved to India, where he joined the Superior Telegraph Engineering Branch, Posts & Telegraph Service on 23rd November 1923. He became an Assistant Divisional Engineer of North West Frontier Province and the same appointment in the Punjab in October 1932, Burma in 1934 and of the Punjab & North West Frontier Province in 1937. He was promoted to Divisional Engineer of North West Frontier Province in 1940. While employed in Calcutta a rifle he was using jammed and a cartridge exploded in his face. An immediate operation saved his eyesight and prevented any lasting damage.

Roland married Amelia Rowe (1900–68), born at Cannock, Staffordshire, at Holborn Register Office, London on 7th July 1933. They were both living at the Hotel Russell, Russell Square, Bloomsbury at the time. She was living with her parents at 15 Alma Street, Wolverhampton in 1901. She was described as a domestic when she travelled from Southampton, Hampshire to the USA aboard SS *Caronia*, departing Southampton on 2nd October 1926 and arriving at New York on 9th October. She returned from New York to Plymouth, Devon or London aboard SS *Tuscania*, arriving on 23rd May 1927. Amelia was living at 34 Lower Wood End, Wolverhampton, Staffordshire in 1928 when she travelled to India aboard the P&O liner RMS *Maloja*, departing London on 21st September 1928. She returned aboard TSS *Jervis Bay*, departing Colombo and arriving in England on 6th April 1929.

They lived at 12 Goldthorn Road, Wolverhampton before sailing for India aboard RMS *Maloja*, departing London on 6th April 1934. Amelia returned to England with her daughter aboard SS *City of Canterbury* from Karachi, arriving at Plymouth, Devon on 14th April 1937, giving her intended place of residence as Florence House, Vicarage Road, Wednesfield, Staffordshire. They returned to Bombay aboard RMS *Viceroy of India*, departing London on 27th August 1938,

RMS *Maloja* was a P&O liner built by Harland & Wolff in Belfast. The previous SS *Maloja* was sunk by a German mine in 1916. RMS *Maloja* was launched on 19th April 1923 and, with her sister ship RMS *Mooltan*, gained a reputation for comfort and reliability. The two sister ships were the largest that could comfortably pass through the Suez Canal at the time. RMS *Maloja* commenced her maiden voyage on 2nd November. The two ships ran a fortnightly service between Tilbury and Sydney via Colombo and Melbourne. On 11th September 1939 *Maloja* was requisitioned by the Admiralty and converted into an armed merchant cruiser in Bombay, India. She joined the Northern Patrol between Shetland and Iceland as HMS *Maloja* (F26). On 13th March 1940 *Maloja* intercepted a ship southeast of Iceland claiming to be the Japanese *Taki Maru*. Adverse weather prevented a boarding party investigating but, when it cleared, it became clear that the vessel was the German *La Coruña*. The German crew scuttled her and were picked up by the British ship. On 6th November 1941 *Maloja* began troopship duty. She was part of a large convoy from Liverpool on 28th July 1942, bound for Calcutta, arriving on 19th September. In December she took Allied troops to North Africa after the Operation Torch landings. On 15th January 1947 *Maloja* was returned to P&O and underwent a refit at Royal Albert Dock, London. Following the independence of Indonesia in 1948, *Maloja* helped to repatriate Dutch civilians to the Netherlands until 1951. On 19th January 1954 *Maloja* arrived at Tilbury after her last voyage. She was broken for scrap at Inverkeithing, Scotland.

giving their address in England as 527 Stafford Road, Wolverhampton. They had a daughter:

- June Elcock (14th March 1934–1975) was born at Wolverhampton, Staffordshire. She sailed for England without her parents aboard SS *Mulbera* under the care of Mrs Mary Christina Gregory (see under her sister, Doris June Rowe, below), departing Calcutta, India and arriving at London in April 1935. Their intended address was Homeles, 158 Neachells Lane, Wednesfield, near Wolverhampton. They returned to Bombay aboard RMS *Strathmore*, departing London on 28th March 1936. June married Derek Owen (15th August 1935–January 2002), born at Stoke-on-Trent, in 1955 at Newcastle under Lyme, Staffordshire. He was living with his parents at 16 Trent Terrace, Stoke-on-Trent in 1939. Derek married Pauline I Heath née Cubley (born 1941) in October 1979. They lived at 64 Elldawn Avenue in later life. Pauline had married Frank Heath (9th March 1937–1978) in 1962. They were living at 135 Doxey Road, Stafford at the time of Frank's death there. Frank and Pauline had a son, Gary I Heath, in 1964. June and Derek had five children all born at Stoke-on-Trent, Staffordshire:
    - Robert P Owen (born 1956).
    - Christine A Owen (born 1957) is believed to have married Christopher Kinsella (born 1951) in 1980. They had a son, Christopher Marc Kinsella, in 1981.

- Peter J Owen (born 1959).
- Simon D Owen (born 1960) married Julie E Delves (born 1959) in 1979.
- Christopher Dominic Owen (born 1969) served in 1st Royal Scots (24794611) during the 1991 Gulf War.

Amelia's father, Samuel Walter Rowe (9th September 1876–17th December 1950), born at Ironbridge, Shropshire, married Florence née Fox (1876–1929), born at Brettell Lane, Wolverhampton, in 1898 at Cannock, Staffordshire. He was a coal hewer in 1901, when they were boarding at 15 Alma Street, Wolverhampton. By 1911 they had moved to 34 Lower Wood End, Wednesfield, Wolverhampton. He was described as a mining engineer when Amelia married in 1933. Samuel died at Handsworth, Birmingham, Warwickshire and Florence at Wolverhampton. In addition to Amelia they had another nine children:

- Alice Louisa Rowe (1898–1909), born at Cannock and died at Dudley, Staffordshire.
- Possibly Annie Rowe (born and died 1899), born at Cannock.
- Olive Rowe (26th March 1903–1982), born at Wolverhampton, married Robert Vincent Whittall (10th June 1899–1942) in 1925. He was living with his parents at 2 Hall Street, Sedgley, Staffordshire in 1911. He was a packer and she was a battery worker in 1939, when they were living at 54 Ridge Land, Wednesfield, Staffordshire. They had two children – Ada L Whittall (1925) and Dennis R Whittall (12th April 1930).
- Possibly Ernest Rowe (born and died 1905), born at Wolverhampton.
- May Rowe (6th May 1906–1972) married Thomas Turner (11th August 1905–20th March 1963) in 1928. They were living at 282 Wood End Road, Wednesfield in 1939, when he was a volunteer with Wednesfield Auxiliary Fire Service. They were living at 114 Mattox Road, Wednesfield at the time of his death there. Her death was registered at Wolverhampton. They had a son, William G Turner (18th April 1930).
- Eveline Ivy Rowe (born 1908), born at Dudley.
- George Rowe (2nd April 1911–1964), born at Wolverhampton, married Edith Gill (2nd December 1914–1985) in 1937 at Bilston, Staffordshire. He was an engineer's fitter in 1939, when they were living at 187 Wood End Road, Wednesfield. He was also a volunteer with the Wednesfield Auxiliary Fire Service. They had a daughter, Doris Rowe (born 22nd June 1919), a domestic servant in 1939, who later married as Gregory.
- Samuel Rowe (19th July 1915–1967) married Violet Florence Elkin (24th November 1911–February 1987) in 1938 at Wolverhampton. They were living with her mother at 77 First Avenue, Wolverhampton in 1939, by when Samuel was a heavy pump tester. They had a son, Christopher S Rowe, in 1947.

St Thomas's Church was built in 1840 and is the oldest church in Dehradun. It was constructed by thirteen soldiers of the East India Company in the Gothic style. In October 1940 Harry Rodger Webb was baptised in the church. He is better known as the singer, actor and philanthropist, Sir Cliff Richard.

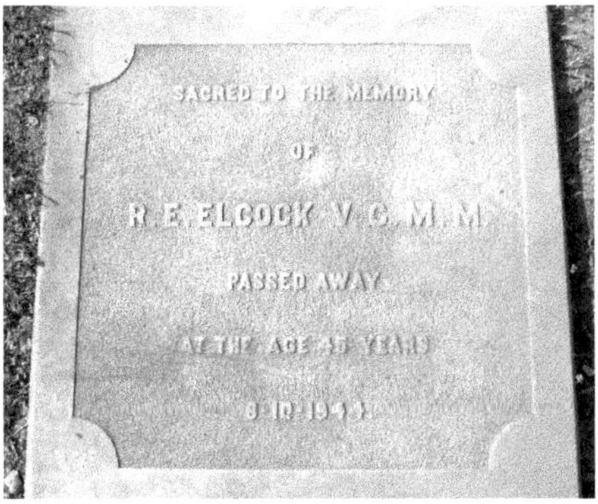

Roland Elcock's grave in St Thomas's Churchyard (Memorials to Valour).

- Doris June Rowe (22nd June 1919–October 1985) was a domestic servant in 1939, living with her brother, George and wife Edith. She married Percival 'Percy' Anderson Gregory (24th June 1912–July 1985), born at Medway, Kent, in 1941 at Bilston. He was the son of Charles Leonard Gregory, who served in the Royal Navy (1875–1956) and Mary Christina Anderson (1874–1963). George was a carpenter and joiner, living with his parents at 158 St Michael, Wednesfield in 1939. Doris and George had two children – John Anderson Gregory (2nd July 1941–9th July 2000) and June A Gregory (1945).

Roland Elcock died at Dehra Dun, North West Frontier Province, India on 6th October 1944. He is buried in St Thomas's Churchyard, Dehra Dun (Dehradun). He is commemorated in a number of other places:

- Wolverhampton
    - Roland Elcock House, Barnfield Road.
    - Book of Remembrance and VC Memorial in the concourse of the Civic Centre, St Peter's Square.

    - A Department for Communities and Local Government commemorative paving stone was dedicated at the Cenotaph, St Peter's Church Gardens, Exchange Street, on 15th October 2018.
- Edinburgh
    - A commemorative paver dedicated at The Royal Scots Club, 29 Abercromby Place by the Princess Royal on 11th March 2019 to mark the centenary of the Royal Scots Club.
    - Display at the Museum of the Royal Scots (The Royal Regiment), Edinburgh Castle.

The Department for Communities and Local Government commemorative paving stone in St Peter's Church Gardens, Wolverhampton (Memorials to Valour).

Amelia and June returned to England aboard RMS *Maloja*, departing Bombay and arriving at Southampton, Hampshire on 22nd October 1945. Their proposed address was 158 Neachells Lane, Wednesfield. Amelia undertook domestic work to earn a living. She died at Wolverhampton.

The Royal Scots Club in Edinburgh. The commemorative paver is outside the open door.

The King George V Silver Jubilee Medal commemorated the 25th anniversary of the coronation. 85,235 medals were issued, with a proportion to each Commonwealth country. The medals were awarded at the discretion of the local government, but in general went to members of the Royal Family and household, ministers, government and local government officials and members of the armed forces.

The Royal Scots Museum within Edinburgh Castle.

In addition to the VC and MM he was awarded the 1914–15 Star, British War Medal 1914–20, Victory Medal 1914–19, George V Silver Jubilee Medal 1935 and George VI Coronation Medal 1937. His daughter sold the medals to help with her mother's expenses. They were purchased by Major General Reginald Johnstone at Christie's on behalf of the Royal Scots for £650 on 18th February 1958. The VC is held by the Museum of the Royal Scots (The Royal Regiment), The Castle, Edinburgh, Midlothian, Scotland.

LIEUTENANT ROBERT VAUGHAN GORLE
A Battery, 50th Brigade, Royal Field Artillery

Robert Gorle was born on 6th May 1896 at 67 Victoria Road South, Southsea, Hampshire. His father, Major Harry Vaughan Gorle DSO (8th September 1868–28th December 1951), born at Poughill, Cornwall, was educated privately and joined the Royal Berkshire Regiment (Princess Charlotte of Wales's) from 4th (Militia) Battalion, Lincolnshire Regiment on 28th June 1890. He was promoted lieutenant on 29th September 1893 and transferred to the Army Service Corps on 1st October. Harry married Ethel Catherine née Archdall (26th September 1873–23rd November 1904), born at Queenstown, Co Cork, Ireland, on 27th June 1895 at Cork, where she subsequently died. He was promoted captain on 1st April 1898 and served in the South African War as Deputy Assistant Adjutant General October 1899–15th February 1900 and from 24th March 1902. He was present at the defence of Kimberley, where he was in charge of civilian and military supply services. He was also on operations in Orange River Colony May–29th November 1900, Cape Colony, north of the Orange River, in Orange River Colony March–31st May 1902 and Cape Colony 30th November 1900–March 1902. Harry was mentioned in Lieutenant Colonel Robert Kekewich's (Kimberley garrison commander) despatch of 15th February 1900 for the exceedingly onerous task of arranging victualling and supply of the garrison and 50,000 people in the town, LG 6th May 1900. He was also mentioned in Lord Roberts' despatch of 4th September 1901, LG 10th September 1901 and was awarded the DSO, LG 27th September 1901. This was presented by the Officer Commanding Troops, Kroonstad on 14th September 1902. Harry sailed from Cape Town for Southampton, Hampshire aboard RMS *Briton*, arriving on 5th November. He was promoted major on 3rd February 1905 and retired on 6th June 1908. He returned to South Africa and sailed for London from Durban aboard SS *Commonwealth*, arriving on 28th April 1914. Harry married Edith Mary Francis

(14th May 1877–22nd November 1954), born at St Thomas, Exeter, Devon, on 2nd June 1914 at Bridestowe, near Okehampton, Devon. She was the daughter of the Reverend John Loveband Francis (1844–1933), Rector of Bridestowe and Laura Jane Davies (1848–1918). Harry returned to South Africa again and sailed from Cape Town to Plymouth, Devon aboard SS *Llandovery Castle*, arriving on 13th November 1914. He was recalled, embarked aboard HT *Minnewaska* at Devonport, Devon on 9th August 1916, disembarked at Salonika on 20th August and served there with 37th Reserve Park (later 238th Company (14th South African Horse Transport Company)) from 22nd August. He was granted twenty-one days leave in Britain and proceeded to the Base Command Depot on 5th February 1918. He embarked aboard HT *Rose* for Taranto, Italy on 7th February and returned on the same ship, disembarking at Salonika from Taranto on 26th March. He rejoined 238th Company on 28th March. On 28th June he joined the Base Horse Transport Depot, Salonika for posting and embarked for Britain via Taranto on 3rd July. Harry was Mentioned in Despatches again, LG 11th June 1918. He was living in Northern Rhodesia (now Zambia) in March 1922. They were living at Oak Cottage, Beyton, Suffolk in 1939, when he was Head Warden of the Beyton Air Raid Precautions and she was in the Women's Voluntary Service. They were living at Marl Cottage, Beyton at the time of his death there. Edith was living at 205 Kentwood Hill, Tilehurst, near Reading, Berkshire at the time of her death at 10 Southcote Road, Reading. Harry Gorle had two other children from his second marriage:

Robert Gorle was born at 67 Victoria Road South, Southsea, on the right (The Move Market).

Poughill is mentioned in the Domesday Book. St Olaf's Church dates from the 14th century. There are a number of listed buildings in the village, including Burshill Manor and Church House, which date from the early 16th century. The Battle of Stamford Hill or Battle of Stratton, was fought during the Civil War on 16th May 1643 on the outskirts of Poughill. Each year, on the closest weekend to the anniversary, there is a re-enactment of the battle and a procession through the streets of Stratton village.

Cork or Cobh was known as Queenstown from 1849 until 1920 to commemorate a visit by Queen Victoria. The name changed to Cobh during the Irish War of Independence. The Royal Cork Yacht Club, established in 1720, is the oldest in the world. Cobh developed rapidly in the early 19th century. The harbour was an important naval base during the Napoleonic Wars and Great War. During the latter conflict the port was used by British and American vessels operating against U-boats. Q-ships also operated from there and it is believed that they were named because many were fitted out in Queenstown The Irish Naval Service still uses the port facilities. After the French wars the town became a health resort. Cobh saw the departure of the first steamship to sail from Ireland to England in 1821 and the first steamship to cross the Atlantic, the *Sirius*, in 1838. Cobh became a major transatlantic port and the departure point for two and a half million of the six million Irish who emigrated to America 1848–1950. On 11th April 1912 RMS *Titanic* made her final port call before setting out across the Atlantic and disaster. Of the 123 passengers who boarded at Queenstown, only forty-four survived. When RMS *Lusitania* was torpedoed and sunk off the Old Head of Kinsale on 7th May 1915, the survivors and the dead were brought to Queenstown. Over one hundred of the 1,198 who died in the disaster are buried in the Old Church Cemetery. Frederick Edwards (1894–1964), who was also awarded the VC in the Great War, was born in Queenstown. Cobh is also the birthplace of Roy Maurice Keane (born 10th August 1971), the joint (with Denis Irwin) most successful Irish footballer of all time. He won nineteen major trophies in his club career, seventeen of them with Manchester United.

- Joan Mary Partridge Gorle (1915–c.2008), born at Portsmouth, Hampshire, married Geoffrey Shaw Vincent (born 9th March 1896), a bank manager born at Clocolan, Free State Province, South Africa, in the mid to late 1930s. He arrived at Southampton aboard MV *Llangibby Castle* on 14th November 1932 from Mombasa, Kenya, giving his address in Britain as 84 Hillside Road, Streatham Hill, London. Joan and Geoffrey arrived at

The Distinguished Service Order, instituted by Queen Victoria on 6th September 1886, is usually awarded to majors (or equivalent) or above. In the past it was occasionally awarded to valorous junior officers. There were 8,981 awards in the Great War. The order recognised meritorious or distinguished service in war. Prior to 1943 the order could only be given to someone mentioned in despatches. Since 1993 the order has been restricted solely to distinguished service and not for gallantry. Although the DSO is now open to all ranks, it has yet to be awarded to a non-commissioned rank.

St Thomas (St Thomas the Apostle's) is a parish of Exeter on the western side of the River Exe. St Thomas became an urban district in 1894 and lasted until 1974. The mediaeval parish church was burned down in 1645 during the Civil War and had been rebuilt by 1657. An arcade survived from the earlier church of 1412. Additions were made c.1810 and 1829.

Bridestowe, where Harry Gorle married Edith Francis in 1914, is about ten kilometres southwest of Okehampton, on the edge of Dartmoor. St Bridget's Church has some Norman work but is mainly 13th and 15th century. Millaton House was the childhood home of Peter Alexander Rupert Carington, 6th Baron Carrington, Baron Carrington of Upton KG GCMG CH MC PC DL (6th June 1919 – 9th July 2018), Conservative politician and peer who served as Defence Secretary 1970–74, Foreign Secretary 1979–82 and NATO Secretary-General 1984–88.

Southampton aboard RMS *Pretoria Castle* on 17th March 1950, giving their address as c/o Major Gorle DSO, Earl Cottage, Beyton, near Bury St Edmunds. Geoffrey was described as a civil servant. They arrived at Southampton aboard RMMV *Capetown Castle* on 25th April 1952, giving their address as c/o Mrs Gorle, Earl Cottage, Beyton. They were living in Northern Rhodesia in 1952 and at 15 Oak Tree Road, Reading, Berkshire in 1955. Geoffrey predeceased Joan. She married her cousin, Richmond Ambrose Gorle (1910–71) in 1970 at Nuneaton, Warwickshire – see the fifth child of the paternal grandparents below. Joan later married Duncan Howson, who predeceased her. Joan had four children from her first marriage:

- David Vincent (born 1939) married Sue. They were living at Harare, Zimbabwe when his mother moved in with them after the death of her third husband. Sue was a widow living in Cape Province, South Africa by 2015.
- Diana Vincent (born 1941).
- Twins Josephine and Jacqueline Vincent (born 1949).

- Michael John Vaughan Gorle (1917–10th August 1945), born at Havant, Hampshire, was educated at Imperial Service College, Windsor, Berkshire, where he was a lance corporal in the Officers' Training Corps. He was commissioned in the Royal Berkshire Regiment, Supplementary Reserve of Officers on 3rd November 1937 and was granted a temporary commission in the Royal Army Service Corps on 19th June 1939 (73360). Michael was promoted lieutenant on 1st January 1941 and war substantive captain and temporary major on 16th January 1943. He relinquished his commission on account of ill-health on 18th July 1944 and was granted the honorary rank of major. He last appears in the Army List in September 1944. He was living at Oak Cottage, Beyton, Suffolk at the time of his death at Papworth Sanatorium, Cambridge and is buried in All Saints Churchyard, Church Road, Beyton. He is commemorated with five other men on a plaque in All Saints Church, which was dedicated on 10th October 1948. Although he appears on this war memorial, he is not commemorated by the CWGC.

Robert's paternal grandfather, Captain John Taylor/Tayler Gorle (26th September 1822–2nd August 1888), born at Birmingham, Warwickshire, was commissioned as an ensign in 10th Regiment of Foot. He was promoted lieutenant by purchase in 1842 and served in the Sutlej Campaign 1846, including the Battle of Sobraon. He was promoted captain by purchase on exchange into 28th Regiment of Foot on 17th December 1847. He exchanged into 40th Regiment of Foot on 17th May 1850. John married Frances née Moore (12th May 1826–24th December 1900), born at Saharanpur, India, on 15th November 1848 at Kempsey, Worcestershire. They were living at Ferryside, Carmarthen in 1857, at Welsh Street, Chepstow in 1859 and at Napleton House, Kempsey in 1861. John was appointed Commissioner for Land

In the early 19th century the Sikh Kingdom of the Punjab bordered the possessions of the British East India Company. From 1839 onwards persistent mutinies amongst the Sikh soldiers led the Company to build up forces on the border at Ferozepur. Diplomatic relations deteriorated and on 11th December 1845 the Sikhs crossed the Sutlej River in a pre-emptive attack. Initially the British were outnumbered and undersupplied, but the Sikhs did not press their advantage before the British reinforced their position. They drove the Sikhs back in a series of battles known as the Sutlej Campaign 1845–46 or the First Anglo-Sikh War. The Treaty of Lahore of 22nd February 1846 forced the Sikh Kingdom to surrender Kashmir to the East India Company and a British resident was established in Lahore. However, Sikh resentment resulted in a new war in 1847. The Sutlej Medal was issued to officers and men of the British Army and Honourable East India Company who served in the Sutlej Campaign 1845–46. The medal was the first to use clasps to denote different battles and the first in which the recipient is shown on the reverse of the medal. Further battles are indicated by a clasp. As Moodkee was the first battle no clasp was produced. Three clasps were awarded for Ferozeshuhur, Aliwal and Sobraon.

The distant Himalayas seen from Saharanpur in Uttar Pradesh, which is named after Saint Shah Haroon Chishti. The Maratha Army invaded the Saharanpur region in 1757 and it was ruled by the Maratha Empire until defeated by the British East India Company in 1803.

Tax on 6th August 1866 at Poughill, Cornwall. They moved to New Zealand and had a farm named Winterfold at Courtenay, Canterbury, where Frances played the organ in the church. They both died at their home at Metherell Tower, Bratton Clovelly, Devon. In addition to Harry they had ten other children:

- Henrietta Ann Gorle (March 1850–27th July 1929), born at Plymouth, Devon, married Thomas Hamilton Anson (27th March 1842–14th June 1894), born at Loodiana (Ludhiana), India (or Simla, Bengal, India), in New Zealand on 20th February 1872. He was the son of Major Frederick Walpole Anson (1806–48) and Catherine Hanson (1808–80), who married on 25th July 1827 at Agra, India. Frederick was the son of Lieutenant General Sir George Anson GCB, Governor of the Royal Hospital Chelsea (1769–1849) and Frances Constance Hamilton (1779–1834). Sir George commanded a cavalry brigade under the Duke of Wellington during the Peninsula War 1809–13 and was the Whig MP for Lichfield 1806–41. Frederick was commissioned in the Honourable East India Company and served for twenty-five years in India, ending up in 18th Bengal Native Infantry. Frederick died at Chelsea, London and is buried in the Royal Hospital Chelsea burial ground. Catherine and her son, Thomas, were boarding at 1 Bath Place, Bath Road, Cheltenham, Gloucestershire in 1851. Thomas was educated at Eton. He and his mother emigrated to Canterbury, New Zealand aboard the *Cressy* about 1860. Catherine subsequently died at The Desert, Courtenay, Canterbury. Thomas worked on Mr CJ Harper's Lake Coleridge station. About 1863 he entered into a partnership with John Karslake Karslake (1839–21st June 1872). They purchased the Waireka run in the Malvern district and a block of country on the Broken River from CJ Harper. They ran the property for two years before selling it in 1868 to Messrs Foster and Moore. They then purchased Mount Torlesse Station and ran it until Karslake's death. Thomas then ran Winterfold

Kempsey in the Malvern Hills District has a long history, with Iron Age and Roman remains in the area. Its name derives from Kemys, a Saxon chief, and the area was part of the Kingdom of Mercia. The village was recorded in the Domesday Book. The church of St Mary was built between the 12th and 15th centuries. A number of English Kings visited Kempsey, including Henry II in 1186. Henry III was there on 2nd August 1265, as a prisoner of Simon de Montfort, and Bishop Walter de Cantelupe said Mass for him in Kempsey church next morning. The death of de Montfort at the Battle of Evesham on 4th August 1265 ended the baronial opposition to Henry III. Edward I visited in 1276 and 1281. The population of Kempsey was reduced drastically during the Black Death, from 600 in 1299 to eighty-six in 1327. There were skirmishes in the area during the Civil War. A local tradition has it that Cromwell supervised the battering down of the old church and flattened the nose of every statue. There are bullet marks of the south side of the Church tower. The composer Sir Edward Elgar (1857–1934) lived in the village 1923–27.

Napleton House, built in the early 18th century, is reputed to be on the site of a Roman villa. The Georgian house was remodelled in Victorian times and was owned at one time by the Marquess of Blandford (BusinessLive).

at Courtenay, Rakaia, Canterbury with his family. He was chairman of the Courtenay School Committee 1873–74 and was appointed Commissioner of the Peace (NZ Gazette 8th March 1887). He held a number of other appointments including – Chairman of the Courtenay Road Board, President of the Courtenay Agricultural and Pastoral Association, member of the Selwyn Licensing Committee, Selwyn County Council, North Canterbury Education Board (chairman for two years) and the Appointments Committee of the Board. He was also a layman of Courtenay Anglican Church and conducted services there following the resignation of Reverend Collins. He twice contested elections for the House of Representatives unsuccessfully. In May 1894 Thomas discovered some oat sheaves on his property were alight at about 11.00 p.m. He fought the fire overnight and was drenched in the process. He left his home to attend a meeting of the Board of Education on 7th June but felt unwell and spent the night at Halswell. He joined the meeting the following morning but was taken seriously ill soon after and was moved to the home of James Brett at Fendalton. Dr Nedwill arrived shortly afterwards but, despite all efforts to save him, he died there on 14th June. Henrietta was living with some of her children at 41 Idris Road, Riccarton, Canterbury by 1928. She subsequently died there and was buried with her husband and daughter, Rachel, in St Matthews Courtenay Anglican Churchyard, Halkett Road, Christchurch. They had eleven children:

St Matthew's Church, Courtenay, where Frances played the organ.

- George Edward Northey Anson (18th March 1873–25th February 1940) married Margaret Emily Greenstreet (1864–1942) in 1891. They had a daughter, Janet Margaret Anson, in 1898.
- Violet Frances Woodville Anson (13th January 1875–2nd January 1938) married George Thompson Mulcock (1870–1944) in 1897. They had nine children – Alice Rubina Mulcock 1898, George Eric Mulcock 1899, Thirza Anson Mulcock 1901, Dorothy Heneretta Mulcock 1903, Helen Frances Mulcock 1905, Violet Rebecca Mulcock 1908, Barbara Everard Mulcock 1912, Georgina Beryl Mulcock 1913 and Lorna Jeanette Mulcock 1917.
- Aubrey Vernon Anson (27th October 1876–5th August 1956), a farmer, died at the public hospital in Christchurch. He left everything to his sister, Lorna Brook Anson. He and Lorna were living at 64 Jeffreys Road, Fendlaton when he made a will on 18th December 1930.
- Catherine Rose Hamilton Anson (22nd July 1881–22nd August 1948).
- Thomas Henry Karslake Anson (4th February 1883–11th November 1956) married Agnes Ida Dunlop (1893–24th October 1966) in 1914. They had at least three children – Rex Anson 1916, Agnes Joy Anson 1918 and Norman Ralph Anson 1920.
- Barbara Aimee Hope Anson (1885–1st June 1949) married Philip Tresillian Shand (1879–1965) in 1908. They had at least three children – Nora Frances Shand 1912, Philip Anson Shand 1915 and Ernest John Tressillian Shand 1920.
- Henrietta Rachael/Rachel Anson (9th September 1886–3rd May 1889).
- Alice Nona Anson (5th March 1888–16th March 1962) married John Harington Heathcote Dunkley (1878–1930) in 1917.
- Lorna Brooke Anson (9th November 1890–21st October 1965), a twin with Frederick, never married.
- Frederick John Granby Anson (9th November 1890–20th September 1978), a twin with Lorna, married Annie Elizabeth Bradbury at Christchurch on 17th January 1916. They lived at Bridle Path Road, Heathcote Valley, Canterbury and later at 136 Nayland Street, Sumners, Christchurch. He

enlisted at Christchurch on 8th February 1917 (53996), declaring previous service in A Company, Canterbury Infantry. He was described as a farmer, working for T Davies at Taneatau, 5′ 10″ tall, weighing 159 lbs, with light brown hair, blue eyes, fair complexion and his religious denomination was Church of England. He joined C Company, 28th Reinforcements on 30th April and G Company, 27th Reinforcements on 29th June. He forfeited one day's pay for being absent without leave 14th-15th July. On 16th July he embarked aboard HMNZT 11 *Athenic* (Troopship 88) at Wellington and disembarked at Liverpool on 16th September. He was posted to A Company, 5th (Reserve) Rifle Brigade, New Zealand Rifle Brigade, Tidworth, Hampshire the same day. He proceeded overseas from Brocton, Cannock Chase, Staffordshire on 23rd October and joined the New Zealand Infantry & General Base Depot, Étaples on 26th October. He joined C Company, 1st Rifle Brigade, NZRB on 2nd November. On 22nd November he was admitted to 7th General Hospital, St Omer from 3rd New Zealand Field Ambulance with measles and transferred to 7th Convalescent Depot on 3rd December. He was attached to the New Zealand Infantry & General Base Depot on 15th December and rejoined the Battalion on 13th January 1918. He was detached to 1st Field Company New Zealand Engineers on 12th March and rejoined the Battalion on 22nd March. He was wounded on 2nd September but initially remained with the Battalion. He was treated at 1st New Zealand Field Ambulance on 4th September. He was wounded again on 8th October and was admitted to 2nd and 3rd New Zealand Field Ambulance before rejoining the Battalion on 19th October. On 26th October he was admitted to 1st New Zealand Field Ambulance with diarrhoea and rejoined the Battalion on 2nd November. Frederick was granted leave in Britain 13th November–1st December and returned to Britain on 19th February 1919, joining at Sling Camp, Bulford, Wiltshire on 3rd March. A discharge medical there on 26th March found no disability from his war service. On 1st April he embarked aboard HMNZT 10 *Arawa* for return to New Zealand, arriving on 15th May. He was discharged on 12th June 1919. He was living at 101 Waghorne Street, Ahuriri, Napier in May 1965, when he applied for replacement medals.

- Ralph Whakatane Anson (11th June 1892–8th October 1918) enlisted in the New Zealand Expeditionary Force on 3rd October 1917 at Christchurch (72052). He was described as a dairy farmer, 5′ 8½″ tall, weighing 126 lbs, with fresh complexion, blue eyes and his religious denomination was Church of England. He was serving in 1st Canterbury Regiment and his address was Bridle Path Road, Heathcote Valley. He was granted leave to 12th November and was then on home service at Trentham. His service reckoned from 4th February 1918 with A/38th and he transferred to A/37th on 26 April. He commenced active service on 2nd May and embarked at

Wellington aboard HMNZT 103 *Maunganui* on 9th May, disembarking at Liverpool on 24th June. He joined the New Zealand Rifle Brigade Reserve Depot at Brocton, Cannock Chase, Staffordshire the same day and went to France on 11th September. He joined the Depot, Étaples on 13th September and A Company, 1st Battalion NZRB on 17th September. Ralph was killed in action on 8th October and was buried on 20th October in Hilltop Cemetery, 6,400m south-southeast of Cambrai. His remains were later moved to Naves Communal Cemetery Extension, France – III C 15.

The grave of Robert's cousin, Ralph Whakatane Anson, in Naves Communal Cemetery Extension.

- Frances Elizabeth Gorle (1851–28th February 1933), birth registered at Upton upon Severn, Worcestershire. Inexplicably her birthplace was recorded as Sardinia, Nice (the former part of Italy and the latter in France) in the 1861 Census, as Nice, France in 1901 and Italy in 1911. In each case her age consistently indicates birth c.1853 and one source gives the date as 27th April 1853. The discrepancy cannot be explained. She accompanied her parents to Upper Riccarton, Christchurch, New Zealand and married Henry Vernon Anson (20th February 1852–29th May 1914), an accountant born at Longford, Derbyshire, at Courtenay on 10th March 1875. They returned to England and were living at 8 Diamond Terrace, Greenwich, London in 1901 and at 88 Vanbrugh Park, Blackheath, London in 1911, by when he was a civil servant. He died at Kidbrook Nursing Home, Shooters Hill, Blackheath and she at Kempsey, Worcestershire. They had seven children, six of them born at Christchurch, New Zealand:
  - John Anchitel Anson (16th May 1876–9th May 1966) was an engineer in 1911 living with his parents. He was commissioned in the Royal Engineers (Militia), Western Division (Submarine Miners) and embodied on 11th June 1900. He was disembodied on 13th October and was employed at Home 5th February–27th March 1901. He was seconded for service with the Mounted Infantry in South Africa 28th March or 6th May 1901–6th December 1902. Promoted lieutenant on 19th October 1901 and was returned to the establishment on 7th December 1902. John attended fifty-days days training in 1903 and again in 1904. Assistant Electrical Engineer, Public Works Department, Southern Nigeria 21st March 1908. He last appears in the Army List in January 1908 and transferred to the Special Reserve on 26th August 1908. Promoted captain on 11th June 1910. Re-employed in the Army from 5th August 1914. He was assigned to HMS *Victory* for the Royal Naval Division on 7th October 1914 but this was cancelled on 28th October.

He was living at Brookholme, Vanbrugh Park, Blackheath, London in 1916. He served with the Egyptian Army from 29th March 1918. Promoted major on 27th August 1918 and last appears in the Army List in March 1925. In the 1939 Register he is recorded as having served for seven years as a major with the Egyptian Army prior to 1939. At the time he was living with his sisters, Mildred and Mabel, at Melbury, New Road, Upton upon Severn, Worcestershire. John married Winifred Gilbanks (28th October 1902–10th September 1992), born at Market Bosworth, Leicestershire, on 18th October 1955 at Kempsey, Worcestershire. He was living at 73 Main Road, Kempsey at the time of his death there.

- Henry Percy Richmond Anson (20th October 1877–25th May 1915) married Lilian Mary Daw (30th August 1888–24th November 1977), born at Buttevant, Co Cork, Ireland, on 28th July 1909 at St John the Evangelist, Blackheath, Kent. She was the daughter of Thomas Daw MBE (1859–1920). Henry and Lilian lived at Little Felcourt, East Grinstead, Sussex. Henry was appointed ensign in 3rd Middlesex (Militia) on 8th January 1900 and was granted a regular commission on 21st April. He served in the East Indies from 14th September 1900 and was promoted lieutenant on 26th February 1901. He was appointed acting paymaster 26th May 1901–31st March 1904 and completed the Controllers Class in Madras, qualifying as a paymaster on 30th July 1901. He qualified for mounted infantry at Bangalore. He was acting paymaster again 1st July–31st August 1904 and acting adjutant at Meiktila 19th November 1904–11th March 1905. After being granted leave in Britain 13th March–9th August 1905, he returned to India and was appointed adjutant 20th August 1905–19th August 1908. Promoted captain on 4th July 1906 and joined the Regimental Depot on 5th November 1908. Henry was appointed Adjutant, 8th Battalion (TF) on 2nd January 1912 and went to France with 1/8th Middlesex on 8th March 1915. He was killed in action on 25th May 1915 and is buried in Potijze Chateau Lawn Cemetery, Belgium – A4. Lilian never remarried and died at Faithfull House Care Home, Suffolk Square, Cheltenham, Gloucestershire. Henry and Lilian had a son, Patrick Anchitel Richmond Anson (1914–29th September 1944). Patrick was commissioned from the Royal Military College, Sandhurst into the Middlesex Regiment on 1st February 1934 (62643) and was promoted lieutenant on 1st February 1937 and captain on 1st February 1942. He undertook parachute training at RAF Ringway (now Manchester Airport) 10th-24th February 1942 with the newly formed 4th Parachute Battalion and joined 10th Battalion, The Parachute Regiment at Kabrit Air Base, Egypt in January 1943. He commanded A Company, 10th Battalion on Operation Market Garden, during which his Dakota transport aircraft was shot down near Dodewaard, Netherlands on 18th September 1944. He jumped from the stricken aircraft and made his way over the Rhine on the night of 24th/25th

September. He was wounded during the crossing and was taken prisoner. Patrick died of wounds at Stalag XIB, Fallingbostel, Germany and was buried in a cemetery near the camp. His remains were moved later to Becklingen War Cemetery, Germany (4 E 12).

The grave of Robert's cousin, Henry Percy Richmond Anson, in Potijze Chateau Lawn Cemetery.

- Frances Octavia Anson (born 9th April 1879) was living with her parents in 1901. She married Edwin Turner (born c.1887), an engineer, on 12th July 1908 at St Matthew Church, Hammersmith, London.
- George Okeover Anson (8th August 1880–20th November 1977), a bank clerk and later a bank manager, was living with his parents in 1901 and 1911. He was employed at the London & Westminster Bank, Bank House, Russell Hill Road, Purley, Surrey (later 106a High Road, Kilburn, London), when he joined the Royal Naval Reserve on 17th May 1904 as acting assistant paymaster. He was examined for confirmation in rank on 24th November 1905. George was under instruction aboard various ships – HMS *Empress of India* 15th August–4th September 1904, *Cornwallis* 21st July–8th August 1905, *Prince George* 25th October–10th November 1906, *Hindustan* 6th-26th March 1907 and 23rd July–7th August 1908, under instruction 18th-29th October 1909, *Agamemnon* from 20th March 1910, *Africa* 14th September–4th October 1911, *Orion* 12th-25th May 1912, *St Vincent* 19th July–3rd August 1913, Mercantile Fleet Auxiliary *Bristol* 2nd August 1914 and *Scilly Isles* from 5th September 1915. Appointed paymaster 2nd May 1917 antedated to 17th May 1914. He was demobilised on 2nd June 1919 and was awarded the Decoration for Officers of the Royal Naval Reserve on 4th February 1921. George served aboard HMS *Valiant* 20th May–2nd June 1922 and was promoted paymaster commander on 30th June. He served aboard HMS *Dido* 8th-21st August 1925, *Marlborough* 20th August–2nd September 1928 and transferred to the Retired List due to age on 8th August 1930. George married Margaret Hazelrigg (11th August 1885–19th November 1956), born at Noseley Hall, Noseley, Billesdon, Leicestershire, on 10th October 1914 at Greenwich, London. They were living at 126 Goring Road, Worthing, Sussex in 1939, where Margaret subsequently died. George was living at Briar Patch, Treluswell, near Penryn, Cornwall at the time of his death there.
- Archibald Anson (8th March 1882–31st August 1965), a bank clerk, was living with his parents in 1901. He married Mabel Biggs (27th January

1888–1959), born at Bromley, Kent, at St Matthew's Church, Denmark Hill, London on 24th December 1907. He was an inscribed stock clerk with the London County & Westminster Bank Ltd head office when he enlisted in the Inns of Court OTC, 10 Stone Buildings, Lincoln's Inn, London on 8th December 1916 (9824) and transferred to the Army Reserve next day. He was mobilised on 1st November and applied for a commission on 8th December, described as 5′ 7¼″ tall and weighing 120 lbs. Mabel was living at 7 Dacre Park, Lee, London. Archibald joined the Army Service Corps Cadet School, Grove Park, Lee on 12th February 1917 and was commissioned in the ASC on 11th April. He joined the Mechanical Transport Depot, Bulford, Wiltshire on 18 April. On 20th April he embarked at Southampton, disembarked at Le Havre next day and embarked aboard HT *Transylvania* at Marseille on 3rd May. *Transylvania* was torpedoed and sunk next day with the loss of 412 lives. Archibald was rescued and taken to Savona, Italy. He embarked aboard HMS *Kashmir* at Marseille on 3rd June and disembarked at Alexandria on 11th June. He joined 907th Mechanical Transport (Auxiliary Petrol) Company ASC, Egyptian Expeditionary Force and moved with the unit to Alexandria on 12th June and to Palestine on 31st October. Promoted lieutenant on 11th October. He joined the Base Horse Transport Depot, 137th Company, Kantara on 13th June 1919 and was treated for dysentery at 24th Stationary Hospital 26th June–5th July. On 19th July he embarked for demobilisation aboard HT *Goentoer* at Port Said. Archibald was demobilised from the Dispersal Unit, Crystal Palace on 5th August 1919, giving his address as 22 Queen's Road, Tunbridge Wells, Kent. He relinquished his commission on 1st September 1921, retaining the rank of lieutenant. Archibald was a bank custodian in 1939, when they were living at Farnborough Hill, Hill Brow, Orpington, Kent. Her death was registered at Eastbourne, Sussex. He was living at 15a Headland Avenue, Seaford, Sussex at the time of his death at 10 Park Road, Seaford on 31st August 1965. They had four children – Dahlia Anson (23rd September 1908–4th June 1986), Donald Archibald Vernon Anson (15th April 1910–25th April 1995), who was commissioned in the King's Royal Rifle Corps in February 1940 (117900), Anchitel Vivian Anson (28th February 1912–24th March 2011) and Iris Mabel Anson (29th August 1925–2001).

  - Mildred Anson (7th January 1885–13th November 1964) never married and was living at 71 Main Road, Kempsey at the time of her death there.
  - Mabel Muriel Gladys Anson (11th November 1891–13th December 1983), born at Plymouth, Devon, never married and was living at 49 Hanley Road, Malvern Wells, Worcestershire at the time of her death there.

- John Macartney Gorle (born 1855), born on the Isle of Wight, Hampshire, is believed to have died young.

- Rachel Mary Gorle (1857–13th June 1931), born in Carmarthenshire, was baptised on 7th April 1857 at St Ishmael's Church, Ferryside. She was living with her brother, Richmond, in 1901. She never married and was living at Napleton, Zeal Monachorum, Devon at the time of her death there.
- Richmond Edward Gorle (December 1858–30th December 1935), born at Chepstow, Monmouthshire, was a farmer, living at Metherell Tower, Bratton Clovelly, Devon in 1901 and 1911. He married Hilda Mary Heath (22nd May 1880–2nd December 1960) born at St Leonards, near Hastings, Sussex, in 1909, registered at Okehampton. She was living with her parents at 16 Warrior Square, Hastings in 1881 and 29 Warrior Square in 1891. Richmond and Hilda were living at Rosehill, North Tawton, Devon at the time of his death there. She was still living there in 1939, by when her bachelor brother, Wilfrid Heath (1884–1971), had joined her. He was involved with Air Raid Precautions. Hilda died at Kenwyn Nursing Home, Crediton, Devon. Richmond and Hilda had a son:
    - Richmond Ambrose Gorle (17th February 1910–28th March 1971), born at Bratton, Devon, was a cadet at the Royal Military Academy, Woolwich and was commissioned in the Royal Artillery on 30th January 1930 (44862). He was promoted lieutenant on 30th January 1933, captain on 1st August 1938, major on 1st July 1946 and lieutenant colonel on 12th April 1952. He was a captain serving with the RA Coast Artillery Training Centre, Royal Citadel, Plymouth, Devon in 1939, living at 1 Hoe Park Terrace, Plymouth, Devon. He was Mentioned in Despatches for gallant and distinguished service in the Middle East, LG 6th April 1944 and was awarded the MC for gallant and distinguished service in North West Europe, LG 5th April 1945. He retired on retired pay on account of disability on 11th December 1957. Richmond married Frances Audrey Hawkshaw Croysdale (born 29th February 1908), born at Walton-on-Thames, Surrey, in 1935 at Okehampton, Devon. She was known as Audrey and was living with her parents at Canfield, Esher Avenue, Walton-on-Thames, Surrey in 1911 and Beara Court, Highampton, North Devon in 1917. Her father, John Hawkshaw Croysdale (1878–1957), a retired barrister, enlisted in the Devonshire Regiment at Okehampton on 28th August 1916 (38071) and transferred to the Army Reserve on 29th August. He was mobilised on 18th September and transferred to the Army Pay Corps (8694). He was commissioned in the Army Service Corps on 29th July 1917 and served in France from 7th August with No.9 Detail Issue Store and No.7 Lines of Communication Supply Company. He was demobilised from the Dispersal Unit, Crystal Palace and relinquished his commission on 17th October 1919, retaining the rank of lieutenant. At the time of the 1939 Register Frances was living with her parents at Lambert House, Okehampton. Audrey and Richmond had three children – Rosemary Ann Ruth Gorle (1936–2016), Peter John Taylor Gorle (born 1938) and Felicity M Heather Gorle (born 1944). When Audrey arrived at Southampton from

New York, aboard the Cunard-White Star liner RMS *Queen Elizabeth*, on 4th April 1950 with three of her children, her address was given as Widemouth Bay, Bude, Cornwall. Richmond married his cousin, Joan Mary Partridge Gorle, in 1970 at Nuneaton, Warwickshire. He died at Bramcote Barracks, Nuneaton, Warwickshire.

- Rosa Myra Gorle (1860–14th February 1937), birth registered at Upton upon Severn, was a spinster living at Napleton, Zeal Monachorum at the time of her death there.
- Ambrose Gorle (1862–6th September 1930), a twin with Elinor, whose birth was registered at Stratton, Cornwall, was a farmer in 1901 living with his brother, Richmond. He married Hilda Mary Moore (January 1871–30th December 1958) on 25th September 1907 at Romiley, Cheshire, where she was born. They were living at Desford, Leicestershire in 1911. He was living at Wickland Farm, Forest Green, near Ockley, Surrey at the time of his death there. She was still living at Wickland Farm at the time of her death at the Surrey County Hospital, Guildford, Surrey. They had two daughters:
  - Dorothy Gorle (19th November 1909–1979) never married.
  - Eleanor Gorle (1913–52) never married.
- Elinor Gorle (born and died 1862), a twin with Ambrose.
- Phyllis Gorle (9th October 1864–18th February 1948), born at Poughill, Cornwall, married the Reverend Henry Collins (22nd April 1849–22nd February 1895), born at Hampstead, London, in New Zealand on 16th September 1882. They returned to England and he was Rector of Luffincott, Devon at the time of his death at St Andrew's Hospital, St Giles. Phyllis was living with her children at Breach House, Westbourne, Sussex in 1901 and was still with them in 1939, living at Pages Farm, Glen Faba, Roydon, Essex. She subsequently died there. They had three children:
  - Henry John Collins (born 17th April 1885), born at Smithfield, New Zealand, was a divorced dairy farmer in 1939.
  - Rachael Frances Myra Collins (31st March 1887–1955), born at Rakaia, New Zealand, died a spinster at Margaret's Hospital, Epping, Essex, while living at Glen Faba, Low Hill, Roydon, Essex.
  - Phyllis Muriel Collins (25th August 1889–1962), also born at Rakaia, was a spinster in 1955.
- Louisa Gorle (10th December 1866–16th September 1903), birth registered at Stratton, Cornwall, was a spinster living at Metherell Tower at the time of her death there.

His maternal grandfather, the Reverend Canon William Frederick Archdall (4th February 1835–19th November 1916), born at Wicklow, Ireland, was the son of Lieutenant William Frederick Archdall and Elizabeth Henry. The surname has also been seen as Archdale. He graduated from Trinity College, Dublin University (MA)

Trinity College Dublin dates back to 1592. In the 18th century it was regarded as a Protestant establishment. Catholics were allowed to apply for admission from 1793, but it was not until 1873 that religious tests were abolished. Irish Catholic bishops imposed a ban on Catholics entering Trinity College, which was not rescinded until 1970. Women were admitted as full members in 1904. Following independence, Trinity College had a cool relationship with the new Irish state but thrives today, with student numbers doubling by the 1990s. In 1991 Thomas Noel Mitchell became the first Roman Catholic elected Provost of Trinity College.

and was ordained deacon in 1861 and priest in 1862. He was appointed Curate at Portadown, Co Armagh in 1861, at Lislee, Co Cork in 1863, at Kanturk, Co Cork in 1869 and at Clonmel, Co Cork in 1872. He was the Rector of Glanmire, Rathcooney, Co Cork 1874–1913 and was Prebendary of Killaspugmullane in 1883. William married Constance/Constancia Riall Sarah née Smith (16th November 1843–23rd July 1910), born at Stradbally with Clones & Ballylanheen, Co Waterford, Ireland, on 8th October 1872 at Queenstown, Co Cork. They were living at Dunkettle, Cork in 1901 and 1911. She died at Glanmire Rectory, Rathcooney, Co Cork and he was living at The Grove House, Pembroke, Passage West, Cork at the time of his death there. In addition to Ethel they had at least two other children:

- Constance Henrietta Archdall (born 10th May 1877), born at Glanmire Rectory, was a spinster in 1916.
- Grace Ramsay Archdall (4th May 1880–24th June 1938) married Captain John William Dustan (1st December 1873–2nd July 1917), born at Malta, at Glanmire Church, Rathcooney, Co Cork on 31st December 1902. He was living with his widowed mother at Paul Mill Road, Oak Land, St Saviour's, Jersey, Channel Islands in 1891. He was commissioned in the Royal Marine Light Infantry on 1st September 1892 and attended the Royal Naval College 30th September 1892–30th June 1893. He joined the Chatham Division and was promoted lieutenant on 1st July 1893. John served aboard HMS *Resolution* in the Channel from 5th December 1895 and rejoined the Chatham Division on 18th December 1897. He embarked aboard SS *Ceylon* for service on the China Station with HMS *Centurion* on 17th September 1898. He was promoted captain on 15th March 1900 and was mentioned in Commander-in-Chief, China Station's despatch of 8th July 1900 (LG 5th October 1900). John was also awarded the China War Medal 1900 with clasp 'Relief of Pekin'. He joined the Portsmouth Division on 27th July 1901, HMS *Empress of India* for *Thames* on 23rd April 1902 and HMS *Aeolus* (Queenstown) on 16th September. He

returned to the Portsmouth Division on 19th June 1903 and joined HMS *Suffolk*, Channel Fleet on 28th June 1904 and HMS *Vulcan* in the Mediterranean on 6th February 1905. He returned to the Portsmouth Division on 21st February 1905 and joined HMS *Duncan*, Channel and Atlantic Fleets, on 7th June 1906 before returning to the Portsmouth Division again on 6th March 1908. He joined HMS *Cormorant* as Commandant Ascension Island on 4th April 1908 and returned to the Portsmouth Division on 13th May 1910. Promoted major on 17th May 1911. Grace and John were living at Brockenhurst, Hampshire that year. He joined the Chatham Division on 1st November 1911, HMS *St Vincent*, 1st Battle Squadron, Grand Fleet on 10th January 1913 and the Chatham Division on 13th October 1915. John retired on 11th January 1917 due to ill-health contracted on active service and was granted retired pay of £260 p.a. He died at his home at The Patch, Hunton Bridge, Abbots Langley, Hertfordshire. Grace was living at Lavaglan, Newberry Road, Combe, Martin, Ilfracombe, Devonshire at the time of her death there. They had a son:

- John Anthony Ramsay Dustan (born 27th December 1903–c. 1978).

Robert was educated at The Wells House, Malvern Wells, Worcestershire and Rugby School, Warwickshire until August 1911. He became a farmer in the Transvaal, South Africa and returned to Britain on the outbreak of war.

The Wells House School was a preparatory school founded in 1860 by the Reverend William Wilberforce Gedge. Originally in Cheltenham and named Stamford House, he moved the School to Malvern Wells in 1870, to occupy a hotel and took its name from it, The Wells House. Edward Elgar was a music teacher there. Gedge remained Head until 1889. Ownership of the school was transferred to an educational trust in 1961 and girls were admitted from 1974. The School closed in 1991 and has been converted into apartments. Famous alumni include chef Rick Stein and Lord Robin Janvrin, who was the Queen's Private Secretary. The School is the large building halfway up the surrounding Malvern Hills.

Rugby School was founded in 1567 as a free grammar school for local boys and is one of the oldest independent schools in Britain. It was transformed by Headmaster Thomas Arnold 1828–41 and was regarded as the forerunner of the Victorian public school. In 1845 a committee of Rugby schoolboys wrote the 'Laws of Football as Played at Rugby School', the first published laws for any code of football. The School was regulated as one of the seven schools included in the Public Schools Act 1868. In 1975 the first girls were admitted. School legend has it that pupil William Webb Ellis was the first to pick up a football and run with it, thus inventing the sport of rugby. However, there is only one source for the story, a former pupil who was not a contemporary of Webb Ellis. There were no standard rules for football in Webb Ellis's time at Rugby (1816–25) and most varieties involved carrying the ball. Rugby Fives, a handball game derived from Wessex Fives, is still played. The School has produced a number of Test and County cricketers. Amongst its other famous alumni are numerous senior military men, the poet Rupert Brooke, actor Sir Anthony Quayle, explorer Frederick Courteney Selous, statesman Austen Chamberlain and Prime Minister Neville Chamberlain. Amongst famous sportsmen are Chris Brasher, the 1956 Olympic gold medallist, pace-setter for Roger Bannister's first sub-four minute mile and co-founder of the London Marathon. Tom Wills, who invented Australian Rules football also attended the School. As did Thomas Hughes who wrote the semi-autobiographical *Tom Brown's Schooldays*, which included the fictional character Harry Flashman.

Robert applied for a commission on 19th April 1915 and was commissioned on 15th May into 161st Brigade, Royal Field Artillery, 31st Division. He was described as 6′ 1½″ tall and weighed 156 lbs. Before 31st Division embarked for Egypt, all the artillery units left it on 2nd December and assembled at Larkhill, Wiltshire. Between 30th December 1915 and 3rd January 1916 they moved to France to join 32nd Division. Robert sailed for France on 31st December 1915. He was wounded by a gunshot in the left arm on 3rd July 1916 and was evacuated to England the next day on HMHS *Egypt* from Le Havre to Southampton, arriving on 5th July. He was treated at 1st London General Hospital, Camberwell from 6th July. A medical board there on 31st July found him unfit for any service for two months and he was granted leave until 30th September at The Grove, Passage West, Co Cork. He then transferred to Assistant Director Medical Services, Cork District, Irish Command. A medical board at the Central Military Hospital, Cork on 9th October found him unfit for General Service for one month but fit for Home Service. On 23rd October he joined 23rd Artillery, 5th B Reserve Brigade at Ballincollig, Ireland. A medical board at the Central Military Hospital, Cork on 9th November found him fit for General Service. He was promoted lieutenant on 1st July 1917.

On 5th October he was wounded by a shell in the right back and top of the right arm near Ypres. A fragment was removed at 5th British Red Cross Hospital, Wimereux on 10th October. It is not known when Robert transferred to 50th Brigade

SS *Egypt* (7,912 tons) was built by Caird & Co at Greenock on the Clyde for the Peninsular & Oriental Steam Navigation Co. She was launched in 1897 and ran between Britain and India, carrying 301 first and 208 second class passengers. She was converted into a hospital ship during the Great War. After being refitted, she re-entered service in 1921. On 20th May 1922 *Egypt* collided with SS *Seine* in dense fog off Ushant. *Egypt* sank in twenty minutes with the loss of eighty-six lives. Gold bullion valued at £1,054,000 (£61.2M in 2023) was also lost. The wreck was found in 1930 and an Italian company undertook the salvage operation. Because of the deep water a diver in an armoured suit placed explosives to blast through the ship and then used a grab to pick up the gold and silver. The salvage operation continued until 1935, by when ninety-eight percent of the contents of the strong room had been recovered.

RFA in 9th Division. However, it must have been before he was wounded because 32nd Division was not involved in the Third Battle of Ypres but 9th Division was. He was evacuated to England via Boulogne to Dover on 14th October and was treated at Prince of Wales's Hospital for Officers, Marylebone Road, London. A medical board there on 24th October found him unfit for General Service for three months, Home Service for two months and light duties for one month. He was granted leave. A medical board there on 28th November found him unfit for General Service for two months, Home Service for one month and recommended he be posted to a command depot. A medical board at the Royal Artillery Command Depot, South Camp, Ripon,

1st London General Hospital was installed in St Gabriel's College in August 1914. It was a large modern building, built in 1900, and temporary administrative offices were erected in the grounds, while extensive work was carried out on the sanitary arrangements. All the toilets were at the top of the building and there were only two bathrooms for every fifty patients. Nearby Cormont Secondary School was prepared for convalescent cases, but it had no bathrooms and these had to be added. The Hospital was completed within three months, with the former College and School connected by a covered passage. Medical and nursing staff were seconded from St Bartholemew's Hospital. In April 1915, 71 Upper Tulse Hill was leased as a relief hospital, adding twenty beds. In December huts were erected in Myatt's Fields to accommodate 520 more patients. By 1917 the Hospital had 231 beds for officers and 1,038 for other ranks. In April 1918 the King and Queen visited and the Hospital closed in 1919. The main building is now an apartment block and Cormont Secondary School is now the Charles Edward Brooke Girls' School.

Sir Robert Hadfield (1858–1940) founded and supported 5th British Red Cross Hospital at Wimereux with one hundred beds. The hospital was organised by Lady Hadfield (Frances Belt Wickersham (1862–1949) born in Philadelphia, Pennsylvania, USA) and cost £75,000 (£4.4M in 2023). The hospital, which was also known as Lady Hadfield's Hospital and the Anglo-American Hospital, opened on 14th December 1914. By the time that it closed on 10th January 1919, 16,000 casualties had passed through it. During the war, Sir Robert's company, Hadfield's Steel of Sheffield, produced £36,000,000 (£2,092M in 2023) worth of armaments.

The Prince of Wales Hospital at 222 Marylebone Road, London opened in 1916 in the 700-bed Great Central Hotel and closed in July 1919. During its time as an officers' hospital it had a bad reputation. The food was poor and patients were not allowed to leave the hospital before 1 p.m. nor attend theatre matinees without permission. The Commandant required those fit enough to attend military lectures for two hours on alternate mornings or afternoons. The hotel was a convalescent hospital during the Second World War and later became headquarters of the British Railways Board; the staff knew it as the Kremlin. In the 1980s the building became a hotel again.

Yorkshire on 28th December found him unfit for General Service for one month but fit for Home Service and he was granted leave until 18th January 1918.

On 19th January he transferred to the Royal Artillery and Tank Corps Command Depot, Catterick, Yorkshire. Medical boards there on 25th January and 25th February found him unfit for General Service for one month but a medical board on 26th March found him fit for General Service and he subsequently returned to France. **Awarded the VC for his actions at Ledeghem, Belgium on 1st October 1918, LG 14th December 1918.** The VC was presented by the King in the quadrangle of Buckingham Palace on 14th June 1919. He was demobilised from the Officers' Wing, Repatriation Camp, Pirbright and resigned his commission on 25th July 1919, retaining the rank of lieutenant.

Robert returned to farming near Fort Jameson, North-Eastern Rhodesia (now Chipata, Zambia) and lived at Sinoia, Southern Rhodesia (now Zimbabwe) at some

The Fourth Legislative Assembly of the Southern Rhodesia Parliament in 1935. Robert Gorle, the Sergeant-at-Arms, is in the second row, eighth from the left, holding the mace.

time. He was part of the Second Legislative Assembly in Southern Rhodesia in 1929, the Fourth Legislative Assembly in 1935 and was appointed Sergeant-at-Arms and librarian for the Southern Rhodesia Parliament.

Robert Gorle married Ruth Thomas (died 1971), born in Rhodesia, on 9th July 1924 at Plumtree, Southern Rhodesia. She spoke the Ndebele language fluently and had a thorough understanding of local customs. They lived at Salisbury, Rhodesia. In November 1928, after hours of persuasion by a salesman, she ordered a copy of *The Great Controversy* by Ellen G White (1827–1915). Robert and Ruth were going to present it to a more religiously inclined relative but decided to read it first. It left a marked impression on them and they were eventually baptised and became charter members of the Salisbury Seventh-day Adventist Church. They pressed for a church school to be established but the church could not afford it. The Gorles paid the teacher's salary from their own meagre resources and the school flourished. After Robert's death, Ruth moved to Somerset West, Western Cape, South Africa in 1937. She joined Helderberg College (BA & MA) and taught there in the English Department. In 1950 she was also appointed the librarian. She transferred to Solusi College, near Bulawayo, Rhodesia in 1957 after her son was appointed Principal there. She was closely connected with the college training programme in the Trans-African Division. She subsequently died at Bulawayo. Ruth is the subject of the book *Ruth Gorle: Makhumalo: Mother of Leaders*, by her daughter, Drusilla Hertogs, published in 1997. Robert and Ruth had three children:

- Drusilla Gorle (19th August 1925–2nd March 2003) became a doctor and set up a practice in East Africa. She married Errol Hertogs and they lived on Mauritius. The island was devastated by Cyclone Carol in February 1960 but they escaped injury and with only slight damage to their property. They helped to establish the Rosie Le Même Adventist Nursing Home, 77 Avenue Telfair, Quatre-Bornes,

Mauritius, to house homeless and elderly persons. It was registered on 11th February 1963 and opened in March. Drusilla moved to England and was working at St Albans' Better Living Centre, Hertfordshire in 1984. She was Senior Clinical Medical Officer at Tower Hamlets Health Authority, London, when she published a paper on measles immunisation initiative 1987–88. In 1998 she was living at 211 Church Road, Earley, Berkshire. She died at Reading, Berkshire. Drusilla had at least a daughter:

    ◦ Marian Celia Hertogs (1st December 1954–3rd June 2003) married Rolf Fredheim in 1976, registered at Watford, Hertfordshire. They were living at Llanddulas, Abergele, Denbighshire, Wales at the time of her death there. They had two children.

• Timothy Vaughan Gorle (25th September 1928–4th April 2020), a twin with Penelope, was

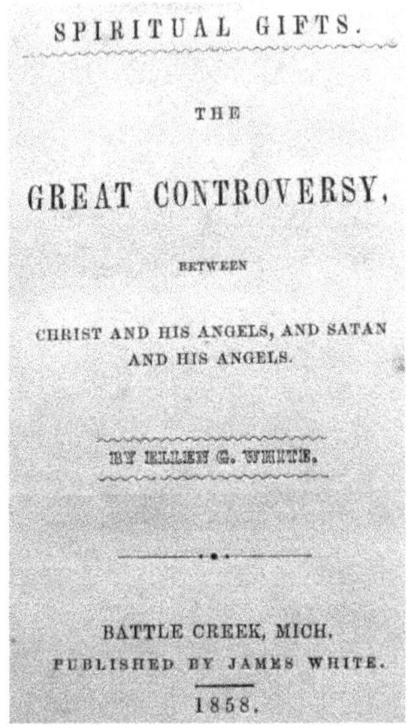

The Great Controversy by Ellen G White.

Claremont Union College, the first Seventh-day Adventist College outside North America, was established in Cape Town in 1893. It is part of the Seventh-day Adventist education system, the world's second largest Christian school system. The College was open to all races and religious affiliations. Only half the students were Seventh-day Adventists. In 1919 it moved to a mission station thirty-two kilometres from Ladysmith, Natal, and became the South African Training College. In 1922 it became Spion Kop College, but the remote location and inaccessibility were insurmountable problems. A new location was found at a farm named Bakkerskloof at Somerset West, below Helderberg Mountain, near Cape Town. The move there took place in 1928 and the establishment became Helderberg College. Student numbers grew and in 1951 it became a senior college and began to offer degree courses. It became Helderberg College of Higher Education in November 2017. The College includes a local research centre of the Ellen G White Estate.

appointed Principal of Solusi College, near Bulawayo, Rhodesia. He married Magdalena Johanna Jeanette (born 1st February 1930). He became a missionary, travelling from Southampton, England to New York, USA aboard SS *United States*, arriving on 2nd April 1954 and 8th February 1959. Their address in 1959 was 19 Charing Cross, London. They emigrated to New South Wales, Australia and were living at 23 College Drive, Cooranbong, Lake Macquarie, where he was a minister at Gateway Seventh-day Adventist Church, 119 Avondale Road, Cooranbong. They were living at 23 College Drive, Cooranbong in 1980. They had a son, Robert Vaughan Gorle (born 9th June 1953).

The book written by Drusilla Hertogs about her mother.

- Penelope Ellen Jane Gorle (25th September 1928–1929) was a twin with Timothy.

Ruth's father, William Elliot Thomas JP (c.1865–12th May 1944), born at Inyati, Bubi, Matabeleland North Province, was the son of the Reverend Thomas Morgan Thomas. Thomas was a missionary for the London Missionary Society, who arrived in Rhodesia in the early 1850s, and Caroline Hutchinson. Thomas worked for many years among the Matabele and became a friend and adviser of Mzilikazi Khumalo (c.1790–1868), King of the Mthwakazi Kingdom, now Matabeleland, Zimbabwe. William was made a member of an Impi of the Khumalo clan and in later years became a counsellor to and acquaintance of Lobengula Khumalo (c.1845-c.1894), son of Mzilikazi. He married Ellen 'Helen' Prynne née Poultney (3rd March 1859–24th November 1907), born at Aliwal North, Cape, South Africa, in 1887. Ellen had married Charles Emly Spranger (16th April 1853–23rd July 1879), an agriculture and cattle farmer born at Tenby, Pembrokeshire, c.1878 in South Africa. They were living at Welbedacht Farm, near Zeerust, Marico, Transvaal, South Africa when he died at the South African National Tuberculosis Settlement, Eastern Cape. Ellen died at the Memorial Hospital, Bulawayo, Matabeleland. In addition to Ruth, she had four other children from her two marriages:

- Charlotte Emily Adelaide Rose Spranger (1st November 1879–7th November 1950) married Thomas E Spreight. She died at Gadzema, Rhodesia.
- Gwendoline Althea Thomas (1887–1960) born at Zeerust, Marico, Transvaal, South Africa and died at Pietermaritzburg, KwaZulu-Natal, South Africa.
- Walter Eric Thomas (born 16th July 1889) was educated at South African College, Cape Town, South Africa and Brasenose College, Oxford as a Rhodes Scholar in 1910. He played rugby for Oxford in the Oxford v Cambridge Varsity

matches 1911–13. He joined the Rhodesian Civil Service in 1914 and was commissioned in 2nd Rhodesia Regiment, serving in the East African Campaign 1915–17. He arrived in Britain with a draft of other officers from South Rhodesia on 11th October 1917 and was granted a temporary commission as a captain in the King's Royal Rifle Corps on 29th January 1918, retaining previous seniority. He went to France on 4th February. Awarded the MC (LG 30th May 1919). Walter was released from service on returning to South Rhodesia on 5th August 1919. He relinquished his commission on 15th December 1920. Walter was attached to 1st King's Royal Rifle Corps in France as a temporary captain 1917–18. He was appointed Legal Adviser, Southern Rhodesian Government 1928, Solicitor General 1933, King's Counsel, Attorney General, Southern Rhodesia 1934, Judge of the High Court of Southern Rhodesia 1944 and Senior Puisne Judge of the High Court, Southern Rhodesia. He was awarded the OBE (LG 2nd January 1939), CMG (LG 8th June 1950) and was knighted on 10th June 1954 (LG 9th July 1954). Walter married Margaret Halcro Fairbairn (1900–1st February 1982) in 1925 at Hampstead, London, where she was born. She was living with her parents at 9 Eldon Road, Hampstead in 1911. They lived at Harari, Mount Pleasant, Salisbury, Southern Rhodesia. Margaret was living at 1 Ashton Road, Alexandra Park, Salisbury, Zimbabwe at the time of her death there. They had two children – Heather Fairbairn Thomas (15th May 1927–2007) and James Thomas (born c.1929).

The SKETCH

Lobengula on the front page of The Sketch in November 1893.

- Evan Morgan Thomas.

Robert did not receive an invitation to attend the Prince of Wales's dinner at the House of Lords in 1929, probably because his whereabouts in Southern Rhodesia were not known. He wrote to the War Office in 1930 requesting that his VC particulars be entered in the Army List. He also mentioned that he had not received an invitation to the dinner and asked for a copy of the invitation. The War Office agreed to amend the Army List. Robert was on holiday on his own at Durban, Natal when he was admitted to the Government Hospital there suffering from emphysema and pneumonia. He died there eight days later, on 10th January 1937. He is buried in Stellawood Cemetery, Durban, South Africa (Section K, Grave 144). A memorial was placed over the grave in 1939 by the Urban Branch of the British Empire Service League. Robert is commemorated in a number of other places:

Robert Gorle's grave in Stellawood Cemetery, Durban, South Africa (Memorials to Valour).

St George's Chapel, Woolwich before and after the V1 strike in 1944. The Royal Artillery VC Memorial is on the curved wall behind the altar.

- Gorle Road, Larkhill, Wiltshire.
- The Royal Artillery VC Memorial in the ruins of St George's Chapel, the former Garrison Church at Woolwich, Grand Depot Road, which was reduced to a roofless shell by a V1 in 1944.
- Named on one of eleven plaques honouring 175 men from overseas awarded the VC for the Great War. The plaques were unveiled by the Senior Minister of State at the Foreign & Commonwealth Office and Minister for Faith and Communities, Baroness Warsi, at a reception at Lancaster House, London on 26th June 2014 attended by The Duke of Kent and relatives of the VC recipients. The South African plaque is at the Castle of Good Hope, Cape Town.
- Memorial plaque at the Royal Artillery Tercentenary Chapel and Cloister, Larkhill, Wiltshire unveiled by Queen Elizabeth II on 26th May 2016.
- Memorial plaque at Rugby School, Warwickshire, unveiled in 2017.
- A Department for Communities and Local Government commemorative paving stone was dedicated at the junction of Victoria Avenue South and Merton Road, Southsea, Hampshire, close to his birthplace, on 1st October 2018.

The Castle of Good Hope, Cape Town.

The Royal Artillery VC memorial plaque is on the far wall of the Royal Artillery Tercentenary Chapel at Larkhill.

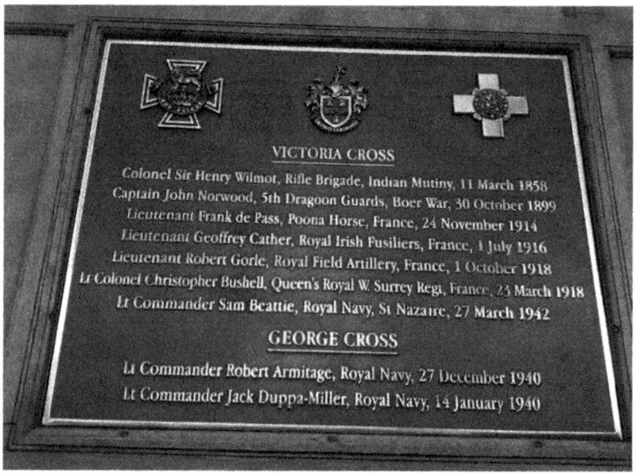

The VC and GC memorial at Rugby School (Memorials to Valour).

The Victory Medal (or Inter-Allied Victory Medal) was first proposed by French Marshal Ferdinand Foch as a common award for all the nations allied against the Central Powers. Regardless of nationality, each medal is 36mm in diameter, the ribbon is a double rainbow and the obverse shows winged victory (except Japan and Siam where winged victory has no relevance). For British Empire forces the medal was issued to all who received the 1914 or 1914–15 Star and to almost all who received the British War Medal. The British alone struck 6,335,000 Victory Medals. These three medals were known as Pip, Squeak and Wilfred after a popular newspaper comic strip. To qualify for the Victory Medal recipients had to be mobilised for war service and have entered a theatre of war between 5th August 1914 and 11th November 1918, plus Russia 1919–20 and mine clearance in the North Sea until 30th November 1919. Those Mentioned in Despatches wore an oakleaf on the Victory Medal ribbon as shown here.

In addition to the VC he was awarded the 1914–15 Star, British War Medal 1914–20 and Victory Medal 1914–19. A blog online, dated 30th March 2015, claimed that Robert Gorle's VC group and his father's DSO group passed to Joan Howson and were stolen in the 1980s. The allegation has not been verified. The VC group was owned by Kevin Patience of Bahrain 1987–91 and was purchased by Lord Ashcroft in a private sale in 1993. The VC is held by the Michael Ashcroft Trust, the holding institution for the Lord Ashcroft Victoria Cross Collection and is displayed in the Imperial War Museum's Lord Ashcroft Gallery.

42954 PRIVATE NORMAN HARVEY
1st Battalion, The Royal Inniskilling Fusiliers

Norman Harvey was born on 6th April 1899 at Newton-le-Willows, Lancashire. His father, Charles William Harvey (1872–1959), born at Standon, Hertfordshire, was baptised on 8th September 1872. He was an orphan by 1881, living with his uncle and aunt, James and Eliza Tew, at Mill End, Standon. He was a packer in 1893 and later a platelayer on the railways. Charles married Mary née Beesley (1871–1953), a smoother in a plate glass works born at St Helens, Lancashire, in 1893 at Prescot, Lancashire. By 1911 they were living at 6 Golborne Dale Road, Newton-le-Willows and had moved to 2 Parkside, Old Station Buildings by 1919. Norman had ten siblings:

- Mary Ellen Harvey (6th August 1893–1971), born at Newton-le-Willows, married Edward Snape (14th February 1892–October 1978), a warder, on 7th December 1916 at St Peter's Church, Newton in Makerfield. He was living with his parents at 15 Bridge Street, Bamber Bridge in 1911. Edward was the brother of Mary Elizabeth Snape who married Mary's brother Charles (see below). Edward served in the Army during the Great War. He was a mental nurse in 1939, when they were living at 12 Larch Avenue, Newton-le-Willows. They had a son:
    - Charles W Snape (born 1922) married Winifred York (born 1923) in 1944 at Newton-le-Willows. She was living with her parents at 44 Tamworth Street, Newton-le-Willows in 1939. Her father, Francis York, served in the Lancashire Fusiliers (11/13780) and was discharged on 26th May 1916. Winifred and Charles had two children – Charles Snape 1947 and Gillian Snape 1950.

Newton-le-Willows, a market town between Manchester and St Helens, was also known as Newton in Makerfield. The lord of the manor was Edward the Confessor at the time of his death in 1066. Neweton was mentioned in the Domesday Book. One of the last battles of the Second English Civil War was close to Newton. The town's two railway stations are amongst the oldest in the country and Parkside was the site of the world's first fatal rail accident. Amongst the famous people associated with the town are:

- Richard Paul 'Rick' Astley (born 1966), the singer and songwriter best known for his signature song *Never Gonna Give You Up*, was born at Newton-le-Willows.
- Andrew Murray 'Andy' Burnham (born 1970), Labour politician who served in Prime Minister Gordon Brown's Cabinet as Chief Secretary to the Treasury 2007–08, Culture Secretary 2008–09 and Health Secretary 2009–10, was educated at Newton-le-Willows. He became Mayor of Greater Manchester in 2017.
- Sir John Turton Randall (1905–84), the physicist who radically improved the cavity magnetron, a critically important component of centimetric radar, a significant technology in winning the Second World War, was born in Newton-le-Willows. The cavity magnetron is a major component of microwave ovens.
- Colin Welland, born Colin Edward Williams (1934–2015), the actor and screenwriter who won the BAFTA for Best Supporting Actor for the film *Kes* (1969) and the Academy Award for Best Original Screenplay for the film *Chariots of Fire* (1981). He was educated at Newton-le-Willows Grammar School.

- Charles William Harvey (1st August 1895–25th January 1964), born at Lowton, Lancashire, was a toffee maker in 1911. He married Mary Elizabeth Snape (8th January 1899–January 1978), born at Bamber Bridge, Lancashire, in 1929 at Preston, Lancashire. She was living with her parents at 11 Bridge Street, Bamber Bridge in 1911. Mary's brother, Edward Snape, married Charles' sister Mary Ellen (see above). Charles was a platelayer in 1939, when they were living at 3 Parkside Road, Newton-le-Willows. They had a daughter:

Standon parish, which includes the village of Puckeridge, is first mentioned in a Saxon charter of 944–46. Arthur Martin-Leake, one of only three men awarded the VC twice, was born at High Cross, just south of the village. His story is related in the first book in this series, *Victoria Crosses on the Western front – Mons to Hill 60 August 1914–April 1915*.

St Helens, historically in the county of Lancashire, is now part of Merseyside. The first recorded settlements are in the Domesday Book in 1086. The name St Helens came from a chapel of ease dedicated to St Elyn and the earliest documented reference to it is in 1552. The area developed significantly during the Industrial Revolution. By 1838 the town was responsible for administering the townships of Eccleston, Parr, Sutton and Windle. St Helens became a municipal borough in 1868, a county borough in 1887 and a metropolitan borough in 1974. The Industrial Revolution brought coal mining, glass making, copper smelting, cotton and linen works and other industrial processes to the area.

Coal seams were mentioned in 1556 and digging for it developed into the main industry. In the early years shallow mining operations scarred the landscape and the shafts were prone to flooding and collapse. However, St Helens' location close to developing industrial areas in Liverpool and elsewhere led to a massive expansion in coal extraction. The development of steam engines allowed water to be pumped efficiently, leading to the exploitation of deeper seams. Up to 5,000 men were still employed in coal mining in the 1970s. The last deep coal mine, Sutton Manor Colliery, closed in May 1991.

Transport links became vital to the life of the town, in order to shift its products, particularly coal. The Sankey Canal linked St Helens to the Mersey in 1757 and it was extended in 1775 to transport coal to Liverpool. The Liverpool and Manchester Railway opened in 1830 and passed through the southern edge of the town. As transport links improved, there was an influx of other industries to what had been a relatively sparsely populated area.

The abundance of local coal, sand and salt, made the area ideal for glass making and works are known to have existed from at least 1688. The Pilkington Brothers works, founded in 1826, still produces all the UK's flat glass, although it is no longer the major employer that it once was.

Thomas Beecham (1820–1907) moved to Wigan in 1847, where he sold a laxative, Beecham's Pills. By 1859 he was based in St Helens and expanded his business by opening his first factory there. His son, Sir Joseph Beecham (1848–1916), expanded the business and was also mayor 1889–99 and 1910–12. His son, Sir Thomas Beecham (1879–1961), was a conductor best known for his association with the London Philharmonic and Royal Philharmonic Orchestras.

  - Kathleen Harvey (16th December 1931–1970) married Leonard Johnson in 1956 at Newton. They are believed to have had a son, Paul A Johnson, in 1962.
- Harold Harvey (5th May 1897–1966) was an under gardener in 1911. He married Emily Rose (13th November 1897–4th November 1993), born at Lowton, in 1920 at Leigh, Lancashire. He was a gardener and she was a temporary nurse attendant in 1939, when they were living at Ivy Cottage, 99 Twiss Green Lane, Culcheth, Lancashire.
- Jack Harvey (born 20th April 1901) married Nellie Clare (23rd April 1901–May 1996), born at Pendlebury, Lancashire, in 1927 at Barton upon Irwell, Lancashire. He was a permanent way ganger in 1939, when they were living at 24 Cedar Crescent, Newton-le-Willows. They had a son, Alan William Harvey (2nd April 1930–1950).
- Esther Harvey (23rd May 1903–1975) was baptised on 1st November 1903 at St Peter's Church, Newton-in-Makerfield. She married Peter Taylor (born 19th April 1897), a police constable, on 24th September 1924 at St Peter's Church, Newton-le-Willows. He was living at 2 Birchley Street, St Helens at the time. He was living with his parents at 111 Crow Lane Nest, Newton-le-Willows in 1901. He was a police sergeant in 1939, when they were living at 134 Broad Oak Road, St Helens. Her death was registered at Wigan. They had two children:
  - Olive Taylor (born 30th September 1925) married Stanley Richard Marsh (12th April 1926–August 2001) on 8th August 1948 at St Helens. He was living with his parents at 107 Fry Street, St Helens in 1939. His death was registered in Wigan. They are believed to have had four children – Lynne Marsh 1952, Neil Marsh 1953, Keith Marsh 1955 and Brendon Marsh 1957.
  - Peter Gerald Taylor (29th June 1939–May 1955).
- Tom Harvey (14th July 1905–January 1986) was baptised on 8th March 1908 at St Peter's Church, Newton-in-Makerfield. He married Edna Miller (29th September 1910–January 1994) in 1935 at Leigh. He was a farm horseman in 1939, when they were living at 6 Heath Lane, Golborne, Lancashire. He was also an Air Raid Precautions Warden. They had four children, all registered at Leigh:
  - Joan Harvey (born 15th March 1937) married David E McCall (born 20th May 1938), born at Liverpool, in 1959. They had two children – Beverley D McCall 1960 and Nicholas McCall 1962.
  - James E Harvey (born 1941) is believed to have married Norah Fearnley (born 1938) in 1960. She was living with her parents at 107 Wordsworth Avenue, Leigh in 1939. They had two children – Clive E Harvey 1961 and Simon G Harvey 1963.
  - Michael J Harvey (1950) is believed to have married Mary M Murphy (born 1954) in 1970. They had two children – Claire Mary Harvey 1973 and Matthew James Harvey 1978.

 - David Harvey (born 1955) is believed to have married Karen D Halford (born 1958), born at Liverpool, in 1977. They had a son, Nicholas David Harvey in 1977.
- Joseph Harvey (5th November 1907–January 1983) was baptised on 8th March 1908 at St Peter's Church, Newton-in-Makerfield. He married Phyllis Hodson (30th June 1906–April 1970) in 1930. He was a bakery van driver at the time of the 1939 register, when he was a patient at Leigh Hospital. Phyllis was living with her children at 102 East Lancashire Road, Golborne. They had four children:
  - Ethel Harvey (1930–39).
  - Leonard Harvey (born 1931).
  - Marjory Harvey (born 1934).
  - Eric Harvey (born 1935) married Maureen Fawcett (born 1936) in 1958 at Warrington. They had three children – Geoffrey E Harvey 1959, David J Harvey 1962 and Maria Patricia Harvey 1968.
- Ada Harvey (31st August 1909–9th October 2007) married Arthur Savage (6th June 1906–October 1971) in 1936. He was living with his parents at 11 Booth Street, Warrington in 1911. He was a steam hammer driver for a wire screen manufacturer in 1939, when they were living at 12 Dale Street, Warrington.
- Lily Harvey (26th March 1912–January 1960) married John William Bellis (8th September 1913–April 1972), born at Chester-le Street, Co Durham, in 1937. He was a maker-up in textiles in 1939, when they were living at 13 Worsley Street, Golborne. Their deaths were registered at Leigh. They had a son, Brian William Bellis (26th July 1938–14th October 1989), who was living at 13 Worsley Street, Golborne at the time of his death there.
- Ethel Harvey (13th January 1915–4th January 1999) married Thomas A Wharton (born 1913) in 1936. They had two daughters both registered at Hawarden – Ethel M Wharton 1937 and Margaret Wharton 1939.

Norman's paternal grandfather, Charles Harvey (c.1835–25th May 1879), an agricultural labourer, married Ellen née Bird (c.1837–12th December 1875) at Standon, Hertfordshire, where they were both born, in 1858, registered at Ware, Hertfordshire. They were living at Stortford Road, Standon in 1861 and both subsequently died at Standon. In addition to Charles they had three other children:

- Esther Harvey (1st October 1862–1948) married Charles Swallow (4th March 1860–4th December 1946), a farm labourer, on 23rd November 1878 at Standon, where he was born. They were living at Standon Street, Standon in 1881 and 1891. By 1901 they had moved to High Street, Standon and he was a factory labourer. He was a farm labourer again by 1911 and they were still at High Street in 1939. They both subsequently died there. Esther had two daughters:
  - Emily Harvey (1878–26th May 1942), baptised on 13th October 1878, married George John Cobb (1877–1958) in 1899. She died at Napsbury

Hospital, St Albans, Hertfordshire and his death was registered at Edmonton, Middlesex.
  - Ada Swallow (22nd October 1880–13th August 1944) married Sidney Charles Roper (12th January 1879–1970) in 1904, registered at Ware. They had at least two children – Sidney Charles Roper 1906 and Gertrude E Roper 1912.
- Sarah Harvey (30th July 1865–1949) married William George Barrick (24th May 1868–5th April 1941), born at Pancras, London, on 14th April 1890 at St Mary's, Walthamstow, London. He was a milk carrier in 1911, when they were living at 5 Beulah Road, Walthamstow. Later he was a window cleaner. They were living in retirement at 5 Beulah Road in 1939 and were still living there at the time of his death at Western House Hospital, Ware, Hertfordshire. She died in Essex. They had three children:
  - William Frederick Charles Barrick (27th May 1893–1973), born at West Ham, was a window cleaner in 1911, living with his parents. He married Ellen M Preedy in 1913 at West Ham. He was a milk roundsman in 1941. William's death was registered at Waltham Forest. They had eight children – Maud E S Barrick 1914, William FC Barrick 1915, Lily M Barrick 1919, Helen H Barrick 1921, Gladys I Barrick 1922, Phyllis D Barrick 1923, Joan I Barrick 1925 and Joyce P Barrick 1927.
  - Charles Barrick (1895–1941) was an assistant milk carrier in 1911 living with his parents. He enlisted in C Company, 3/7th Essex (4323 & 301182) on 26th January 1916 and was living at 36a Wingfield Road, Walthamstow at the time. He was described as 5′ 5¾″ tall and his religious denomination was Church of England. He was absent from 7.00 p.m. on 14th June until tattoo on 17th June, for which he was fined six days' pay. On 10th July he was posted to B Company, 1/7th Essex and embarked aboard HMT *Huntsgreen* at Devonport on 13th July. He disembarked at Alexandria on 24th July and joined the unit at Ballybunion, on the Sinai side of the Suez Canal, on 15th August. He was confined to barracks for three days for having a dirty rifle on guard mounting on 2nd August and for four days for inattention on parade on 20th August. On 6th November Charles was admitted to hospital at Suez 'not yet diagnosed' and was transferred to 27th General Hospital, Cairo with psoriasis on 10th November He was transferred to 19th General Hospital, Alexandria on 11th November and to the Recovery Hospital, Mustapha next day. On 15th January 1917 he was discharged to a base depot at Mustapha and rejoined the unit at Bir-El-Abd on 7th February. He was wounded in the left leg on 27th March and was transferred to hospital in Cairo on 4th April and Abbassia on 17th April. He rejoined his unit on 29th May and was attached to a light trench mortar battery on 15th June. From 20th September onwards he was in various hospitals, including 34th Stationary and 71st General. On 6th October he was admitted to hospital

with tonsillitis. On 5th October 1919 Charles had a discharge medical at Khartoum and embarked aboard SS *Himalaya* on 29th October for return to Britain. He was demobilised from the Dispersal Unit, Crystal Palace on 12th November, giving his address as 5 Beulah Road, Walthamstow. Charles was disembodied on 9th December 1919. He married Bessie E Gould at West Ham in 1923. They had five children – Josephine I Barrick 1924, Nellie K Barrick 1926, Lilian P Barrick 1928, Doreen P Barrick 1933 and Jean M Barrick 1938.

  - Nathaniel Barrick (1st April 1897–1974) was an assistant milk carrier in 1911 living with his parents. He married Jane A Deeks at West Ham in 1922. They had six children – Gwendoline A Barrick 1923, Eileen N Barrick 1924, Iris D Barrick 1926, Jean V Barrick 1928, Mavis H Barrick 1932 and Alan A Barrick 1938.

- Emily Harvey (8th November 1868–24th September 1901) married Nehemiah Tew (17th February 1870–3rd May 1928), an agricultural labourer, on 1st June 1890. They were living at Stortford Road, Standon in 1891. By 1901 he was a public works crane driver and they were living at 14 Islington Green, Islington, London. She died at Standon. Emily had four children:
  - Ellen Harvey (born 1889).
  - Alfred Richard Tew (30th August 1891–1964) married Gertrude MD Tew née Jordan (23rd October 1894–June 1979) in 1921, registered at Ware. His death was registered at Edmonton and hers at Hertford. They had a daughter, Sylvia F Tew, in 1937, registered at Edmonton.
  - David James Tew (25th November 1894–1920) married Gertrude MD Tew née Jordan (23rd October 1894–June 1979) at Edmonton in 1919. They had a daughter, Hazel GC Tew, later that year. After David's death, Gertrude married his brother, Alfred.
  - Emily Maud Tew (15th December 1897–1960), birth registered at Pancras, London and death, unmarried, at Hertford.

  Nehemiah married Esther Mary Ann Meyer (26th July 1873–1950), born at Bow, London, in 1920 at Greenwich, London. Nehemiah subsequently died there. Esther was living at 31 Allas Road, Bethnal Green, London in 1945 and was still there at the time of her death.

His maternal grandfather, Joseph Beesley (1840–1910), born at St Helens, Lancashire, married Mary née Cunliffe (1840–92), also born at St Helens, on 28th January 1861 at the Chapel of Rainford, Prescot, Lancashire. He was a glass polisher in 1861, living with his wife at Raven Street, St Helens. They had moved to 14 Crosfield Street by 1871, by when he was a plate glass polisher. By 1891 he was a general labourer and they were living at 48 Lyon Street. At the time of the 1901 Census, Joseph was visiting his daughter, Ann Naylor and family, at 22 Lyon Street,

A chapel of ease existed at Rainford at the time of the Reformation and was built because of the distance to the mother church at Prescot. The first known curate was Laurence Roby in 1541, when the Diocese of Chester was established. Before then Prescot was in the Diocese of Lichfield. Despite the Reformation, the chapel remained Roman Catholic for a while, as did much of this part of Lancashire. However, in the first half of the 17th century the chapel was served by Puritan curates appointed by the Vicar of Prescot. Later Prescot lost some control and the inhabitants appointed Presbyterian ministers of their own choosing. Following the Act of Toleration, the chapel was registered as a meeting place for Protestant Dissenters in July 1689 but, in 1702, it was recovered by the established Church of England. The chapel suffered from lack of endowment and in 1758 the south side had to be pulled down and rebuilt. As the village expanded, so the congregation grew and the chapel was extended. In 1787 the vestry was rebuilt and enlarged. In 1869 Rainford became a parish, served by a vicar rather than a curate. However, it was recognised that a new church was required to accommodate the rapidly increasing population. Work commenced in April 1877 a few yards south of the old chapel, which is seen here, and the new building was consecrated on All Saints Day 1878. A tower was added in 1903. The old chapel, which had stood for over 300 years, was then demolished.

together with his daughters, Beatrice and Ada. In addition to Mary they had ten other children, all born at St Helens:

- Edwin Beesley (1862–1933), a plate glass cutter, married Esther Griffiths (1866–1902) in 1887. He was living with his children at 132 Chapel Lane, St Helens in 1911. They had three children:
    - Edwin Beesley (born 1892) was a clerk in a glass works in 1911, living with his father. He married Florence Smith in 1918. They had three children – Ernest E Beesley 1924, Lawrence L Beesley 1931 and Valentine V Beesley 1933.
    - Mary Beesley (born 1893).
    - Esther Beesley (born 1895).
- Margaret Beesley (26th October 1863–28th March 1941) married William Aspinwall (1861–19th April 1935), a gardener, on 14th November 1887 at Christ Church, Eccleston, where he lived. He was a coal dealer in 1911, when they were living at Pleasant View, Kiln Lane, St Helens. They were still there at the time of his death. She was living at 100 Kiln Lane, St Helens in 1939 and subsequently died there. They had seven children:
    - William Aspinwall (1888–1956) was a house painter, living with his parents in 1911. He was a painter working for Greenhall Whitley Brewers when he enlisted in 5th (Reserve) Battalion, South Lancashire Regiment at St Helens

on 21st November 1914 (3462 & 241243). He was just 5′3″ tall. William went to France on 28th March 1915 with 1/5th Battalion. He received a gunshot wound to the left foot on 13th August 1916 and returned to Britain on 21st August. A medical board on 21st November 1917 at Wellington Road Auxiliary Hospital, Liverpool found he was no longer physically fit for war service due to ankylosis of the ankle and he was discharged on 12th December.

- Ann Aspinwall (born 1890).
- John Aspinwall (1892–1962) was a glass maker living with his parents in 1911. He is believed to have married Alice Chapman in 1919 and they had a daughter, Vera Aspinwall, in 1920.
- Joseph Beesley Aspinwall (13th June 1894–18th February 1949) was a glass maker living with his parents in 1911. He never married and was a coal dealer in 1939 living with his mother.
- Doris Aspinwall (13th October 1896–1979) was a wages clerk in 1939 living with her mother. She never married.
- Mary Frances Aspinwall (1st January 1899–1975) married Robert Greener (6th October 1903–1989) in 1926. They had a daughter, Eileen M Greener, later that year.
- Bertha Aspinwall (10th July 1908–10th September 1994) was employed in domestic duties in 1939. She married John E Bone at Prescot in 1956.

- Ann Beesley (1866–1933) married Herbert Naylor (1866–1920) in 1890. He was a witness at the marriage of Ann's sister, Alice. In 1901 he was a brewer's labourer, when they were living at 22 Lyon Street, St Helens. Ann's father, Joseph Beesley, and her sisters, Beatrice and Ada, were visiting at the time of the 1901 Census. Ann and Herbert were living at 18 Hanover Street, St Helens in 1911. They had three children:
  - Phoebe Naylor (18th October 1891–1947) married George Cole (15th April 1889–1973) in 1909. They were living at 62 Chamberlain Street, St Helens in 1911, when he was a sheet glass cutter and she was a milliner. They were living at 22 Gamble Avenue, St Helens in 1939. They had three children – Horace Cole 1910, George Cole 1915 and Phyllis Cole 1918.
  - John Herbert Naylor (1894) was a glass bevellor in 1911, living with parents. He enlisted in 3rd West Lancashire Field Ambulance RAMC (1167 & 20274) at St Helens on 23rd November 1911. He was 5′5½″ tall and was a member of the Church Lads' Brigade. He attended annual camp at Kirkham 4th-18th August 1912 and at Denbigh 17th-31st August 1913. On 18th January 1914 he enrolled in the Special Reserve for three years. He was embodied for service with 18th Field Ambulance on 5th August 1914, when he was living at 151 Albion Street, St Helens. He embarked at Southampton on 9th September and disembarked at St Nazaire the next day. He was admitted to hospital with piles 26th-29th January 1915 and to 18th Field

Ambulance with pyrexia 2nd-6th November 1916. He was granted leave 29th November–9th December and was appointed to the Nursing Section on 11th May 1917. John was confined to barracks for three days for being absent from 9.00 p.m. until 10.00 p.m. on 18th July. He was granted leave 6th-19th January 1918, 10th July–9th August and 8th-22nd May 1919. John returned to Britain on 4th June and transferred to the Class Z Reserve on 2nd July. He was discharged on 31st March 1920.
  - Mona Naylor (1896–1945) married Charles WF Bryer (24th December 1896–1973) in 1919. They had two children – Muriel F Bryer 1920 and Norman C Bryer 1926.
- Phoebe Beesley (1867–88).
- Joseph Beesley (1870–88).
- Alice Beesley (26th October 1873–1954) married Richard Pearce (17th July 1873–5th February 1937) on 24th June 1894 at St Helens Parish Church. He was a glassmaker, living at 30 Lowe Street, St Helens and she was living at 113 Frederick Street, St Helens at the time. They were living at 72 Chamberlain Street, St Helens in 1911. They were living at 25 Leslie Road, St Helens at the time of his death at 1 Warrington Road, Whiston, Lancashire. Alice was still living there in 1939. They had six children:
  - Mary Emily Pearce (1894–96).
  - Ada Pearce (7th August 1896–1982) married James Morris Earl (22nd September 1892–1990) in 1926. They had a daughter, Margaret A Earl, in 1930.
  - Marion Pearce (27th February 1898–12th February 1991) was a certified assistant teacher in 1939, living with her mother.
  - Edith Pearce (9th October 1900–6th January 1990) was a certified assistant teacher in 1939, living with her mother.
  - Richard Pearce (11th June 1904–1980) married Agnes Green in 1921. They had three children – George L Pearce 1921, Norman Pearce 1925 and John Pearce 1934.
  - George Arthur Pearce (23rd April 1916–1983) was incapacitated in 1939, living with his mother.
- William Beesley (19th December 1875–1903) was a warehouse boy in 1891. He married Louisa Warren (9th August 1874–1947) in 1895. William was an electric tram car conductor in 1901, when they were living at 21 Rigby Street, St Helens. Louisa married James Wilson (12th March 1882–1959) in 1905. He was a glass beveller in 1911, when they were living at 29 Clyde Street, St Helens. They were living at 35 Queen Street in 1939, when he was a glass warehouse labourer and a volunteer with the Ambulance Auxiliary Service. Louisa had eight children from her two marriages and other relationships:
  - Constantine Thomas Warren (12th July 1892–1953) was a general labourer in a plate glass works in 1911, living with his mother.

  - Joseph Beesley (1896–1905).
  - Thomas Redvers Beesley (10th August 1900–1960) married Gladys Roberts in 1920.
  - James Beesley (10th April 1904–13th February 1974), appears as James Wilson in the 1911 Census.
  - Joseph Wilson (25th July 1906–1962) married May Pierce (born 2nd May 1904) in 1937. He was an electric crane driver in 1939, when they were living with his parents. They had two daughters – Dorothy Wilson 1928 and Jean H Wilson 1946.
  - Lily Wilson (born 1908).
  - Doris Wilson (born 1910).
  - Francis Wilson (born and died 1913).
- Thomas Beesley (born 1879) was a splitter in a glass works in 1891.
- Beatrice Maud Beesley (27th May 1882–1919) was baptised on 28th June 1882 at St Thomas, Eccleston. She married William Parr (8th August 1880–1952) in 1901 at Prescot. He was a wood sawyer for a cabinetmaker in 1911, when they were living at 53 Witham Road, Skelmersdale, Lancashire. William enlisted in the West Lancashire Division, Royal Engineers (Territorial Force) on 4th August 1915 at St Helens (8435 & 430211). He was described as 5′ 2¼″ tall, weighing 120 lbs, of good physical development and his religious denomination was Roman Catholic. He was absent from check parade at Maidstone, Kent on 4th November but the charge was dismissed. He was confined to barracks for two days for being absent from billets on roll call at 10.00 p.m. on 6th May at Herne, Kent. William went to France on 5th May 1917, arriving on 8th May and joined 5th Reinforcement Company from the Base on 6th June. He transferred to 479th Field Company RE (61st Division) on 27th June and to 421st Field Company RE (57th Division) on 2nd August. He was granted leave in Britain 25th January–8th February 1918 and was in hospital 13th-17th August. William was appointed acting paid lance corporal on 1st November. He was granted leave in Britain and while there was retained for demobilisation. William transferred to the Class Z Reserve from Heaton Park, Manchester on 25th February 1919. Beatrice almost certainly died following complications with the birth of Harold. They had eight children:
  - William Parr (born 2nd December 1902).
  - Joseph Beesley Parr (24th July 1903–30th December 1981) married Elsie Dennett in 1935.
  - Margaret Gertrude Parr (1906–22nd March 1992).
  - Thomas Parr (5th November 1907–1967)
  - Mary Beatrice Parr (1910–11).
  - Beatrice Parr (born 1912) married Vincent Harris in 1935. They had six children – Patricia M Harris 1936, Peter Harris 1941, Joan M Harris 1948, Pauline Harris 1950, Diane Harris 1953 and Kathryn A Harris 1959.

    - John Parr (born 1914).
    - Harold Parr (4th December 1919–May 1994).

  William Parr married Janet Collins (27th March 1887–4th December 1963) in 1925. William was a wood machinist in 1939, when they were living at 86 Birchley Street, St Helens. Janet died at Winwick County Hospital, Warrington. They had a daughter, Janet Clarkson Parr (born 6th June 1925) who married James H Sharrock in 1954. They had two children – James Sharrock 1957 and Robert A Sharrock 1960.
- Ada Beesley (27th December 1884–18th February 1975) married Samuel Topping (31st January 1887–1961) on 25th December 1908. He was living at 13 Canal Bank East, St Helens in 1901. He was a sheet glass maker in 1911, when they were living at 90 Albion Street, St Helens. They were living at 68 Grant Street, St Helens when he enlisted in the Royal Garrison Artillery on 9th November 1915 (4876). He was 5′ 10″ tall and had served in 5th South Lancashire Regiment (Territorial Force) for six years. He was discharged five days later on 13th November at the Citadel, Plymouth, Devon, having joined there on 11th November, on the grounds that he was not likely to make an efficient soldier. They were living at 231 Elephant Lane, St Helens in 1939, when he was an Air Raid Precautions Warden involved with first aid. Ada was living at 125 Broadway, Eccleston at the time of her death there. They had five children:
    - Ada Topping (9th June 1909–1923).
    - Samuel James Topping (31st December 1911–5th April 2003) married Elsie Golding in 1935. They had four children – Brian Topping 1936, Patricia Topping 1937, Kathleen Topping 1938 and Janet Topping 1946.
    - Winifred Topping (1st February 1914–1997).
    - Marion Topping (1926–69).
    - Eunice Topping (born 1929) married Kenneth T Stevenson in 1955.

Norman was educated at St Peter's Church of England School, Newton-le-Willows and was a member of the Church Lads' Brigade. He worked for Messrs Randall and later for Caulfield's at Newton. He enlisted, aged fifteen, in the South Lancashire Regiment in November 1914 (3036), giving his date of birth as 7th May 1897. He went to France on 6th August 1915 and was slightly wounded later that year. He was seriously wounded in 1917 and was evacuated to Britain, where he was retained when his true age was discovered. He attended a physical training and bayonet fighting course at Portsmouth, Hampshire and qualified as an instructor, before returning to France in the spring of 1918 to join 1st Royal Inniskilling Fusiliers (42954).

Awarded the VC for his actions near Ingoyghem, Belgium on 25th October 1918, LG 6th January 1919. The Battalion CO presented the VC ribbon to Norman on 26th December before the award had been gazetted. The VC was presented by the King in the quadrangle at Buckingham Palace on 15th May 1919.

St Matthew's Church was built in the Early English style in 1871, with the tower being completed in 1875. A vestry was added in 1884–85 and a lean-to on the west end in 1900. The building is Grade II listed.

Norman was presented with an illuminated address and £100 in War Bonds at a ceremony in Newton-le-Willows. He was promoted lance corporal in early 1919 and was discharged from the Army on 27th May 1921. He then worked on the railways.

Norman Harvey married Nora Osmond Treadwell (19th April 1901–May 1972), born at Blaby, Leicestershire, on 4th September 1919 at St Matthew's Church, Dyffryn, Bryncoch, near Neath, Glamorganshire. His address was 2 Parkside, Oldstation, Newton le Willows and hers was Primrose Barns, Dyffryn. Nora and Norman had four children:

- Avril Joyce Treadwell Harvey (8th April 1920–30th December 2000), birth registered at Neath, South Wales, married Edward Bibby (20th June 1913–October 1989), born at Wigan, in 1938 at Newton-le-Willows, Lancashire. He was a centre lathe turner and an ARP fire watcher in 1939, when they were living at 33 Wood Street, Newton-le-Willows. They lived in Sierra Leone for a period, where he was a gas works manager. Her address was 47 Viaduct Street, Newton-le-Willows, when she arrived with her son, Gordon, at Liverpool aboard RMMV *Accra* on 19th September 1949 from Freetown, Sierra Leone. She embarked aboard SS *Sansu* at Liverpool on 17th August 1956, with her children

Barbara and Gordon, bound for Freetown. She arrived with her son, Gordon, at Newcastle aboard SS *Cochrane* on 24th March 1957 and her address was still 47 Viaduct Street. She embarked aboard RMV *Apapa* with her son, Gordon, at Liverpool on 24th July 1958 bound for Freetown, Sierra Leone. She and Edward disembarked from RMV *Apapa* at Liverpool on 23rd March 1959 from Freetown, Sierra Leone. He was an assistant works manager and they were living at 69 Mill Lane, Stockton Heath, Cheshire. Both their deaths were registered at Warrington, Cheshire. They had four children, possibly six:

- ◦ Avril S Bibby (born 1938), born at Newton-le-Willows, married George E Skeech (born 1936) there in 1960. His birth was registered at Warrington and he was living with his parents at 61 Athol Street, Newton-le-Willows in 1939. Avril and George had a son, Ian Michael Skeech, in 1967.
- ◦ Barbara Anne Bibby (24th November 1939–13th February 2014), birth registered at Warrington, married Paul Compton Kirkbride (24th August 1936–13th September 2007), born at Lancaster, Lancashire, in 1967 at Newton-le-Willows. He was living with his parents at 11 Lonsdale Place, Lancaster in 1939. Barbara and Paul had two children – Alastair Harvey Kirkbride 1971 and Sarah Jane Kirkbride 1973. Paul had married Joan Burrows (died 2020) in 1958 and they had five children – Susan A Kirkbride 1959, twins Andrew D and Linda E Kirkbride 1961, Ian F Kirkbride 1962 and Stephen Kirkbride 1965. They divorced and Joan is believed to have married John P Tootle in 1967. Barbara and Paul are also believed to have divorced. Barbara died at Barnet, London. Paul married Hanne-Lore Leichenring née Hagen (1st September 1935–2003), registered at Wandsworth in April 1978. Hanne-Lore was born at Hamburg, West Germany. They were living at Flat 45, Palmerston House, Strasburg Road, London at the time of their deaths.
- ◦ Gordon Edward Bibby (born 27th January 1941) married Lynda Powell at Rochdale in 1976. They had two children – Hayley Suzanne Bibby 1977 and Jamie David Bibby 1981.
- ◦ Possibly Anne Bibby (born 1944), registered at Brentford.
- ◦ Possibly Anthony Bibby (born 1945), registered at Stockport.
- ◦ Sarah Bibby (born 1946), registered at Hove, Sussex.

- Patricia Harvey (14th July 1922–18th March 2016), birth registered at Neath, is understood to have married George Leslie Johnson (9th March 1920–20th June 2001) in 1942 at Newton-le-Willows. In 1939 he was a steel turner, living with his parents at 10 Chandos Street, Newton-le-Willows. They had three children:
    - ◦ Gary M Johnson (born 1944) married Shirley J Morritt in 1968.
    - ◦ Keith Johnson (born 1948).
    - ◦ Neil L Johnson (born 1951).
- Norman Harvey (born 10th June 1924).

- Geraldine Harvey (born 17th July 1933) is believed to have married Stephen Clark in 1960 at Newton-le-Willows. This couple are understood to have had three children, all registered at Birkenhead – Stephen H Clark 1962, David N Clark 1963 and Susan Wendy Clark 1966.

Nora's father, George King Treadwell (1869–1935), a gamekeeper born at Chalkshire Farm, Aylesbury, Buckinghamshire, married Jane née Osmond (1869–1931), born at Halberton, Devon, in 1897 at Tiverton, Devon. They were living at Knoll Farm, Blaby, Leicestershire in 1901. In 1911 they were living at Tynyrheol Cottages, Bryncoch, Neath, Glamorganshire, by when he was a horse keeper underground. They had moved to 1 Primrose Bank, Bryncoch, Neath by 1915. Both their deaths were registered at Neath. In addition to Nora they had five other children:

- Gordon Treadwell (23rd August 1897–1st August 1955), born at Halberton, Devon, was a collier when he enlisted in the Welsh Guards (4727) on 11th December 1915 at Bridgend, Glamorgan. He was described as 6' tall, weighing 146 lbs, with fresh complexion, slightly flat-feet and his religious denomination was Wesleyan. He transferred to the Army Reserve next day and was mobilised in the Reserve Battalion, Welsh Guards on 18th April 1918. He joined at Caterham, Surrey next day. Gordon disembarked at Boulogne, France from Folkestone, Kent on 10th November, joining 1st Battalion on 17th November. He was admitted to No.4 Casualty Clearing Station with influenza on 25th November. He returned to Britain on 3rd January 1919 and was transferred to the Class Z Reserve on 13th January, recording his next-of-kin as Rhoda Morgan, 27 Coedcae Road, Abertridwr, Caerphilly. He was discharged on 31st March 1920. Gordon married Florence Clarke (10th September 1896–10th July 1958) in 1921 at Neath. He was a coal hewer (on compensation – silicosis) in 1939, when they were living at 1 Queens Row, Neath. They were living at Penlan, Tynyrheol Terrace, Bryncoch at the time of his death there. She was living at 53 Main Road, Tynyrheol at the time of her death at Glanrhyd Hospital, Tondu Road, Pen-y-Fai, Bridgend, Glamorgan. They had two children – Betty Treadwell 1922 and Dennis Treadwell 1924.
- Allan Kenneth Treadwell (21st September 1898–1958) was a collier, living with his parents when he enlisted in 3rd Royal Scots Fusiliers on 8th February 1915 at Neath (17186), described as nineteen years and four months old and 5′ 6″ tall. He joined at Ayr the same day and went to France on 23rd March 1915 to join 2nd Battalion. He was wounded on 17th May and was evacuated to Britain on 21st May, on the strength of the Depot next day. He was discharged on 22nd July 1915 having overstated his age on enlistment. Allan married Rose May Hatfield (14th May 1899–1981), born at Leintwardine, Herefordshire, on 30th March 1918 at Cilybebyll Church, Glamorgan. She was living with her mother and siblings at

Llewllech, Pontardawe in 1911. Allan and Rose were living at 85 Gwyn Street, Pontardawe, Glamorgan in 1939. They had four children:
  - George K Treadwell (born 1919) married Catherine N Byrne (born 1920) in 1939. They had four children – Lancelot K Treadwell 1939, Mavis N Treadwell 1942, Pauline K Treadwell 1943 and Alanna J Treadwell 1958.
  - Terence Treadwell (born 1921) married Sarah M Powell (born 1926) in 1948. They had at least one child, Anne Treadwell, in 1949.
  - Miriam Iris Treadwell (30th August 1924–1995) married Rheinallt M Jones (born 1922) in 1952. They had three children – William A Jones 1953, Sharon A Jones 1958 and John R Jones 1961.
  - Gladys M Treadwell (born 14th September 1930) married Peter J Parsons in 1952. They had two children – Dorothy E Parsons 1956 and Brian KJ Parsons 1958.
- Richard Samuel Treadwell (11th December 1899–11th December 1958) was a brick worker when he joined the Royal Navy on 10th January 1918. He joined HMS *Vivid II* (Stokers and Engine Room Artificers School) at Devonport, as a stoker class II (K48313). He was described as 5′ 3½″ tall, with brown hair, grey eyes and fresh complexion. Richard transferred to the battleship, HMS *Collingwood* on 5th April. He was appointed stoker class I on 30th January 1919 and was demobilised on 12th March. He was a coalminer hewer in 1939, living with his sister, Kathleen, at 1 Primrose Bank, Bryncoch. He never married and subsequently died there.
- Kathleen Treadwell (15th December 1902–27th March 1981), born at Blaby, Leicestershire, never married and was living at 1 Primrose Bank, Bryncoch at the time of her death there.
- Una Marian Treadwell (26th September 1906–22nd October 1978), birth registered at Market Harborough, Leicestershire, married Arthur Ansell (28th February 1876–1941), born at Ampthill, Bedfordshire. No trace of the marriage has been found. He was working for the Automobile Association in 1939, when they were living at 2 Robeston Back, Narberth, Pembrokeshire. Arthur had married Kate Catherine (sic) Wright (c.1880–January 1911), born at Crowland, Lincolnshire, on 18th February 1901 at Bolsover Parish Church, Derbyshire. Arthur was a platelayer at the time. Kate's death was registered at Chesterfield, Derbyshire. Arthur was a sawyer's labourer in a colliery at the time of the 1911 Census, living with his children at 14 Lower Grove Road, Chesterfield. Arthur and Kate had four children, including Christopher Edward Ansell (16th November 1901–1973), Percy Harold Ansell (1903–22) and Lillian Maud Ansell (1905). Una married Harry Burrows on 19th April 1950 at Manchester. She is believed to have married for a third time in 1972 as Plowman but no trace of this marriage has been found. She was living at 9 Hulme Hall Crescent, Cheadle Hulme, Greater Manchester at the time of her death. Una and Arthur had five children:

- Malcolm P Ansell (born 1929).
- Gerald A Ansell (born 1930) is believed to have married Elizabeth H Thomas (born 1935) at Pembroke in 1957. They had three children – Christine T Ansell 1961, Tracey E Ansell 1963 and Thomas Barry Ansell 1967.
- Daphne J Ansell (born 1931).
- Mavis P Ansell (1934) is understood to have married Brian Lakin at Manchester in 1957. They had two sons – Ian G Lakin 1961 and Mark A Lakin 1964.
- Bernard Colin Ansell (13th January 1937–1996) married Carol L Nowell (born 1940) at Pembroke in 1961. They had two children – Michael C Ansell 1962 and Janet Ansell 1963.

Norman enlisted as a blacksmith's striker in the Royal Engineers (Territorial Army) on 11th September 1925 (6973652). He attended the VC Dinner at the Royal Gallery of the House of Lords, London on 9th November 1929. In 1934 he was invited to attend the opening of the Mersey Tunnel by King George V.

Norman in 1941 (Charles Snape).

Norman was embodied on 1st September 1939 and was promoted lance corporal on 25th September. He served in France 28th January–18th June 1940 and was promoted corporal on 16th February, lance sergeant on 16th April 1940 and sergeant on 30th July. He served in Palestine from 6th October 1940 and was appointed company quartermaster sergeant (warrant officer class II) on 24th April 1941 while serving with 199th Railway Workshop Company RE.

Norman committed suicide at Haifa, Palestine on 16th February 1942 by shooting himself with a rifle. An inquest on 13th March and a court of inquiry on 30th April concluded that he was temporarily of unsound mind. He is buried at Khayat Beach War Cemetery, Haifa (now Sharon), Israel (A A 4). He is commemorated in a number of other places:

- Newton-le-Willows
  - Harvey Avenue.
  - Named on the War Memorial.
  - A Department for Communities and Local Government commemorative paving stone was dedicated at Newton-le-Willows & Earlestown War Memorial, Market Street, Earlestown, Merseyside on 27th October 2018.

Khayat Beach War Cemetery in Israel, where Norman is buried.

Newton-le-Willows War Memorial, at the Town Hall, Market Street, Earlestown, was unveiled by Lord Newton on 19th April 1905 following the Second Boer War 1899–1902. Memorial panels were added following the Great War and Second World War. In front of the memorial is Norman Harvey's Department for Communities and Local Government commemorative paving stone (Memorials to Valour).

The statue of Norman Harvey in Mesnes Park Remembrance Meadow.

The 1939–45 Star, for operational service between 3rd September 1939 and 2nd September 1945 (8th May 1945 in Europe), was the only campaign star covering the full duration of the Second World War. The Battle of Britain Clasp was awarded to 2,936 fighter aircrew who took part in the Battle of Britain 10th July–31st October 1940. The Bomber Command Clasp was instituted on 26th February 2013 for aircrew who participated in at least one operational sortie in a Bomber Command operational unit. The 1939–45 Star was awarded in general for 180 days service. There were exceptions, such as airborne troops, who qualified if they had participated in any airborne operation and had completed sixty days service in an operational unit. Aircrew qualified after sixty days service in an operational unit, including at least one operational sortie. The award of a gallantry medal or MID qualified the recipient for the 1939–45 Star, regardless of service duration, as did service terminated prematurely by death or disability. In some circumstances only one day's service was required when not covered by another star and some notable examples are:

Battle of France 10th May – 19th June 1940.
St Nazaire Raid 22nd – 28th March 1942.
Dieppe Raid 19th August 1942.
Anglo-Iraq War 10th April – 25th May 1941.
Japanese conquest of Burma 22nd February – 15th May 1942.
Battle of Madagascar 5th May – 5th November 1942.

  - Statue in Mesnes Park Remembrance Meadow, dedicated on 27th October 2018, with his daughter, Geraldine, in attendance.
- Belfast, Co Antrim, Northern Ireland
  - Named on a memorial to the VCs of former Irish Regiments in St Anne's Cathedral.
  - Named on 36th (Ulster) Division Memorial Garden, St Leonard's Crescent off Newtonards Road.
- A memorial stone at Ulster Tower, Thiepval, France, naming all the VCs of 36th (Ulster) Division, was dedicated on 1st July 1991 by the Royal Irish Rangers.
- National Memorial Arboretum, Alrewas, Staffordshire

The Defence Medal was instituted in May 1945 for non-operational military and certain types of civilian war service (Home Guard, Civil Defence, Royal Observer Corps, Fire Service and other approved civilian services) from 3rd September 1939 to 8th May 1945 and for the Pacific Theatre until 2nd September 1945. In the United Kingdom military personnel in headquarters, training units and airfields were eligible for the award. Qualifying service varied. In the United Kingdom the requirement was three years or three months in a Mine and Bomb Disposal Unit. In a non-operational area, not subjected to air attack and not closely threatened, the requirement was one year's service overseas outside the individual's country of residence. In a non-operational area subjected to air attack or closely threatened, the requirement was six months.

- Twenty-two Berberis shrubs representing the twenty-two members of the Church Lads' Brigade who were awarded the VC were planted in the Church Lads & Church Girls Brigade Memorial Plot.
- Named on the Irish Regiments VC Memorial.

The War Medal 1939–45 was instituted on 16th August 1945 and was awarded to all full-time personnel of the armed forces and Merchant Navy for serving for twenty-eight days, irrespective of where they were serving, between 3rd September 1939 and 2nd September 1945.

In addition to the VC he was awarded the 1914–15 Star, British War Medal 1914–20, Victory Medal 1914–19, 1939–45 Star, Defence Medal, War Medal 1939–45 and George VI Coronation Medal 1937. The medals were purchased at Sotheby's on 26th November 1980 for £9,000. The VC is held by the Royal Inniskilling Fusiliers Regimental Museum, The Castle, Enniskillen, Co Fermanagh, Northern Ireland.

LIEUTENANT DAVID STUART MCGREGOR
6th Battalion, The Royal Scots (Lothian Regiment), attached 29th Battalion, Machine Gun Corps

David McGregor was born on 16th October 1895 at 112 Marchmont Road, Edinburgh, Midlothian, Scotland. His father, David McGregor (1st November 1849–4th March 1934), a tailor born at Auchterless, Aberdeenshire, married Annie Stewart née McDonald (2nd December 1855–26th June 1942) on 15th June 1888 at Grandtully, Dull, Perthshire, where she was born. They were living at 130 Marchmont Road, Edinburgh in 1891, at 140 Marchmont Road in 1901 and at 125 Warrender Park Road, Edinburgh in 1922. David senior died at Ferragon, Craigs Road, Corstorphine, Edinburgh. Annie was living at 9 Craigs Road, Corstorphine at the time of her death at 35 Grange Loan, Edinburgh. David junior had three siblings:

- James McDonald McGregor (5th June 1890–29th June 1976), born at 130 Marchmont Road, Edinburgh, was a master clothier. He was commissioned in 6th Seaforth Highlanders on 16th August 1915 and was promoted lieutenant on 1st

July 1917. He last appears in the Army List in October 1921. James married Janet 'Nettie' Douglas Banks (22nd February 1895–13th October 1978), born at 5 Edina Place, Edinburgh, on 28th April 1923 at St Margaret's Parish Church, Restalrig, Edinburgh. He was living at 125 Warrender Park Road, Edinburgh and she at 4 Abercorn Crescent, Edinburgh at the time. She was living with her parents at 3 Wolseley Terrace, Canongate, Edinburgh in 1901. James died at Woodbrae, Hamilton Road, Gullane, East Lothian and Janet at North Berwick.

140 Marchmont Road is the building with the awning over the ground floor shop. JK Rowling, author of the Harry Potter books, lived there in 1993.

- Marjorie Isobel Stuart McGregor (13th January 1893–1968), born at 130 Marchmont Road, Edinburgh, enrolled in the Scottish Education Department to study nursing in March 1911. She qualified as a State Registered Nurse at the School of Medicine, Royal College of Edinburgh on 24th October. Marjorie studied medicine at the Royal College of Surgeons of Edinburgh and the University of Edinburgh (MB ChB). She was a medical officer at Dundee War Hospital, house physician at Leith General Hospital, Edinburgh and house surgeon at Eggington Hall Military Hospital, Derby, Derbyshire. Marjorie married Louis Cecil Wood (6th May 1888–30th September 1962), born at Woolston, New Zealand, on 8th February 1917 at 120 Warrender Park Road, Edinburgh. She was living at 125 Warrender Park Road at the time. His parents were living at The Esplanade, Summer, Christchurch, New Zealand. Louis served in the Mountain Rifles (Voluntary) School Cadets and was a stock buyer at the time of his enlistment on 17th August 1914 at Kensington, Sydney, New South

Auchterless is traditionally known as Kirkton of Auchterless. The history of the area dates back to prehistoric times, with the remains of stone circles and earthen huts. Towie-Barclay farm, which incorporates Tolly Castle, was built in the 14th century but most of the remains are 16th century. Auchterless (New Parish) Church, built in 1879, incorporates parts of the previous church into the tower wall. Auchterless station was opened in 1857 by the Banff Macduff & Turriff Junction Railway on the Inveramsay to Macduff line. It closed to passengers in 1951 and to goods in 1966.

Dull, now in Perth and Kinross, is paired with Boring, Oregon, USA and Bland, New South Wales, Australia in the League of Extraordinary Communities. Dull is in the Scottish Highlands on the River Tay. The parish church is on the site of an early monastery founded by St Adomnan, Abbot of Iona, who died in 704. The surrounding district was known as the Appin of Dull, which refers to the former monastic estate. Four undecorated crosses, of which three survive, one at Dull, stood around the monastic precinct to define an area of sanctuary. The village was in decline throughout the 20th century, with its church and school going out of use. In 1951 the population was over 2,000 but by 2012 was under one hundred.

Wales, Australia into A Company, 3rd Battalion AIF (194). He was described as 5′ 10½″ tall, weighing 170 lbs, with fair complexion, brown eyes, brown hair and his religious denomination was Church of England. He sailed from Sydney on 20th October 1914 aboard HMAT A14 *Euripides*. He embarked aboard SS *Derflinger* on 5th April 1915 to join the Mediterranean Expeditionary Force. He received a gunshot wound to the left foot at Gallipoli on 25th April 1915 and was evacuated aboard HMHS *Delta* on 2nd May. He arrived at Southampton and was admitted to No.1 Southern General Hospital, Dudley Road, Birmingham, Warwickshire on 12th May, from where he was discharged on seven days' leave on 17th May. On 26th May he was admitted to 5th Southern General Hospital, Portsmouth with an abscess on the left foot and was discharged on 3rd June. He transferred to Monte Video Camp, Weymouth, Dorset for convalescence on 21st June. He forfeited four days' pay for breaking out of camp and being drunk at 7.00 a.m. on 26th June until apprehended at 6.30 p.m. on 29th June. On 21st July he embarked at Weymouth and disembarked at Alexandria, Egypt from HMT *Grampion* on 2nd August. Next day he was taken on the strength of the Overseas Base, Mustapha and embarked aboard HMT *Cawdor Castle* for the front on 10th August. Louis rejoined his unit on 16th August. He was admitted to 1st Australian Field Ambulance, Sarpi Camp, Mudros and transferred to 3rd Australian General Hospital and 2nd Australian Stationary Hospital, Mudros with gastro-enteritis on 18th September. He was embarked aboard RMS *Aquitania* on 19th October, sailing on 21st October, and was admitted to New End Military Hospital, Hampstead, London with dysentery on 28th October. He was discharged to duty on 3rd November but was admitted to Tooting Military Hospital with typhoid (relapse) on 16th November and was discharged to duty on 10th February 1916. Louis was absent without leave 11th–14th February, for which he was in detention for three days and forfeited four days' pay. He embarked for return to Egypt aboard SS *Minnetonka* on 25th March and was taken on the strength of 1st Training Battalion, Tel-el-Kebir, Egypt on 10th April. He transferred to 55th Battalion AIF at Ferry Post on 20th April and joined next day. On 19th June he embarked aboard HMT *Caledonian* and disembarked at Marseille, France on 29th June. He was promoted lance corporal on 10th July and corporal on 24th July. He attended a school of instruction 24th August–3rd September, then rejoined the Battalion. **Awarded the MM for his actions at Fleurbaix, France on the night of 30th September/1st October during a raid on a German strongpoint north of Bas Maisnil. On entering the enemy trenches, he attacked and killed a German soldier and destroyed an enemy machine gun emplacement before returning with valuable information about a listening post in the enemy wire, LG 21st December 1916.** Louis was taken ill on 10th October and was admitted to 14th then 15th Australian Field Ambulance. He was transferred to No.1 Australian Casualty Clearing Station next day and to 35th General Hospital, Calais on 16th October. He embarked aboard HMHS *Dieppe* at Calais for evacuation to England and was admitted to 5th Northern General Hospital, Leicester with pneumonia on 21st October. He transferred to No.2 Command Depot, Weymouth on 17th November and was granted leave on 20th November from No.1 Command Depot, Perham Down. He was admitted to Eggington Hall Red Cross Hospital, Derbyshire on 24th November, where he met Marjorie. He joined No.1 Command Depot, Perham Down on 1st January 1917. On 10th March he joined the Australian Army Medical Corps Training Depot, Parkhouse Camp, Tidworth, Wiltshire and was appointed acting RSM of the Convalescent Training Depot, Parkhouse Camp on 13th May. Louis was posted to 6th Officer Cadet Battalion, Oxford on 3rd November and joined on 9th November. He qualified on 26th March 1918 and retained the appointment of cadet until commissioned. On 8th April he was appointed extra duty paid sergeant and acting RSM of 14th Training Battalion, Codford, Wiltshire. Louis was commissioned on 1st May, joined the General Infantry Reinforcements and went to France via Southampton on 9th May. He joined the Australian Infantry Base Depot on 11th May and was taken on the strength of 55th Battalion on 16th May. On 2nd July he was admitted to 15th Australian Field Ambulance with influenza. He attended the Australian Corps Gas School 20th–26th July and rejoined the Battalion. Promoted lieutenant 1st September and attended the Lewis Gun School 3rd-25th October. He was granted leave in Britain on 28th October and seventy-five days' long service leave abroad on 12th November. Louis embarked aboard HMT *Orsova* at Liverpool for return to Australia on 8th January 1919 and arrived at Sydney on 3rd March. A discharge medical next day found him two-thirds incapacitated for general labour. He was discharged on 2nd May 1919. His address was initially Head Street, Summer, Christchurch, New Zealand. By August 1920 it was 26 Ladies Mile, Remuera, Auckland and in September it was 4 Kitirawa Road, Remuera, Auckland. Marjorie embarked aboard SS *Pakeha* at Southampton, Hampshire on 9th December 1920. Their address in January 1921 was 15 Bennett Street, Paparui, Christchurch. Louis served again during the Second World War as a temporary lieutenant on 1st August 1941 with the Waipara Battalion. They were living at Hawarden, North Canterbury in 1942. Marjorie and Louis divorced in 1952 at Christchurch. Marjorie embarked aboard SS *Southern Cross* at Wellington, arriving at Southampton on 20th May 1957. Her intended residence was Eastcott House, Easterton, near Devizes, Wiltshire. She returned to New Zealand on 10th December and subsequently died at Christchurch. They had four children:

- Marjorie Anne Louise Wood (born 14th August 1918), born at Morningside, Edinburgh, was living with her mother at Hawarden in 1943.
- Dorothy Mabel Wood (12th April 1920–1st October 2013), born at Christchurch, New Zealand, was living with her mother at Hawarden in 1943. She married Laurence Gregory Oxley (15th November 1923–7th January 2007) on 19th April 1948 in New Zealand. Laurence was a bank clerk with the Bank of New South Wales, Hereford Street, Christchurch when he enlisted in 21st Battalion, 2nd New Zealand Expeditionary Force on 20th January 1942 (619802). He also served in J Force (New Zealand element of the British Commonwealth Occupation Force in Japan) post Second World War with 4th Base Ordnance Depot. They were living at 17 Greers Road, Canterbury in 1981, when he was a banker. They both died at Christchurch. They had three children – Michael Oxley, Victoria Oxley and Sarah Oxley.
- Moira Isobel Stuart McGregor Wood (9th December 1921–16th March 2011) married Peter Lochhead Kennedy (12th May 1924–2nd January 1992), a medical practitioner, c.1949. He was commissioned as a pilot officer in the Royal New Zealand Air Force and was promoted flying officer on 19th September 1944. They had four children – Paul Kennedy (1950–4th October 2001), Stuart Kennedy (1953), Hamish Kennedy and Belinda Kennedy. The marriage ended in divorce c.1974. Moira married Kenneth Askin Rutherford (26th October 1918–24th March 1998), born at Waipara, New Zealand, after 1976. Ken enlisted in the RNZAF and was promoted to warrant officer. He was commissioned as a pilot officer on 4th August 1943 (NZ 404469) and was promoted flying officer on 4th February 1944 and flight lieutenant on 4th August 1945. **Awarded the DFC while serving with No.17 Squadron RNZAF. He had completed a very large number of sorties including attacks against river craft, rolling stock, buildings and installations. On one occasion, he engaged a formation of enemy fighters that was attacking our ground forces. He dispersed them and harried them for over sixty miles, only breaking off the engagement when running short of petrol. The skill and gallantry of this officer were an inspiration to his fellow pilots, LG 25th September 1945.** He also served in No.67 Squadron RAF. They were living at Whites Road, Ohoka,

Waimakariri, Canterbury in 1981, by when he was a farmer. Kenneth had married Adrienne Mary Warren (14th July 1926–17th July 1976) in 1948 and they had four children – Mimi Rutherford, Dugald Rutherford, Gregor Rutherford and Alastair Rutherford. Peter Kennedy married again on 3rd April 1976 and subsequently died at Christchurch.

  - Stuart 'Ernest' McGregor Wood (23rd December 1923–25th December 2006) married Josephine Anne Lawrence (14th April 1926–11th September 2010) in 1950. He was awarded the Queen's Service Medal. They had four children.

- Ronald Malcolm McGregor (20th September 1898–1972), born at 112 Marchmont Road, Edinburgh, was educated at George Heriot's School (OTC October 1913–July 1916) and Edinburgh University (OTC November 1916–February 1917). He enlisted on 19th September 1916 (TR/2/5104), described as 5′7¾″ tall and weighing 127 lbs. He transferred to the Army Reserve next day and was mobilised on 30th March 1917 to join 53rd Training Reserve Battalion, Kinghorn, Fife next day. He applied for a commission on 16th June, which had to be signed by his father because he was under twenty-one years old. Ronald was commissioned in the Royal Flying Corps on 27th September 1917 and transferred to the Unemployed List on 14th April 1919. He emigrated to Ashburton, Canterbury, New Zealand in 1920 and became a schoolteacher. He married Helen Thomson (born c.1901) there in 1927 and they were living at 128 Park Street, Ashburton in 1928. They travelled to Sydney, Australia aboard SS *Barrabool* from London, departing on 12th May 1933. Their last address was Elmsworth, Galashiels, Scotland and their intended destination was New Zealand. Ronald was commissioned as a flying officer in the Administrative and Special Duties Branch, Section II, Air Training Corps on 15th October 1942 (480090) and was promoted flight lieutenant on 1st October 1944. They were living at 88 Park Street, Ashburton, Canterbury, New Zealand in 1942 and were still there in 1972. They had at least one son, Ronald Stuart McGregor (born c.1930), who was a student in 1949, living at 10 Rolleston Avenue, Fendalton, Canterbury.

David's paternal grandfather, James McGregor (12th January 1817–11th September 1863), born at Kirkmichael, Banffshire, married Marjory née Stuart (17th July 1820–14th June 1910) on 14th November 1847 at Cromdale and Inverallan, Inverness-shire, where she was born. He was a clothier, grocer and spirit retailer in 1861, when they were living at Kirktown, Inverkeithny, Banffshire. He died there. She was a grocer and innkeeper living at the Railway Station Hotel, Grange, Banffshire in 1871. By 1881 she had moved to 31 Thistle Street, Aberdeen and by 1891 to 9 Gladstone Place, Edinburgh. She settled at 97 Craiglea Drive, Edinburgh before 1901 and subsequently died there. In addition to David they had nine other children:

Kirkmichael, in Moray northwest of Tomintoul, was historically part of Banffshire. The church, St Michael's, gives the parish its name. The current building dates from 1807, with substantial repairs in 1951 following a fire.

- Margaret McGregor (born c.1849), born at Auchterless, Aberdeenshire, was living with her mother in 1871.
- John McGregor (born c.1851) was living with his mother in 1871.
- Grigor Stuart McGregor (born c.1853), born at Old Meldrum, Aberdeenshire, was living with his mother in 1871.
- Marjory McGregor (25th April 1854–24th October 1943), born at Inverkeithny, Banffshire, was a housekeeper living with her mother until at least 1901. She died unmarried at 97 Craiglea Drive, Edinburgh.
- Janet Elizabeth McGregor (20th April 1856–8th February 1949) was living with her mother in 1871 and 1881. She was a supervisor at a student's hostel and died unmarried at 97 Craiglea Drive, Edinburgh.
- Isabella McGregor (25th December 1857–1925) was living with her mother in 1871 and 1881. She married Hendry Davidson (6th June 1860–13th November 1923), a clothier born at St Nicholas, Aberdeen, on 25th April 1889 at 14 Melville Terrace, Edinburgh. He was living with his parents at Fern Lea, King's Gate, Old Machar, Aberdeen. They were living at Glencote, Old Machar in 1891, by when he was a master tailor. They had moved to 46 Don Street, Aberdeen by 1901. They were living at Riverview, Peterculter when he died at Westbank, Peterculter, Aberdeenshire. Isabella's death was registered at Peterculter West. They had three children:
    - Arthur Gerrard Davidson (27th July 1890–9th September 1917), born at Glencote, Bonnymuir, Aberdeen, was educated at Aberdeen Grammar School and became a clothier. He served in 4th Gordon Highlanders (1072) from 22nd December 1910 and attended annual camps 15th-29th July 1911 and 20th July–3rd August 1912. He was described as 5′ 8″ tall and weighed 143 lbs. Arthur transferred to 14th London Regiment (1840) on 24th April 1913 and attended annual camp at Abergavenny. He was embodied on 5th August 1914 and went to France from Southampton on 15th September with 1/14th London. Promoted lance corporal 18th January 1915, acting

Arthur Gerrard Davidson is buried in Zuydcoote Military Cemetery, ten kilometres northeast of Dunkirk. The cemetery was opened in the autumn of 1917. Nos.34 and 36 Casualty Clearing Stations were in the area and most of the graves are men who died in these hospitals. On the west side of the cemetery is Zuydcoote French National Cemetery, created after the Great War.

corporal 1st March, lance sergeant 23rd May and sergeant 8th August. He was treated at 3rd Field Ambulance for boils 5th-11th July and at 2nd Field Ambulance and No.4 Casualty Clearing Station for dental trouble 20th-23rd July. Arthur applied for a commission on 7th August while serving with C Company and returned to Britain on 13th September, where he was commissioned in 4th Gordon Highlanders the next day. He later served with the Royal Flying Corps and was killed in action (Zuydcoote Military Cemetery, France – I B 4).

  - Muriel Davidson (born 13th March 1894) was born at 85 Argyll Place, Aberdeen.
  - Marjory Stuart Davidson (1st December 1896–4th September 1972) was born at 453 Great Western Road, Aberdeen and was living at 2 Cecil Hill Street, Albans, Bournemouth, Hampshire at the time of her death there. She never married.
- Elspet 'Elsie' McGregor (4th July 1859–1936) lived with her mother until her death in 1910. Elsie never married and her death was registered at Morningside.
- James McGregor (born 3rd March 1861).
- Annie McGregor (born 5th December 1862) lived with her mother until her death in 1910.

His maternal grandfather, Peter McDonald (c.1804–7th April 1892) a farmer, married Isabella née Stewart (28th July 1808–19th November 1891). They were living at Lodnockey, Dull, Perthshire in 1841. They were still there in 1851 when he was farming forty-five acres and employing two labourers. He was farming seventy-five acres at Upper Lodnockey, of which fifty-eight acres were arable, in 1871. They were still there in 1881, by when he was farming ninety acres, seventy of them arable, and employing two men and two girls. They both died at Laidneskea, Grandtully, Perthshire. In addition to Annie they had seven other children, all born at Dull:

- John McDonald (born c.1838).
- Margaret McDonald (c.1840–17th February 1908), born at Newbigging, Tibbermore, Perthshire.
- Elizabeth 'Betsy' McDonald (born 1841) was a general servant in 1871 and a farmer's daughter in 1881, living with her parents.
- Isabella McDonald (born c.1844) was a general servant in 1871, living with her parents.
- Catherine McDonald (c.1844–16th December 1919) was a general servant in 1871, living with her parents. She married Donald Thomson (c.1841–1919) at

George Watson's College was first established in 1741 on the instructions of George Watson (1654–1723), who bequeathed the bulk of his fortune to found a school for the provision of post-primary boarding education. The governors bought land known as Heriot's Croft in Edinburgh opposite George Heriot's School and the foundation stone was laid on 22nd May 1738. The school opened as George Watson's Hospital on 17th May 1741, with just eleven boys. This grew to eighty-six pupils by 1842 and similar numbers were maintained until the end of the Hospital system in 1870. The governors were responsible for former pupils up to the age of twenty-five and they were helped to find apprenticeships. Watson's preference was for former pupils to become skilled workers but the governors allowed boys who showed ability to pursue medicine or academia. By the 1860s the hospital school system had fallen into disrepute and the solution was to refound Watson's, and three other hospitals under its governorship, as day schools. Watson's reopened as George Watson's College Schools for Boys on 26th September 1870 as a fee-paying day school with 800 boys. In 1869 the original building was sold to the Royal Infirmary of Edinburgh and the school moved a short distance to the former Merchant Maiden Hospital building in Archibald Place. The last remnants of the original building were demolished in 2004. In 1902 the College was the first prestigious Scottish secondary school to appoint a woman head. After the Great War, Edinburgh Royal Infirmary needed to expand again and the Archibald Place school building was cramped and needed to be modernised. In 1927 the site of Merchiston Castle School was purchased and building work commenced facing Colinton Road in August 1929. The new building was opened on 22nd September 1932. Meanwhile, in February 1871 Melville House in George Square, Edinburgh became the first location of George Watson's College Schools for Young Ladies, originally named George Watson's College for Ladies and George Watson's Ladies College in 1890. In 1967 the decision was taken to combine the two Watson's Colleges into a single co-educational campus in Colinton Road. The first joint assembly of the amalgamated school was held on 1st October 1974. It was the largest co-educational school in Scotland, with over 2,400 pupils. Amongst the College's famous alumni are:

- Baron David Steel of Aikwood KT KBE PC (born 1938), Liberal Party leader.
- Sir Malcolm Rifkind KCMG QC (born 1946), Conservative politician.
- Captain Henry Peel Ritchie VC (1876–1958).
- Andrew Gavin Hastings OBE (born 1962), rugby player with sixty-one caps for Scotland, including twenty as captain.
- Sir Chris Hoy MBE (born 1976), six-times Olympic gold medal winning track cyclist.

Aberfeldy in 1877. He was governor and she was matron of Mull Combination Poorhouse (also known as Dervaig Road Poor House), Kilninian and Kilmore, Tobermory, Argyllshire at the time of the 1891 and 1901 Censuses. They both died at Woodbine Cottage, Strathtay, Perthshire. They had three children, all born in Hong Kong – Margaret I Thomson 1879, George John Thomson 1882 and Robert William Thomson 1883.
- Robert McDonald (c.1848–1909) was a ploughman in 1871 and a farmer's son in 1881, living with his parents.
- Christina McDonald (c.1852–1933) was a thresher in 1871, living with her parents. She never married.

George Heriot's School was established in 1628 as George Heriot's Hospital, by bequest of the royal goldsmith, George Heriot. It is governed by the charity George Heriot's Trust. It opened in 1659 with thirty sickly children and, as its finances grew, it took in other pupils. The construction was completed in time for the building to be occupied by Oliver Cromwell's forces during the English Civil War. By the end of the 18th century the Governors had purchased extensive land for feuing (a form of leasehold), which with other land purchases generated considerable revenue. There were a number of disturbances in the 1840s, culminating in 1846 when fifty-two boys were dismissed. This was mainly due to the almost monastic separation of the boys from home life. An 1836 Act gave the governors the power to use the Trust's surplus to set up schools outside the Hospital. As a result, between 1838 and 1885 the Trust ran thirteen juvenile and eight infant outdoor schools across Edinburgh. At its height in the early 1880s this network of free schools had almost 5,000 pupils. The Balfour Commission in 1885 imposed reform on Heriot's, which became a modern, technically oriented day school, charging modest fees. The outdoor school network was wound up and the resources were used for scholarships and bursaries, some of which provided a path to university education. The most uncontroversial aspect of the Balfour Commission's scheme was the takeover of the Watt Institution and School of Arts by the Trust. It was renamed Heriot-Watt College. The School and College were both under the Heriot Governors until the College required a separation in 1927. In 1966 the College was granted university status as Heriot-Watt University. In 1979 George Heriot's became co-educational. By the early 21st century it had c.1,600 pupils and continued to serve its charitable goal by providing free education to a number of fatherless children. Amongst its famous alumni is the actor Alastair Sim (1900–76).

The Merchants of Edinburgh Golf Club is close to the city centre and was designed by Ben Sayers (1856–1924) in 1907. Sayers was a Scottish professional who became a distinguished golf teacher (including King George V), course designer and manufacturer of golf equipment. Although he won twenty-four top-level tournaments, he never won the Open Championship, his best performance was tying for second place in 1888. The Merchants of Edinburgh golf course was altered by James Braid (1870–1950) in 1936. Braid won the Open Championship in 1901, 1905, 1906, 1908 and 1910. The course is described as challenging, with fantastic views.

David was educated at George Watson's College and George Heriot's School, both in Edinburgh. He served in the Officer Training Corps from October 1911. David joined the Edinburgh Stockbridge branch of the Commercial Bank of Scotland in 1911 and was an Associate of the Scottish Bankers Institute. He enlisted in the Midlothian Battery, 1st Lowland Brigade RFA (TF) on 14th February 1913 (369 & 650089), based at 30 Grindlay Street, Edinburgh, described as 5′ 6½″ tall and weighing 151 lbs. He attended annual training in 1913 and 1914. David was a keen sportsman, particularly swimming, golf and rugby. He was a member of the Merchants of Edinburgh Golf Club.

David was mobilised on 5th August 1914 and was granted four days' leave on 14th March and 3rd October 1915. He applied for a commission on 16th September and was commissioned in 3/6th Royal Scots on 8th October 1915. He sailed for Egypt and disembarked on 18th May 1916. The Battalion landed at Marseille, France on 16th May and it is not known when he caught up with it. However, he was involved in the Battle of the Somme. In September 1916 he volunteered for the Machine Gun Corps and joined the 29th Battalion. David was promoted lieutenant on 1st May 1917.

Awarded the VC for his actions at Hoogmolen, Belgium on 22nd October 1918, LG 14th December 1918. He was killed during the VC action at Hill 66, Hoogmolen and is buried in Stasegem Communal Cemetery, Groendreef, Stasegem, Belgium (A I). The VC was presented to his parents by the King in the ballroom at

David McGregor's grave in Stasegem Communal Cemetery.

David's parents' grave in Corstorphine Hill Cemetery (Memorials to Valour).

Buckingham Palace on 15th February 1919. He is commemorated in a number of other places in Edinburgh, Midlothian:

- On the family headstone, Corstorphine Hill Cemetery.
- George Heriot School War Memorial and the Roll of Honour.
- A Department for Communities and Local Government commemorative paving stone was dedicated in Heriot Place outside George Heriot School on 22nd October 2018.

George Heriot's School War Memorial was dedicated in 1922. Of the 2,657 men connected with the School who served in the Great War, 461 were killed or died, almost one hundred of them under the age of twenty.

- George Watson's College War Memorial, Colinton Road.
- A commemorative paver was dedicated at The Royal Scots Club, 29 Abercromby Place by the Princess Royal on 11th March 2019 to mark the centenary of the Club. There is also a framed picture and VC citation inside the Club.
- Commercial Bank of Scotland Ltd War Memorial at the Royal Bank of Scotland, 36 St Andrews Square.
- His father donated a framed portrait of his son to the Merchants of Edinburgh Golf Club but its current whereabouts are not known. There is a framed photograph and citation, together with that of John Cruickshank VC.

In addition to the VC he was awarded the British War Medal 1914–20 and Victory Medal 1914–19. The VC was donated to the Royal Scots in 1976 by David's brother, James. He was not well enough to attend the ceremony and so the medals were handed over to the Colonel of the Regiment, Major General DT Young, by the Minister of Gullane, East Lothian and a friend of James'. The VC is held by The Museum of The Royal Scots (The Royal Regiment), The Castle, Edinburgh, Midlothian.

The Commercial Bank of Scotland War Memorial (Memorials to Valour).

The George Watson's College War Memorial.

240693 ACTING SERGEANT LOUIS MCGUFFIE
1/5th Battalion, The King's Own Scottish Borderers

(*Mary A Kelly*)

Louis McGuffie was born on 15th February 1893 at High Street, Wigtown, Wigtownshire, Scotland. His father, Edward McGuffie (15th April 1858–20th October 1917), born at Bridge of Bladnoch, Bladnoch, Wigtownshire, was a general labourer. He married Lillias 'Lily' McCallum née McKay (1st June 1851–22nd January 1890), born at Fodderty, Ross & Cromarty, on 25th December 1883 at Wigtown. She had married Benjamin McCallum (8th October 1845–9th July 1879), a shepherd born at Durness, Sutherlandshire, on 14th June 1872 at Fodderty. Benjamin died at Glasserton, Wigtownshire and Lily was living with her children at High Vennel, Wigtown in 1881. Lily and Benjamin had five children – Evander Edward McCallum 1872, David McCallum 1874, Maggie Ann McCallum 1876, Elizabeth Helen McCallum 1878 and Benjamin McCallum 1880. Lily died at High Street, Wigtown. Edward and his sons moved in with his parents at East Side High Vennel, Wigtown and were living there at the time of the 1891 Census. He married Catherine née Gilmour (10th June 1860–24th May 1937), a field worker born at North Side of High Street, Wigtown, on 13th October 1892 at Wigtown. They were living at 20 Low Vennel, Wigtown in 1901, by when he was a ploughman. By 1911 he was a general labourer, living at 21 Low Vennel. Edward died at 19 Low Vennel. He had six sons from his two marriages:

- Thomas McGuffie (4th September 1884–1943), born at Botany Street, Wigtown, served in the Royal Scots Fusiliers in France during the Great War (35004). He married Annie Little MacAulay (1882–1946), born at Glencairn, Dumfriesshire, on 5th June 1908 at Closeburn, Dumfriesshire. Both Thomas and Annie died at Buittle, Kirkcudbrightshire.
- Edward John McGuffie (23rd July 1886–3rd January 1955) served in the Cameron Highlanders during the Great War. He suffered from ankle problems and was eventually discharged medically unfit. Edward married Lillian 'Lily' Ann late Mathieson/Matheson née Hogg (28th October 1876–29th June 1946), born at

High Street Wigtown.

Wigtown, in the former royal burgh of Wigtownshire, is known as Scotland's book town, with its concentration of second-hand book shops and an annual book festival. Settlement of the area dates back to Neolithic times and the most notable remains are the Torhousekie standing stones. A Dominican friary, Blackfriars, was founded north of the mouth of the Bladnoch, southeast of Wigtown in 1267. A castle existed by 1291 but there are now no visible remains. By medieval times the settlement centred around a large broad street. Some streets in the town date back to this time. The town became a burgh under King David II in 1341 and its status was formally recognised in a royal charter in 1457. It was made a royal burgh in 1469. The trading port of Wigtown, and its rival Kircudbright, declined from the end of the 15th century. On 11th May 1685 two Scottish Covenanters, Margaret Maclauchlan aged about sixty-three, and Margaret Wilson, aged about eighteen, were executed by Scottish Episcopalians by tying them to stakes on the town's mudflats and allowing them to drown in the rising tide. It was hoped that the younger woman would change her mind after watching the older woman drown but this failed and both died. They are buried in the local churchyard and there is a memorial obelisk on Windy Hill above the town, from where this view was taken. In addition to its mainly agricultural economy, there was a lively smuggling trade in the 18th century. Wool and cotton manufacturing was introduced in the early 1790s. A creamery and a distillery also opened nearby. The current county buildings were erected in 1862 in an unusual French-style. They were restored in 2002/03. A RAF airfield opened in 1941 and was the home of No.1 Air Observers School, later No.1 Advanced Flying Unit (Observer), and a number of short stay operational squadrons. Although the RAF left in 1948, the station is still in use today by light aircraft and is known as Baldoon Airfield. Amongst the notable people who were born or lived at Wigtown are:

- Helen Carte Boulter, born Susan Helen Couper Black (1852–1913), also known as Helen Lenoir, was the second wife of impresario and hotelier Richard D'Oyly Carte. She attended the University of London 1871–74 and was briefly a teacher and actor. In 1877 she became Richard D'Oyly Carte's assistant and later his business manager. She helped to produce the Gilbert and Sullivan and other Savoy Operas, including the arrangements for American productions and tours. She married Richard in 1888 and, as his health declined, she assumed increasing responsibility. She took full control upon his death in 1901. She remarried in 1902 but continued to own the company and ran most of its business interests. When she died, the Savoy Theatre, hotel business and opera company passed to her stepson, Rupert D'Oyly Carte.
- Paul Laverty (born 1957), born in Calcutta, India, was educated at All Souls' School, Wigtown. He gained philosophy and law degrees before living in Nicaragua for three years, where he worked for a human rights organisation. Thereafter he worked with Ken Loach as his screenplay writer, starting with *Carla's Song* in 1996, which starred Robert Carlyle. Loach and Laverty collaborated on other films, including *The Wind That Shakes the Barley*, set during the Irish War of Independence, which won the Palme d'Or at the Cannes Film Festival in 2006.

Bladnoch was a tiny village of ten or so houses until the Bladnoch Distillery was established in 1817. A ford at the village was replaced by the first bridge in 1728, on the south side of which was a public house known for heavy drinking, rowdy behaviour and fighting. A new bridge was built in 1867 and the stones of the old bridge were used to construct a viaduct for the railway over the river in 1875. By 1877 Bladnoch was a large village with its economy based upon McClelland's Distillery, McClelland's Preserved Potato Manufactory and Farina Mill. Other businesses included a creamery, coach building, an iron foundry, a large bakery, drapery and tailoring. By 1845 twenty workers were employed by the distillery, which was enlarged and modernised in 1878. By 1887 output was 51,000 gallons annually. Despite a reduction in demand, reduction in barley production, rising excise duty and the growth of the temperance movement in the late 19th century, Bladnoch survived. However, whisky production ceased on the outbreak of the Second World War but malt continued to be produced until 1949. The distillery reopened in 1957 and had several owners until it was acquired by Bell's in 1983. In 1987 United Distillers Group took over Bell's. Modernisation resulted in eight times the output of 1887. It closed again in 1993 but reopened in 2000. The company went into administration in 2014 but reopened under new owners in 2017.

Inverness. She had married Peter Hogg in 1895 at Inverness. Her death was registered at Kelton, Kirkcudbrightshire. He died opposite 5 St Andrews Street, Castle Douglas, Kirkcudbrightshire. They had a son:

  - James Dornan McGuffie (31st October 1908–1985), born at 25 High Street, Wigtown, married Mary Wolstencroft (18th October 1914–May 1997) in 1944 at Manchester, Lancashire. She was a machinist shirt maker in 1939, living with her parents at 39 Ascot Road, Manchester. Both their deaths were registered at Manchester. They had two daughters – Janet McGuffie 1947 and Margaret A McGuffie 1949.

- James Dornan McGuffie (28th December 1888–18th January 1965), born at High Street, Wigtown, was a ploughman and later a dairyman. He married Margaret 'Maggie'

Looking along Low Vennel towards the county building on North Main Street. The last building at the end of the street on the right, which sticks out slightly, is 1 North Main Street, where Louis' mother lived later. His paternal grandparents lived on the east side of High Vennel in 1891, which is on the left in this view.

Ann Gloag (1885–1936), a domestic cook born at Gretna Green, Dumfriesshire, on 29th May 1914 at Brookhillbank, Applegarth, Dumfriesshire. James married Isabella Scott Downie née Syme (29th May 1900–1976), born at Kirkcaldy and Abbotshall, Fife, at Cupar in 1939. They lived at Kidston View, Peeblesshire. She had married James Downie in 1920. James McGuffie died at Nether Kidston, Peeblesshire. James had four children to his first marriage:

  - Edward Irvine McGuffie (20th January 1915–2001), born at Powillmount, Kirkbean, Kirkcudbrightshire, was a gamekeeper at the time of his marriage to Mary Middleton (6th May 1919–October 1992), born at Closeburn, Arbuthnott, Kincardineshire, on 18th August 1939 at Masonic Hall, Church Street, Brechin, Angus. He was living at Tannadice House, Finavon, Forfar, Angus and she at Stannochie Farm, Brechin. Mary was the sister of Alexander Jolly Middleton, who married Edward's cousin, Mary 'Molly' Janet McGuffie. He died at Brechin, Angus and she at Blackpool, Lancashire. They had four children – Elsie McGuffie 18th March 1940, Irene McGuffie 30th September 1942, Edward 'Eddie' Irvine McGuffie 25th July 1947 and Mary McGuffie 4th July 1951. Eddie served in the RAF as a corporal 1966–75. He married Joanna Matykowski (born 1949), born at Nottingham, Nottinghamshire, in May 1972 at St Serf's Church, Almondbank, Perthshire. They had four children.
  - Isabella 'Bella' Lilian McGuffie (1916–2005), Wigtown, married James 'Jim' Park Brown (1909–82), born at Kirkden, Angus, in 1939 at St Clement, Dundee. They had a son, James Brown (1941–96). Their deaths were registered at Arbroath, Angus.
  - James Alexander McGuffie (1917–91). His death was registered at Portree, Isle of Skye.
  - Mary 'Molly' Janet McGuffie (31st December 1919–27th March 2015) married Alexander 'Alec/Eck' Jolly Middleton (1916–31st March 2014), born at Montrose, Angus, in 1940 at Fettercairn, Aberdeenshire. They lived at Overkelly Farm, Pittenweem, Fife. Alexander was the brother of Mary Middleton, who married Mary Janet McGuffie's cousin, Edward Irvine McGuffie. They were living at North Esk Road, Edzell, Angus at the time of their deaths there. They had three children including, Alexander James Middleton (1940–2001).

- Alexander Mitchell McGuffie, a twin with Benjamin, (17th August 1895–20th February 1897), was born at 25 High Street and died at 8 High Street, Wigtown.
- Benjamin McCallum McGuffie, a twin with Alexander, (17th August 1895–17th February 1896), born and died at 25 High Street.
- Robert McGuffie (24th November 1897–6th January 1977), born at 18 Botany Street, Wigtown, served in the Royal Scots Fusiliers during the Great War (28538). He was wounded a number of times before losing his right arm in September 1917. Although he later fell on desperate times, he refused to sell

his brother's VC when he inherited it, because he said it was not his to sell. He lived at Seaview, Wigtown. On 4th March 1924 he married Margaret McGhie (14th May 1899–21st February 1980), a domestic servant born at Monreith Home Farm, Mochrum, Wigtownshire, at The Manse, Wigtown. Robert became a wildfowler and they lived at Overkillie, Pittenweem, Fife. Robert spent his final years with his niece, Molly and her husband, at Overkelly Farm and died at Marie Curie Memorial Home, Cupar, Fife and Margaret at Dudgeon House, Dumfries.

Louis' paternal grandfather, Thomas McGuffie (born 28th August 1833), born at Bridge of Bladnoch, Wigtownshire, was an errand boy in 1851, living with his parents at Bank Street, Wigtown. He married Margaret née Rankin (c.1838–2nd May 1892) on 27th March 1857 at Wigtown, where she was born. They were living at East Side High Vennel, Wigtown in 1891. Thomas was a rural postman in 1871, when they were living at Bladnoch. By 1881 he was a post messenger and they were living at 50 High Street, Wigtown. Margaret died at High Vennel, Wigtown. In addition to Edward they had nine other children:

- Jane McGuffie (born 8th April 1860), born at Bridge of Bladnoch, Wigtownshire.
- Lawrence McGuffie (22nd June 1862–1864).
- Thomas Rankin McGuffie (24th October 1864–1946) was an ostler in 1881. He married Mary Bella Hannah (c.1867–1953), possibly born at Kirkcolm, Dumfriesshire, in 1891 at Wigtown. He was a general labourer in 1901, when they were living at 7a High Vennel, Wigtown. They had at least four children:
    - Thomas McGuffie (5th September 1891–1963) married Jane Pretsell (1892–1959) at Wigtown on 28th February 1913. They had at least four children – Mary Ann Scott McGuffie (1913–2003), Margaret Aird McGuffie (1915),

Bank Street, Wigtown.

Jane McGuffie (1920–2006) and Thomas McGuffie (1927–2006). Thomas senior was a horseman, living at 30 Agnew Crescent, Wigtown, when he enlisted in the Army Service Corps (T4/040876) on 7th January 1915, described as 5′6¾″ tall and weighing 163 lbs. He joined at Bradford on 8th January and was posted to 196th Company ASC (24th Division) on 6th February. Appointed acting corporal on 8th March and acting company quartermaster sergeant on 3rd April. The Division went to France in late August 1915. He was granted leave 20th-27th January 1916 and 28th December–7th January 1917, while serving with 3rd Company, 24th Divisional Train. Mentioned in Despatches, LG 10th July 1917. He was granted leave 3rd-17th February 1918. On 3rd April he was granted 3d per day extra pay having served for three years as CQMS. On 26th September he was appointed acting company sergeant major and was granted leave 15th-29th January 1919, extended to 4th February. Thomas returned to Britain on 29th June, was demobilised from the Dispersal Unit, Ripon on 1st July and transferred to the Class Z Reserve on 29th July.
  - Margaretta Aird McGuffie (1893–24th September 1950) was living at 4 Belmont Street, Skipton, Yorkshire, England at the time of her death.
  - Jane McGuffie (born 1896).
  - Mary Bella Hannah McGuffie (1900–69).

- Agnes McCaul McGuffie (29th November 1866–13th August 1938) married James White in 1893 at Wigtown. It is not known what became of him. Agnes married James McCormick More (25th February 1867–6th January 1938), born at Glasserton, Wigtownshire, in 1925 at Wigtown. James had married Helen McCormick Irvine (1867–6th November 1923) on 31st May 1901 at Whithorn, Wigtownshire.
- Matthew Barbour McGuffie (3rd June 1870–1870).
- Ellen/Helen Rankin McGuffie (16th August 1871–22nd July 1897) never married.
- Mary McGuffie (18th April 1873–1906) never married.
- Anne Thomson McGuffie (5th November 1876–1878).
- Margaret 'Maggie' McGuffie (born 10th May 1879) was born in Stranraer Prison.

The castle at Stranraer was probably built by Adair of Kilhilt around 1511. It has had a number of uses since, including a store in the early 20th century, a prison in the 19th century and is now a museum.

His maternal grandfather, John Gilmour (c.1823–2nd February 1886), born in Ireland, was a general

Botany Street, Wigtown.

labourer. He married Agnes née McAllister (born c.1828) c.1851 at Wigtown, where she was born. She was a seamstress at the time of the 1851 Census, visiting the household of John and Mary Long, South Side of Back Road, Wigtown. Also visiting was a John Gilmour, an agricultural labourer born in Ireland, aged forty-five. If this was Agnes' future husband, which seems likely, his age was recorded incorrectly in the census return. Her age varies considerably in censuses returns, giving a range for her birth of 1824–31. Her name has also been seen as Nancy, which may have been a pet name. They were living in Wigtown at North Side High Street in 1861, Botany Street in 1871 and South High Street in 1881. John subsequently died there. Agnes was living with her daughter, Agnes, at South Side of Back Road, Wigtown in 1891. In addition to Catherine they had five other children:

- Margaret Gilmour (born c.1852).
- Agnes Gilmour (c.1855–1910) was a servant and domestic cook in 1881, living with her parents. She was living with her mother in 1891 and alone at 12c North Back Street, Wigtown in 1901, when she was described as an outdoor worker. Agnes never married.
- John Gilmour (7th February 1857–1902) was a general labourer in 1881, living with his parents.
- Thomas Gilmour (23rd November/December 1862–2nd July 1918) was a general labourer in 1881, living with his parents. He married Mary Ireland (c.1873–1945) in 1888 at Wigtown. They were living at High Street, Wigtown in 1891. By 1901 he was a farm labourer and they were living at 19b Botany Street Poorhouse, Wigtown. They had at least eight children:
    - James Douglas Gilmour (born 1891).
    - Sarah Gilmour (born 1895).
    - Mary Gilmour (born and died 1896).
    - Mary Gilmour (born 1897).
    - Thomas Gilmour (1900–61).
    - Nancy Gilmour (1901–95) never married.
    - Norman Sydney Gilmour (31st December 1911–1974) married Williamena Thompson (1906–96) in 1934.
    - Marion Robison Gilmour (12th January 1915–2001) never married.
- Jane Gilmour (8th September 1865–1906) died unmarried.

:own Higher Grade School, now Wigtown Primary School.

Louis' grave in Zantvoorde British Cemetery.

Louis was educated at Wigtown Higher Grade School and was probably employed in farming thereafter. He played for Wigtown United Football Club. He also served in 5th King's Own Scottish Borderers (2255 later 240693) and was mobilised on 4th August 1914. He departed Liverpool with the Battalion on 21st

The entrance archway to the Louis McGuffie VC Memorial Gardens, Wigtown. The commemorative paving stone is below the first step beyond the gateway (Memorials to Valour).

May 1915, disembarked at Mudros on 29th May and landed at Gallipoli on 6th June. He was wounded there in December and returned to Mudros on 7th January 1916. He moved to Egypt on 4th February and accompanied the Battalion to France on 17th April 1918.

Awarded the VC for his actions at Piccadilly Farm, near Wytschaete, Belgium on 28th September 1918, LG 14th December 1918. He was killed by a shell at Kruiseik, Belgium on 4th October 1918. He was buried 630m west-southwest of the church in Kruiseik (Map Sheet 28 grid reference P.5.b.7.4). His remains were exhumed in November 1919 and were reburied in Zantvoorde British Cemetery, Belgium (I D 12). Louis is commemorated in a number of other places:

The brass memorial plaque inside Wigtown Town Hall (Memorials to Valour).

Wigtown County Buildings, also known as Wigtown County Buildings and Town Hall.

- Louis McGuffie VC Memorial Gardens, Wigtown, Dumfries & Galloway.
- A Department for Communities and Local Government commemorative paving stone was dedicated at Louis McGuffie VC Memorial Gardens Arch, Wigtown on 28th September 2018.
- Brass plaque inside Wigtown Town Hall, Dumfries & Galloway, paid for by Sir Peter McClelland and unveiled by Sir Herbert Maxwell, Lord Lieutenant of the County, on 4th December 1920.
- Named on Wigtown War Memorial.
- A first day cover commemorating the centenary of his award was released on 28th September 2018 by the British Forces Philatelic Society, with the Royal Burgh of Wigtown and the King's Own Scottish Borderers Association.
- Memorial dedicated at Glasgow Central Station on 8th May 2022 honouring fifty-five VCs from Glasgow and the West of Scotland.

No.1 North Main Street, Wigtown, where Louis' mother lived. The street to the right is Low Vennel.

Wigtown War Memorial.

The panel on Wigtown War Memorial bearing Louis' name.

The VC was presented to his mother by the King at Buckingham Palace on 17th May 1919. She was given a civic reception when she returned to Wigtown, where she was met by the Provost and other dignitaries and was escorted home by a local band. She was greeted by the Right Honourable Earl of Stair, Provost Dyer, Stranraer, and others in the evening, when they expressed their appreciation of her son's bravery

The 1914–15 Star was instituted in December 1918 for personnel who served in any theatre between 5th August 1914 and 31st December 1915. Those awarded the 1914 Star, Africa General Service Medal or Khedive's Sudan Medal 1910, were ineligible to receive it. The 1914–15 Star was awarded with the British War and Victory Medals, the trio known as *Pip, Squeak and Wilfred* after comic strip characters. 2,366,000 medals were awarded to members of the British, Dominion and Empire forces.

The King's Own Scottish Borderers Museum in Berwick-upon-Tweed is, rather unusually for a Scottish regiment, in England. The Regiment was created in 1689, to defend Edinburgh against the Jacobites, and was recruited in the record time of two hours, as men flocked to safeguard the city. In 2006 the Regiment became part of the Royal Regiment of Scotland. The Museum shares the former Berwick Barracks with Berwick Gymnasium Art Gallery and Berwick Museum and Art Gallery.

and their deep regret that he had not survived the war. The residents of Wigtown subscribed to a special fund for her and the proceeds were handed to her during the ceremony for the unveiling of the memorial plaque at the County Buildings (Wigtown Town Hall). Catherine was living at 1 North Main Street, Wigtown when her son's CWGC cemetery register entry was compiled. She subsequently died at her home at 2 North Main Street, Wigtown.

In addition to the VC he was awarded the 1914–15 Star, British War Medal 1914–20 and Victory Medal 1914–19. The VC was presented to the King's Own Scottish Borderers by his brother, Robert, on 19th August 1971. The VC is held by the King's Own Scottish Borderers Museum, Berwick Barracks, The Parade, Berwick-upon-Tweed, Northumberland.

18321 PRIVATE MARTIN JOSEPH MOFFATT
2nd Battalion, The Prince of Wales's Leinster Regiment (Royal Canadians)

Martin Moffatt was born on 24th April 1884 at Knappagh Road, Sligo, Co Sligo, Connaught, Ireland. His surname has also been seen as Moffat, Moffitt and Moffit. His father, also Martin Moffatt (born c.1856), was living at Barrack Street, Sligo when he married Bridget 'Bessie' née McDonagh (c.1856–23rd January 1912) on 24th February 1879 at Calry, Sligo. They were both born at Sligo. Martin senior was a fireman in a gas yard at Knappagh, Co Sligo in November 1892 and a dock labourer in 1901, when they were living at 25 Knappagh Road, Sligo. By 1911 he was an engineer and they were living at 24 Knappagh Road. They later moved to Barrack Street, Sligo. Martin junior had at least nine siblings, all born at Sligo:

- Catherine 'Kate' Moffatt (born 15th January 1880) is believed to have died before 1901.
- Jane Moffatt (7th November 1881–2nd July 1946), a twin with Mary, was a domestic servant in 1901. She married Alexander Campbell (28th February 1884–21st September 1958) on 27th February 1906 at Elphin, Sligo, where he was born. He was a cabinet maker when he enlisted in the Connaught Rangers on 29th April 1902 at Galway (7430), described as 5′9″ tall, weighing 155 lbs, with fresh complexion, brown eyes, brown hair and his religious denomination was Church of England. He joined at Galway on 3rd May and was posted to 1st Battalion on 16th February. He was awarded a good conduct badge on 29th April

Sligo is a commercial and cultural centre on the west coast of Ireland, noted for its connections to the poet WB Yeats. There are numerous ancient sites around the town, including a Neolithic causewayed enclosure of c.4000 BC at Maugheraboy, the oldest known in the British Isles. The natural harbour was known to Greek, Phoenician and Roman traders. During the early medieval period a monastery was founded eight kilometres to the north at Drumcliff. By the 12th century there was a bridge and small settlement at the site of the present town. The Norman knight Maurice Fitzgerald, Lord Chief Justice of Ireland, established the medieval town and port, building Sligo Castle in 1245. He and the King of Connacht founded a Dominican Friary in 1253. There was fierce competition between Gaelic dynasties for the port duties of Sligo, which resulted in the town being burned, sacked or besieged forty-nine times during the medieval period. The town and port grew in importance, trading with Galway, Bristol, France and Spain. After the Elizabethan conquest, Sligo became the county town for the newly created County of Sligo. Parliamentarian soldiers partially sacked Sligo in 1642. During the Williamite War of 1689–91 the town was captured by the Jacobites, who repulsed a Williamite attempt to retake it. In 1798 a force of the Limerick Militia, Essex Fencibles and local yeomanry were defeated by combined Irish and French forces. Charlotte Blake Thornley, mother of Bram Stoker, may have been born in Sligo in 1818. The town suffered from a cholera outbreak in 1832 and Stoker may have been influenced by her experiences of the epidemic when he wrote *Dracula*. The Great Famine of 1847–51 forced over 30,000 people to emigrate through Sligo and there is a memorial on the Quays. The early years of the 20th century saw a great deal of industrial unrest as workers fought for better pay and conditions. This resulted in two major strikes in 1912 and 1913, both ending in victory for the workers.

1904 and transferred to Section A, Army Reserve on 29th April 1905. He was an engineer in 1911, when they were living on Knappagh Road, Sligo. Alexander re-engaged for the Section D Reserve for four years on 28th April 1914. He was mobilised and went to France on 26th August 1914 to join 2nd Battalion. He was promoted lance corporal on 21st September and acting corporal on 30th September. He received gunshot wounds to the face, left thigh and left arm and was admitted to 11th General Hospital, Boulogne on 4th November. He was evacuated to Britain on 7th November and was held on the strength of the Depot. Alexander transferred to 3rd Battalion on 22nd April 1915 and to 1st Royal Irish Regiment on 28th July (11363). He went to Egypt with the Egyptian Expeditionary Force on 5th September. He received a gunshot wound to the shoulder and was admitted to the Convalescent Depot, Abbassia on 19th May 1916. He returned to Britain, joined the Depot on 24th June, was promoted lance sergeant on 12th August, transferred to 3rd Battalion on 20th November and to 2nd Battalion on 22nd February 1917. Alexander transferred to the Labour Corps on 14th May 1917 (174894) and was posted to 659th Company on 4th August. He reverted to lance corporal on 19th September and was posted to 642nd Company on 1st December and 641st Company on 14th August 1918. Alexander was discharged no longer physically fit for war service on 17th February 1919. Jane and Alexander both died at Sligo. They had nine children including:

- Emily Campbell (born 7th October 1906), a shop assistant, married Thomas Murren on 20th November 1928 at the Cathedral of the Immaculate Conception, Sligo. She was living at Ballydoogan, Co Galway and he at Ballytivnan, Sligo at the time. They had a son and three daughters.
- Margaret Campbell (born 30th January 1908).
- Bridget Campbell (5th–8th August 1909).
- Mary Ettie Campbell, a twin with Ester (born 3rd October 1910) married Valentine Cawley (11th February 1906–19th June 1979) in 1927 at Sligo, where he was born. He was living at 113 Old Chester Road, Chester Green, Derbyshire at the time of his death there. They had ten children including – Martin Valentine Cawley (1931–81), Bernard A Cawley (born and died 1932), Patrick J Cawley (1934–2008), Mary A Cawley (1936), Raymond F Cawley (1938–2011) and Amy Cawley (1940–2010).
- Ester Campbell, a twin with Mary (born 3rd October 1910), probably did not survive infancy as she was not mentioned in her father's service record.
- Martin Francis Campbell (14th September 1913–c.1950).
- Mary Jane Campbell (11th October 1915–11th May 1916).
- Joan Campbell (1920–7th April 1963) married Thomas Callaghan (died 24th October 1986) a motor mechanic, on 19th April 1937 at the Cathedral of the Immaculate Conception, Sligo. He was living at 88 St Joseph's Terrace, Sligo at the time. They both died at 7 St Brigid's Place, Sligo. They had six children including – Mary EV Callaghan (1938–2004).

- Mary Moffatt (7th November 1881–2nd June 1882), a twin with Jane.
- Patrick Moffatt (16th March 1886–August 1971) was a labourer in 1901. He moved to England and married Evelyn Florence Grant (born 11th March 1890), born at 10 Sainsbury Road, Gipsy Hill, Lambeth, London, on 22nd December 1918 at Eastbourne, Sussex. He was a warehouseman in 1920, when they were living at 34 Gipsy Hill, Lambeth. He emigrated to Montréal, Canada and moved to New York, USA on 5th September 1929. He was living at 4282 Park Avenue, New York when he applied for US Citizenship on 25th November 1929 (2-13096), described as a labourer, 5′ 9″ tall, with fair complexion, blue eyes, grey/black hair and weighing 150 lbs. Evelyn and their son Maurice were living at 5 South Vale, Upper Norwood, London when they travelled to New York aboard SS *Tuscania* to join Patrick, arriving on 14th October 1930. Evelyn returned to England and was living at 61 Gipsy Hill, Lambeth in 1939. Patrick died in New York. They had a son prior to their marriage:

    - Maurice Alexander Grant, also registered as Moffatt (2nd June 1918–20th February 2001), born at Lambeth, London. He returned to England and married Joan 'Panda' Mary Smith (born 17th September 1916), born at Daventry, Northamptonshire, at Kensington, London in January 1946. She was living with her parents at The Limes, High Street, Northampton in 1939, when she was a clerk and a Sub-Leader in the Auxiliary Territorial Service. They were living at Harlem, New York when he died at St Vincent, Ottawa, Ontario.
- Bridget Moffatt (31st July–1st August 1888).
- Margaret 'Maggie' Moffatt (born 8th March 1890).
- James Moffatt, a twin with William (born 1st November 1892) was a labourer in 1911.
- William Moffatt, a twin with James (1st November 1892–24th May 1969) was a sailor in 1911. He continued serving in the Merchant Navy during the Great War and was awarded the Mercantile Marine Medal and British War Medal. He married Helena O'Rourke (1895–20th April 1963) in 1917 at Liverpool, Lancashire, where she was born. They emigrated to New York, USA. He was a stationary engineer in 1925, when they were living at 4282 Park Avenue, New York. Also living with them was his brother-in-law, Lawrence O'Rourke (born c.1894), a chauffeur. William was an engineer in a hotel in 1940, when they were living at 56 East 158th Street, New York. He was working for Hydrox Ice Cream Co as an engineer at 47 Van Dam Street, New York and they were living at 320 East 158th Street when he registered for the draft in 1941. They both died at New York. They had three children:
    - Francis Joseph Moffatt (16th November 1919–29th August 1999), born at Liverpool, Lancashire, was an elevator operator in a hotel in 1940, living with his parents. He enlisted in the US Coast Guards on 6th May 1941 (109104798), rising to the rank of coxswain by the time of his discharge on 8th May 1946. He was described as 6' tall, weighing 165 lbs and was living at 320 East 158 Street, Bronx, New York. He died at New Jersey.
    - Helena Moffatt (born c.1925) was born at New York.
    - Veronica 'Ronnie' Moffatt (29th December 1936–26th June 2013) married Thomas J Finn (13th August 1930–16th August 2012) in 1958 at New York, where he was born. They both died at New Jersey. They had two daughters.
- Mary Anne Moffatt (28th May 1895–15th October 1912).

Living with the family at the time of the 1901 Census was a grandson, Michael Flynn (born 24th October 1899). He enlisted as Michael Moffatt in 3rd Royal Dublin Fusiliers on 7th December 1915 at Naas, Co Kildare, Ireland (3/25391). He was described as a general labourer, 5′6″ tall, weighing 130 lbs, with fresh complexion, grey eyes and dark brown hair. He gave his age as nineteen years and one month and his next of kin was Martin Moffatt of Knappagh Road, Sligo. He joined G Company at Cork on 18th December but was discharged on 22nd January 1916 having made a false statement about his age on enlistment.

Martin's paternal grandfather, also Martin Moffatt, married Maria and lived on Barrack Street, Sligo. His maternal grandfather, Michael McDonagh, married Jane.

Martin was educated at St Vincent's National School, Sligo until 1900. He was a fireman aboard SS *Effie Grey* at Liverpool, Lancashire 13th-19th October 1906. He then worked as a local seaman and donkeyman on SS *Sligo* out of Sligo Harbour. He was involved in a strike that commenced on 8th March 1913, when seamen on board demanded more help or higher wages for handling cattle. The strike, in which one man was killed, lasted until 6th May.

Martin enlisted in 6th Connaught Rangers at the outbreak of war (1569). He carried out initial training at Kilworth Camp, Co Cork and later moved to Fermoy, Co Cork. Training was completed at Blackdown Camp, Deepcut, Hampshire, England and the Battalion sailed for France on 17th December 1915. He served with the Battalion on the Somme in 1916 and at Messines Ridge in June 1917. The Battalion suffered heavy casualties in the spring of 1918 and was reduced to a training cadre on 13th April. Five officers and 281 men, including Martin, were transferred to 2nd Leinster (18321) and served with it until the end of the war.

Awarded the VC for his actions at Ledgehem, Belgium on 14th October 1918, LG 26th December 1918. The VC was presented by the King in the quadrangle of Buckingham Palace on 12th June 1919. Martin followed Admiral of the Fleet Sir David Beatty and Field Marshal Sir Douglas Haig, who were both receiving the Order of Merit, and admitted that he was 'all of a fluster' in such illustrious company. Sligo set up a testimonial fund and he was presented with £100 in War Bonds and £30 in cash. His Battalion presented him with an inscribed gold watch and a silver cigarette case bearing the regimental crest. A gold-centered

Kilworth Army Camp traces its origins back to the establishment of a large British garrison in nearby Fermoy in 1806. In the late 19th century Kilworth was identified as an ideal training camp and 14,000 acres were purchased there. Firing ranges opened in 1886 and many soldiers who trained at Kilworth fought in the Boer War 1899–1902 and Great War. In 1922 the camp was taken over by the National Army. It was destroyed during the Civil War and later rebuilt. The camp is still used by the Irish Defence Forces and over 4,500 personnel train there each year. In 2014 Queen's University Belfast archaeologists discovered one of the largest and best-preserved Great War underground dugout and trench systems in Britain and Ireland.

The area around Deepcut was used for training by the Army from the late 19th century. Formal military infrastructure commenced in 1900 when the Royal Engineers built a number of camps, including Blackdown in 1903 to accommodate artillery and infantry units. It was centred on Winchester House, renamed Blackdown House when appropriated by the War Office. The barracks at Blackdown were named Minden, Dettingen, Alma, Frith, Aisne and Marne. The Victorian houses were demolished in the 1950s and the site of Aisne and Marne Barracks was redeveloped for military family housing. The last part of Frith Barracks closed in the late 1970s and the land was then used as a military training area. Between 1967 and 1971 Minden Barracks was demolished and rebuilt as Blackdown Barracks, later renamed Princess Royal Barracks. They were used by the Royal Army Ordnance Corps and the School of Ordnance, until it merged with other cap badges into the Royal Logistic Corps in 1993. Dettingen and Alma Barracks were sold and demolished for housing. In 2013, following the Defence Training Review, it was confirmed that the barracks were to close and much of the area has since been developed for housing. The picture shows the Garrison Church of St Barbara built in 1901. It is a prefabricated 'tin tabernacle', constructed of galvanised corrugated iron on a timber frame. When the church was dedicated, it was initially named St Michael and All Angels. It was re-dedicated to St Barbara, the patron saint of the Royal Army Ordnance Corps, in the 1960s. Although relatively plain internally, there are numerous memorials and art works, some of which were relocated from Hilsea Barracks in 1949. The stained-glass windows range in date and origin. Those at the eastern end were installed in 1922, having been taken from Portobello Barracks, Dublin. The three archangels in the west end were purchased in 1956. The three windows above the choir vestry were re-sited from Hilsea, along with another to the west. Several new windows were added in the 1990s, including one commemorating the millennium. The church is Grade II listed.

silver medal was presented by Mr and Mrs McHugh of George Street, Sligo. **Awarded the Belgian Décoration Militaire avec Croix de Guerre, LG 24th October 1919.** Martin was demobilised in 1919 and became a Sligo harbour policeman, a job he held until a few days before his death.

Martin Moffat's medals with the Belgian Croix de Guerre and Décoration Militaire on the right.

Martin Moffatt married Annie McNiffe (4th April 1895–6th August 1963), born at Pound Street, Sligo, in October 1921. They lived at 21 Emmet Placc, Sligo. They had five children including:

- Evelyn Moffatt married Gerard 'Gerry' Dunleavy (died April 2002), a Sligo postman.
- Teresa Veronica 'Vera' Moffatt (born 2nd August 1937) married as Finan and emigrated to the United States. She was living at 58 Brooke Avenue, Englewood, New Jersey by September 1960. They had a son, Brian.
- Joseph P Moffatt (c.May 1930–17th September 1933).

Annie's father, Michael McNiffe (born c.1856), was a carter in 1881, living at Barrack Street, Sligo and later at Pound Street. He married Ellen O'Gara (born 15th June 1859), born at Blackwater and Killala, Co Wexford, Ireland, on 24th February 1884 at the Roman Catholic Chapel, Sligo. He was a carman in 1901, when they were living at 41 Gallows Hill North, Sligo. By 1911 he was a carter and they were living at 15 Rathquarter, Sligo North. Ellen died between 1901 and 1911. Michael was living at Lynn Place, Sligo when his son, Michael, enlisted in 1914. In addition to Annie they had five other children:

Gallows Hill, Sligo.

- John McNiffe (c.1885–22nd May 1953) was a carter in 1911, living with his father. He married Delia McDonagh (1885–13th September 1961) on 4th June 1908 at the Cathedral of the Immaculate Conception, Sligo. They had at least four children – Patrick Joseph McNiff (18th March 1909), John McNiff (8th May 1911), Thomas McNiff (10th April 1914) and Mary Ann McNiff (31st March 1917). John was a labourer living at Church Hill, Sligo when he enlisted in 7th Royal Irish Regiment on 1st April 1915 (4593 & 29115). He was 5′ 3¼″ tall and joined at Ballyhooly on 3rd April. He was later discharged unfit but the date is not clear in his service record. He re-enlisted in 5th (Home Service) Garrison Battalion, Royal Welsh Fusiliers on 24th April 1917 at Ashton-under-Lyne, Lancashire (64559 & 47960). He was described as a labourer, 5′ 2½″ tall, with fresh complexion, blue eyes, brown hair and his religious denomination was Roman Catholic. His next-of-kin was his wife, Bedelia (also shown as Bridget) McNiff, of Church Hill, Sligo, giving their marriage date as 11th June 1908 at the Cathedral of the Immaculate Conception, Sligo. He joined on 26th April, transferred to 305th Company, 19th Battalion, Royal Defence Corps on 2nd August and to 12th Battalion RDC on 19th August. On 5th February 1918 he was hospitalised at Barrow-in-Furness with haemorrhoids, originally contracted in 1912. He refused an operation, the only viable treatment, and was recommended for discharge by the medical officer on 15th February. He was described as 5′ 5″ tall with sallow complexion when he was discharged physically unfit for war service on 8th March 1918. He was assessed as being 20% disabled and received a £25 gratuity.
- Mary McNiffe (born 14th March 1886).
- Ellen McNiffe (4th March 1890–19th February 1984) was living with her father in 1911. She never married.

- Michael 'Mikey' McNiffe (9th November 1892–25th August 1948) was a carter in 1911, living with his father. He was a labourer when he enlisted in the Connaught Rangers (Special Reserve) (4803) at Sligo on 3rd April 1914. He was described as 5′ 7″ tall, weighing 135 lbs, with hazel eyes, fair hair and his religious denomination was Roman Catholic. He served with 4th Battalion, undertaking recruit training until 1st August and was mobilised on 5th August. He was absent without pass from 1.00 p.m. on 19th January 1915 until 1.00 p.m. on 21st January, for which he was awarded three days field punishment and forfeited two days' pay. On 26th January he went to France to join 1st Battalion and was disciplined for stating a falsehood at Étaples on 5th March. Michael returned to Britain on 23rd June on the strength of the Depot. He was absent from tattoo at Galway on 28th August until 9.50 p.m. on 1st September, for which he forfeited three days' pay for misconduct. He joined 4th Battalion on 18th September. He was absent without pass from Bere Island from tattoo on 26th January 1916 until 5.30 p.m. on 5th February, for which he forfeited eleven days' pay and underwent Field Punishment No.2 for eleven days. On 17th February he returned to France to join 6th Battalion and was granted leave to Britain 15th-25th September. On 12th June 1918 he was admitted to 111th Field Ambulance with pyrexia of unknown origin and was transferred to 3rd Canadian General Hospital, Boulogne the same day. He was transferred to 7th Convalescence Depot there with influenza on 16th June, was discharged to a rest camp on 5th July and to a depot at Calais on 8th July. He rejoined the Battalion on 18th August and was granted leave to Britain 27th October–18th November. Michael returned to Britain on 20th February 1919. He was discharged from Cork surplus to military requirements on 19th March, having suffered impairment (left flat foot) since entry into the service. He married Mary 'Molly' Ann Kivlehan (25th April 1899–11th December 1963), born at Emmet Place, Sligo on 18th February 1922 at the Cathedral of the Immaculate Conception, Sligo. They were both living at Emmet Place, Sligo at the time. He died at Sligo General Hospital and she at 8 Emmet Place, Sligo. They had seven children including – Helen McNiffe (1922–79), Patrick 'Paddy' Joseph McNiffe (1924–2007), Michael 'Mick' McNiffe (1925–78) and James 'Jimmy' McNiffe (1927- 2014).
- Thomas McNiffe (born 10th December 1894) was a general labourer in 1911, living with his father.

Martin attended the VC Garden Party at Buckingham Palace on 26th June 1920 and thc VC Dinner at the Royal Gallery of the House of Lords, London on 9th November 1929. One of the witnesses of his VC action was Father Moran, a Roman Catholic chaplain, whom he met again on 19th September 1934 on the ex-servicemen's Pilgrimage of Peace to Lourdes, France. The two became firm friends. Six other VCs attended the pilgrimage – John Caffrey, Robert Downie, Michael O'Leary, John O'Neill, John Ormsby and Alfred Wilkinson.

Rosses Point, a village near Sligo, is at the entrance to Sligo Harbour from Sligo Bay. There are a number of lighthouses in the area. In 1985 marine archaeologists uncovered the wrecks of three Spanish Armada ships that had been driven onto the coast in a storm in September 1588. The poet, William Butler Yeats, and his artist brother, Jack Butler Yeats, spent their summer holidays at Elsinore House in Rosses Point.

Martin drowned at sea near Rosses Point, Sligo on 5th January 1946, just a week after losing his job with the harbour police. His body was found on 7th January on the beach at Bellyweelin, Rosses Point. An inquest heard that he had suffered from a weak heart and a verdict of 'death from drowning' was recorded. There was no

The Cathedral of the Immaculate Conception of the Roman Catholic Diocese of Elphin on Temple Street, Sligo. The Cathedral was dedicated on 26th July 1874 by Cardinal Paul Cullen of Dublin. It is noted for being the only Romanesque style cathedral built during the 19th century.

Martin Moffatt's grave in Sligo Town Cemetery (Memorials to Valour).

The Irish Regiments VC Memorial at the National Memorial Arboretum.

Front page of the Victor Comic of 25th February 1984.

evidence to show how he entered the water. His funeral was held at the Cathedral of the Immaculate Conception and he is buried in the family grave in Sligo Town Cemetery. He is commemorated in a number of other places:

- A Department for Communities and Local Government commemorative paving stone was dedicated at the Cross of Sacrifice, Glasnevin Cemetery, Dublin, Ireland on 11th November 2018.
- Named on the Irish Regiments VC Memorial, National Memorial Arboretum, Alrewas, Staffordshire.
- His VC action was featured in Issues 638 and 1201 of the Victor Comic, entitled 'Sign Here!' dated 12th May 1973 and 'A True Story of Men at War' dated 25th February 1984.

In addition to the VC he was awarded the 1914–15 Star, British War Medal 1914–20, Victory Medal 1914–19 with Mentioned-in-Despatches Oakleaf, Belgian Croix de Guerre and Belgian Décoration Militaire. The VC was auctioned by Christie's on 21st October 1991 and was purchased by Lord Ashcroft. The VC is held by the Michael Ashcroft Trust, the holding institution for the Lord Ashcroft Victoria Cross Collection, and is displayed in the Imperial War Museum's Lord Ashcroft Gallery. A copy set of medals is displayed at Sligo County Museum on Stephen Street.

4119 SERGEANT JOHN O'NEILL
2nd Battalion, The Prince of Wales's Leinster Regiment (Royal Canadians)

John O'Neill was born on 27th January 1897 at 13 Forsyth Street, Airdrie, Lanarkshire, Scotland. His surname has also been seen as O'Neil and O'Niell. His father, Samuel O'Neill (9th April 1863–24th June 1923), born at Rasharkin, Co Antrim, Ireland, was a coalminer, living at 23 Loudon Street, Airdrie in 1891. He married Agnes née Devan (28th June 1871–30th April 1928), a domestic servant born at Queen Street, Castle Douglas, Kirkcudbrightshire, on 26th August 1891 at the Roman Catholic Church, Girvan, Ayrshire. She was living at 14 Montgomerie Street, Girvan when she married. They were living at 3 South Nimmo Street, New Monkland, Airdrie by 1901 and at 19 Moore Street, Cadzow, Hamilton, Lanarkshire at the time of his death at Kirklands Mental Hospital, Bothwell, Lanarkshire. Agnes died at 19 Moore Street, Cadzow. John had fifteen siblings including:

- Samuel O'Neill (born and died 15th March 1892) born at 75 Johnston Terrace, Airdrie.
- Agnes O'Neill (born and died 31st December 1892) born at Stranraer, Wigtownshire less than nine months after Samuel.
- Charles O'Neill (7th December 1893–25 April 1949), a coalminer born at Stranraer, Wigtownshire, married Margaret Mary Murphy (23rd June 1896–1985), a housekeeper, on 4th October 1924 at St Anne's Roman Catholic Church, Cadzow, Hamilton. She was living with her parents at 59 Eddlewood Row, Hamilton. They both died at Hamilton. They had two children:
    - Mary Ann Bernadette Campbell O'Neill (7th March 1926–2011), born at Beckford Lodge, Hamilton, married John Hayes in 1951.
    - Samuel O'Neill (25th September 1930–1974).

John O'Neill's father was born at Rasharkin in Co Antrim. It lay within the barony of Kilconway and belonged to the MacDonnells in the 17th century. Presbyterians and Catholics in the area were active in the United Irishmen movement, which sought an independent Ireland in the 19th century.

Queen Street, Castle Douglas, Kirkcudbrightshire, where Agnes Devan was born. Castle Douglas has historical traces dating back of prehistoric crannogs on Carlingwark Loch. The Iron Age Torrs Pony-cap and Horns was found in Torrs Loch in 1812. A large bronze cauldron, containing one hundred metal objects, was found in Carlingwark Loch in 1866. North of the town are two Roman forts and nearby is Threave Castle, seat of the Earls of Douglas. Mary Queen of Scots is believed to have stayed at the House of Fuffnock on her way to Port Mary in 1568. The building of a military road through the area improved transportation in the 18th century. Castle Douglas was founded in 1792 by William Douglas, who claimed, but had no close connection with the Douglases of Threave Castle. He created a planned town on the shores of Carlingwark Loch with a grid pattern of streets. He also created a number of industries in Castle Douglas, including hand-woven cotton factories. Robert Burns spent a night at Carlinwark Inn in June 1794. The railway arrived in 1859 and the town developed into a major market for the surrounding area. The railway closed in 1965 but the A75 road was developed along the line of the original military road. Amongst famous people associated with the town are:

- Major General Sir Victor Morven Fortune KBE CB DSO DL (1883–1949) was forced to surrender 51st (Highland) Division to the Germans on 12th June 1940. As a senior British officer in captivity, he worked to improve the conditions of the men under his command. He suffered a stroke in 1944 but refused repatriation and was liberated in April 1945.
- Sir William Henry Veno (1866–1933), who created Veno's Cough Syrup, was the son of a gamekeeper just outside Castle Douglas.
- The father of President Jerry Rawlings (1947–2020) of Ghana came from Castle Douglas.

- James O'Neill (4th February 1895–25th April 1967), born at 24 Loudon Street, Airdrie, emigrated to the United States in 1928. He married Mary Fitzpatrick (18th October 1902–29th July 1961) there on 31st August 1928. She was born in Scotland. They were living at Girard, Trumbull Co, Ohio in 1930 when he was a dyer. They both died at Youngstown, Mahoning Co, Ohio. They had three children born at Girard:
    - James Stanley O'Neill (9th November 1929–25th September 1980) married Mary Elizabeth Calderon in March 1952 and they had three sons. He worked mainly for the City Council at Warren, Ohio and served during the Korean War.
    - Richard Bernard O'Neill (born 14th May 1934) worked for Packard Electric at Warren, Ohio. He married three times and had children. He also served in the Naval Reserve.

John's mother was living at 14 Montgomerie Street, Girvan when she married. The house is the building to the left of North Parish Church.

  - Mary Elizabeth 'Betty' O'Neill (born 10th October 1936) moved to England in April 1969 and settled in Croydon, Surrey. She married John McCaughey (born 14th March 1938) on 14th June 1969 at Mitcham. Mary was an administrative assistant and general secretary. John underwent National Service and was later a Post Office manager. They had an adopted son, Martin McCaughey (born 1972).
- Arthur O'Neill (25th February 1899–1976), born at 3 South Nimmo Street, Airdrie, was a coalminer. He served during the Great War and was wounded on 13th October 1918. He married Mary McGovern (born 1st January 1899), a domestic servant born at Avondale, Lanarkshire and living at 7 Ramsay's Buildings, Hamilton, on 22nd April 1922 at the Roman Catholic Chapel, Hamilton. He was a night porter in 1939, when they were living at 212 Penton Place Buildings, Southwark, London. Also living with them was his brother, John O'Neill VC. Arthur's death was registered at Haringey, London. They had three children:
  - Agnes Devan O'Neill (born 6th April 1926) born at 10 Ramsay's Buildings, Hamilton.
  - Arthur O'Neill (1928–December 2009).
  - Annie O'Neill (born 18th December 1931), born at Beckford Lodge, Hamilton.
- Mary O'Neill (30th March 1901–8th April 1982), born at 3 South Nimmo Street, Airdrie. She married Joseph Walker (7th March 1900–22nd July 1968) on 30th September 1928 at St Anne's Roman Catholic Church, Cadzow, Hamilton. She died at Stonehouse Hospital, Lanarkshire. They had eight children including:
  - Agnes Walker (1928–86) married Francis Burns in 1949.
  - Mary 'Maimie' Walker (25th December 1929–May 1972) married Thomas 'Tommy' McCluskey (11th December 1928–2nd May 2015) in 1951 at Hamilton, where he was born. He served in the Royal Army Medical Corps. They had a daughter.
  - William Walker (born and died 1932).
  - Samuel Gerard Walker (1933–25th December 1976) married Lesley May Mitchell at Hamilton in 1974.
  - Isobel Theresa Walker (1st January 1938–21st June 2004), born at Cadzow Rows, Hamilton, married Thomas Patrick Shaw (26th January 1937–19th

April 1987) at Hamilton, where he was born, in 1959. He died at the Royal Infirmary, Glasgow, Lanarkshire and she at Eddlewood, Hamilton. They had four children.
  - Joseph Matthew Walker (1939–24th January 2009) married Edna Burns in 1961.
  - Thomas John Walker (1st April 1942 –5th January 2009), born at Glasgow, married Catherine A Rattigan (6th January 1940–29th March 2019) in 1962. They had four children, including Edward Walker (born c.1966).
- Annie O'Neill (14th February 1905–February 1984), born at 9 Manse Place, Airdrie, married Robert McNamara at Hamilton in 1923. She died at Stourbridge, West Midlands. They adopted a son named Robert.
- Hugh Patrick O'Neill (born 15th May 1908) was a miner when he emigrated to Montréal, Québec, Canada aboard SS *Montroyal*, departing Greenock on 27th July 1929 and arriving at Québec on 2nd August. Hugh married Janet 'Jenny' Hogg (born 25th May 1905), born in Scotland, on 22nd February 1930 at Hamilton, Wentworth Co, Ontario. He was a case hardener and she was a factory hand at the time. They were living at 104 Cedar Street South, Timmins, Cochrane Co, Ontario at the time of her death on 11th August 1932 at St Mary's Hospital, Timmins. He married Ruth Caroline Bateman (born c.1918) on 12th February 1934 at Timmins. She was living with her parents at 17 Maple Drive, Timmins in 1921. They were living at 3 Bush Street South, Timmins in 1935. He died at Timmins. They had two children:
  - Agnes Ruth O'Neill (born and died on 12th December 1935), born at Timmins.
  - Donald Hugh O'Neill (14th February 1937–26th November 2006), born at Schumacher, Cochrane Co. He died at Oakville, Halton, Ontario.
- Thomas O'Neill (16th July–22nd August 1909) born at 68 Annathill, Airdrie. He died at Airdrie.
- Margaret O'Neill (26th August 1913–15th April 1946), born at 236 Annathill, by Airdrie, emigrated to the United States where she married Alexander 'Alex' McEwan (born 22nd November 1906), a factory worker born at Bellshill, Lanarkshire, on 5th September 1931 at Detroit, Michigan. He was a stock chaser with a Chrysler Corporation automobile factory in 1939, when they were living at 2157 Philip, Detroit and had moved to 1281 Eastlawn Avenue by 1940. He was described as 5′9″ tall, weighing 140 lbs, with blue eyes, black hair and light complexion on his draft registration card. She died at St Claire Shores, Michigan. They had four children–Agnes McEwan (c.1934). Alexander McEwan (c.1936), James McEwan (c.1937) and John McEwan.
- Possibly Catherine O'Neill (1914–19).

John's paternal grandfather, Charles O'Neill, a labourer born in Ireland, married Mary née Hammil or Hamil (born c.1831), probably in Ireland, where she was born.

Charles died before 1871. Mary was living as a widow at 12 Palacecraig Rows, Old Monkland, Airdrie, Lanarkshire in 1871 and at 48 Backrow Faskin, Old Monkland, Airdrie, Lanarkshire in 1881. In addition to Samuel they had four other children, all born in Ireland:

- Charles O'Neill (born c.1850) was a coal miner in 1871.
- John O'Neill (26th August 1849–1900), born at Antrim, Ireland, was a labourer in 1871.
- Ann 'Annie' O'Neill (born 3rd June 1855) was a weaver in a cotton factory in 1871.
- James O'Neill (born 27th June 1858) was a coalminer.

His maternal grandfather, James Devan (c.1843–15th June 1920), born at Stoneykirk, Wigtownshire, married Annie née Boyd (18th April 1841–5th April 1914), born at Co Down, Ireland, at Little Lochand, Inch, Wigtownshire on 9th October 1860. James was a general labourer in 1871, when they were living at King Street, Castle Douglas, Kirkcudbrightshire. By 1881 they had moved to 24 Hanover Square, Stranraer, Wigtownshire. He was a telegraph foreman in 1891 by when they were living at Lochhouse Cottage, Kirkpatrick Juxta, Dumfriesshire. Annie died at 101 George Street, Stranraer, Wigtownshire. James married Jane S 'Jeannie' Rice (born c.1844) in 1919 at Blythswood, Lanarkshire. He was living at 7 Rose Street, Stranraer at the time of his death at Clark's Land, Sheddens, Lanarkshire. In addition to Agnes, James and Annie had ten other children:

- Elizabeth 'Lizzie' Devan (25th August 1861–8th April 1904), born at Inch, married Charles McGhee (10th May 1863–1931), born at Beith, Ayrshire, on

George Street, Stranraer.

16th August 1886 at St Joseph's, Stranraer. He was a stone breaker in 1891, when they were living at 75 Johnston Street, New Monkland, Lanarkshire. By 1901 they had moved to 3 South Nimmo Street, New Monkland. She died at Airdrie, Lanarkshire. They had seven children – Helen 'Ellen' McGhee 1887, James McGhee (1889–1933), Annie McGhee 1891, Catherine McGhee 1892, Agnes McGhee 1894, Patrick McGhee 1898 and Charles McGhee 1901. Their son James married Christina Macfarlane at Glasgow on 27th November 1908 and they had four children – Grace 1909, John 1912, Robert 1914 and David 1916. They were living at 293 Parliamentary Road, Glasgow. James was a motor driver when he enlisted in the Army Service Corps (Motor Transport) on 8th December 1915 (315904 & 198343) and transferred to the Reserve next day. He was 5′ 11″ tall and was mobilised on 20th April 1917 to join the ASC (MT) Reserve Depot, Grove Park on 24th April. He was appointed paid acting lance corporal on 15th May and went to France on 22nd May. He was appointed acting corporal on 28th December. On 6th March 1918 he returned to Britain having lost two fingers on his left hand on 13th February. James was discharged no longer physically fit for war service on 20th September 1918.

- Hugh Devan (13th January 1865–1931) was a tinsmith in 1881. He married Catherine Murray Raverty (c.1868–29th November 1931) on 25th August 1891 at St Patrick's Chapel, Glasgow. He was a telegraph linesman living at 14 Montgomery Street, Girvan, Ayrshire and she was a sewing machine worker living at 19 Shaftesbury Avenue, Glasgow at the time. They were living at 36 Green Street, Ayr when their son, Hugh, enlisted in 1913. They both died at Ayr, Ayrshire. They had eight children:
    - Hugh Devan (1893–1956) was working for the General Post Office as a jointer's mate when he enlisted as a field line telegraphist in the Lowland Divisional Engineers (Territorial Force) at Rutherglen on 18th March 1913 (2486 & 418040). He was 5′ 8½″ tall and transferred to 4th Highland Light Infantry on 11th July. He attended annual camp 18th July–1st August. On 6th June 1914 he transferred to No.1 Section, Lowland Divisional Signal Company RE and qualified as an electrician driver on 23rd June. Having attended annual camp 17th-31st July he was mobilised on 5th August. Hugh re-mustered as a sapper on 1st December and joined the Mediterranean Expeditionary Force on 21st May 1915. He transferred to 155th Brigade Signal Section at Gallipoli on 24th October and returned to 52nd (Lowland) Division Signal Company on 15th February 1916. On 24th March he forfeited three days' pay for disobedience to standing orders. He re-mustered in 52nd (Lowland) Division Signal Company as a telegraphist on 1st January 1917. He was deprived of two days' pay for failing to attend a parade on 8th April 1918 and landed in France from Egypt on 17th April. On 18th May he was granted fourteen days leave in Britain and one month from 28th October. His discharge medical at Nimy, Belgium on 16th March

1919 found no disabilities and he was demobilised from Chatham on 20th March. Hugh was disembodied on 18th April 1919.

  - James Devan (1894–94).
  - Charles Devan (1895–1st April 1917) died on active service with 17th Highland Light Infantry (42371) (Savy British Cemetery, France – I B 9).
  - Ann Devan (1898–1987) married Alfred James Norris (c.1907–1985) at Oxford, England in 1957. Both their deaths were registered at Prestwick, Ayrshire.
  - Thomas Devan (1901–85).
  - Michael Devan (1903–04).
  - John Devan (1906–61).
  - Mary Helen Devan (24th May 1908–1988) married Patrick Devenney (born c.1901) at St Margaret's Church, Ayr on 3rd September 1932. Mary died at Wigan, Lancashire.
- Annie Devan (23rd May 1867–28th July 1890), born at Castle Douglas, Kirkcudbrightshire and died at Stranraer.
- James Devan (22nd August 1869–18th July 1925) married Jane 'Jeanie' Morrison (1870–17th February 1911) at St Joseph's Catholic Church, Lewis Street, Stranraer on 30th April 1889. He was a tinsmith and gasfitter in 1901, when they were living at 102 Queensby Street, Dumfries. They had ten children:
  - Annie Boyd Devan (1889).
  - James Devan (1891–94).
  - William Morrison Devan (1893–5th February 1922).
  - Hugh Devan (1895).
  - Jane Morrison Devan (1897–1968) married Alexander Foley (1896–1989) in 1926.
  - Arthur Devan (born and died 1898).
  - Thomas Devan (1900–71).
  - Charles Devan (1903).
  - James Devan (1906–27th April 1918).
  - Augustus Devan (6th August 1908–1947).
- Thomas Devan (born 12th July 1873–31st December 1929), a twin with John, born at Stranraer, married Mary McMillan (born c.1875), born at Belfast, Ireland, on 30th September 1895 at Campbeltown, Argyll. He was a telephone wireman in 1901, when they were living at 110 Longrow, Campbelltown, Argyll. They had moved to 41 Glynne Street, Orrell, Bootle, Lancashire by 1911. Thomas was a telephone wires inspector when he was deemed to have enlisted in the Royal Engineers Signals (329791) at Liverpool on 18th April 1918. He was called up for service on 29th July and transferred to the Class W Army Reserve next day. He was discharged surplus to military requirements on 14th December 1918. Thomas is believed to have been residing at The Oddfellows Arms, Tottington Road, Bury, Lancashire at the time of his death there.

- John Devan (12th July 1873–1902), a twin with Thomas, was a tailor, living with his sister, Elizabeth and her family, in 1891 and with his brother, Thomas, in 1901.
- Charles Devan (1875–1947), a tailor and clothier, married Annie Kenny (1871–1941) on 29th April 1897 at the Roman Catholic Chapel, Girvan, where she was born. They were living at 122 Dalrymple Street, Girvan in 1901 and at 41 Bridge Street in 1920. They had three children:
    - Annie Devan (1899–1963) married Duncan Kerr Miller (1900–69) in 1937.
    - Elizabeth 'Lizzie' Devan (4th March 1900–1979).
    - Charles Devan (1902–80).
- Arthur Devan (28th April 1878–1879).
- Margaret 'Maggie' Devan (1880–1904) married Bernard Allan (1876–1962), born at Urr, Kirkcudbrightshire, in 1898 at Stranraer. He was a telephone wireman in 1901, when they were living at 30 Hill Street, Springburn, Glasgow. Her death was registered at Dennistoun and his at Dumfries. They had at least one child – Arthur Allan 1900.
- Arthur Devan (1885–1923) married Catherine McCall (1884–1964) at Stranraer in 1904. His death was registered at Morningside, Edinburgh and hers at Ayr.

John was educated at the Roman Catholic School, Airdrie and at Glenboig School, Annathill, Lanarkshire. He worked beside his father as a coalminer at Bedlay Colliery, Coatbridge, Lanarkshire. John enlisted in 2nd Leinster in August 1914 and went to France on 13th April 1915. **Awarded the MM for his actions in the attack on Hill 63, northwest of Ploegsteert Wood, Belgium on 4th September 1918, LG 11th February 1919. Awarded the VC for his actions near Moorseele, Belgium on 14th October 1918 and at Stacaghem, Belgium on 20th October 1918, LG 26th December 1918. Appointed Knight of the Belgian Order of Leopold II, LG 4th July 1919. Awarded the French Médaille Militaire, LG 21 August 1919.** The VC was presented by the King in the quadrangle at Buckingham Palace on 2nd August 1919.

John was a member of a guard of honour for King Albert of Belgium in Brussels. He was granted the Freedom of Hamilton, Lanarkshire on 4th August 1919 and during the ceremony he was presented with £400 by the people of Hamilton. The Prince of Wales, Colonel-in-Chief of the Leinster Regiment, was met by John on the outskirts of Colchester, Essex and escorted to the barracks, where he presented honours and awards to members of the Regiment on 6th February 1920. John was one of the

Glenboig School, Annathill.

Bedlay Colliery was opened in 1905 by William Baird & Co to supply coking coal for the Gartsherrie Iron Works. There were two shafts. The colliery closed on 11th December 1981.

The Military Medal, seen here with a Bar, was awarded to other ranks of the British Army (later extended to other services) and Commonwealth countries for bravery on land. It was established on 25th March 1916 as the other ranks equivalent of the Military Cross, which was awarded to commissioned officers and warrant officers. It was the third level gallantry award, ranking below the Distinguished Conduct Medal. Over 115,000 MMs were awarded during the Great War, as well as 5,700 bars and 180 second bars. Private Ernest Corey, a stretcher-bearer with 55th Australian Infantry Battalion, was awarded three bars. Over 15,000 MMs were awarded during the Second World War. It was discontinued in 1993, since when the Military Cross has been awarded to all ranks within the British honours system. Most Commonwealth nations established their own honours systems after the Second World War and award their own gallantry decorations.

Honour Guard at the burial of the Unknown Warrior at Westminster Abbey on 11th November 1920. He was discharged on 23rd February 1919, having been wounded four times, but re-enlisted on 26th January 1920 and served until 25th January 1922. On 20th June 1921 he was awarded the 2nd Class Army Certificate of Education. John returned to the coalmines and worked at Cadzow Colliery, Hamilton from 23rd January 1922 until 24th February 1923.

John O'Neill married Kathleen O'Neill Flanagan (2nd February 1902–5th April 1982), a dressmaker born at Cape Town, South Africa, on 18th February 1922 at Our Lady and St Anne's, Cadzow, Hamilton. They lived at 19 Moore Street, Cadzow. She was living with her parents at 224 London County Council Flats, Wandsworth, London in 1939, while he was a theatre attendant living with his brother, Arthur, in Southwark. They had three children:

- Michael 'Mikey' John E O'Neill (1925–35), born at Colchester, Essex, was hit by a lorry and died in hospital at Dunfermline, Fife.
- Maureen P O'Neill (born 8th July 1929), birth registered at Sheppey, Kent, emigrated to the United States, where she married Captain Max R Stalbaum. They lived in Texas.
- Patricia M O'Neill (born 1930).

Kathleen's father, Henry Edgar Flanagan (1st December 1877–1939), born at Trincomalee, Ceylon, was living with his parents at St Luke, London in 1891. He enlisted as a boy in the Royal Engineers on 27th July 1892 at St George's Barracks, London (26786), described as 5′ 2½″ tall, weighing 98 lbs, with fair complexion, blue eyes, dark red hair and his religious denomination was Roman Catholic. He attained the 2nd Class Army Certificate of Education and was appointed bugler on 1st October 1893. He was posted to Gibraltar on 12th December and was awarded good conduct pay of 1d per day from 27th July 1894. He was posted to Malta on 20th October 1894 and back to Britain on 27th February 1896. Henry attained the 1st Class Army Certificate of Education and qualified in Superior Drawing in 1897. On 22nd June 1898 he was promoted lance corporal and on 27th July was awarded good conduct pay of 2d per day. Henry was promoted sergeant engineer clerk on 2nd March 1899. On 19th June he married Frances Mary Scurlock née Loveless (1870–31st January 1903), born at Wandsworth, London, at Portsea, Hampshire. Frances had married Charles Frederick Scurlock (1863–19th January 1898), born at Pembroke, Pembrokeshire, at Axminster, Devon in 1895. Charles was a shipwright in the Royal Navy aboard the battleship HMS *Thunderer* at Portsmouth Dockyard, Hampshire in 1891. He died at Kensington, London. Henry was posted to South Africa on 23rd June 1899 (Queen's South Africa Medal with Cape Colony clasp and King's South Africa Medal with clasps South Africa 1901 and South Africa 1902). Promotion to staff sergeant engineer clerk followed on 2nd March 1902 and he re-engaged to complete twenty-one years' service on 2nd April. The family was living at 1a Beach Castle, Cape Town, South Africa when Frances contracted enteric fever leading to heart failure three weeks later. Henry was granted class I service pay from 1st April 1904 and was posted to Britain on 16th April 1905. On 1st October he was promoted quartermaster sergeant engineer clerk and was posted to Gibraltar on 10th March 1908. Henry married Stella Mary Agnes Bennett (26th April 1882–4th January 1973), born at Cheltenham, Gloucestershire, on 24th October 1908 at the Cathedral of St Mary the Crowned, Gibraltar. She was known as Agnes. His request to continue service to complete twenty-one years from the age of eighteen was denied on 31st October 1912 due to unfavourable reports and he returned to Britain on 6th April 1913. However, the request was reviewed by Commander Royal Engineers at Colchester on 11th June and was submitted to Colonel WR Stewart, Assistant Director of Fortifications and Works, RE Records Office, who overruled the original decision and Henry was permitted to continue service from 4th July.

He was a draughtsman in the CRE's Office, Colchester on 1st April 1914. A medical inspection at Colchester on 15th March 1915 found him fit for service abroad and he went to France on 17th March and continued to Egypt on 20th March. The family was living at 30 Harsnett Road, Colchester at the time. He was appointed acting superintending clerk and draughtsman at GHQ Egyptian Expeditionary Force on 23rd November. Continuance in this acting appointment was granted on 16th November 1916 while he was serving with 46th Base Park RE. He was promoted warrant officer class I and superintendent clerk and draughtsman on 2nd May 1917. Continuance under the Military Service Acts was granted from 27th December and he was posted to 389th Advanced Park Company on 4th February 1918. On 23rd February he elected to draw his pension while still serving and on 30th April was granted £5 having been awarded the Good Conduct Medal. On 7th November he was granted a bounty of £25 of which £8/6/8 was paid and the remainder was to be drawn later. Henry returned to Britain on 4th February 1919 and joined G Depot Company. He transferred to the Class Z Reserve on demobilisation from Chatham, Kent on 30th April 1919 and was discharged on 14th January 1920. Henry and Agnes were living in retirement at 224 London County Council Flats, Wandsworth, London in 1939, with his daughters, Kathleen and Maire. Agnes was living at 9 Percy Street, London at the time of her death there. In addition to Kathleen, Henry had three other children from his two marriages:

- Bertie Wannell Flanagan (2nd June 1900–10th January 1924), born at Anchor Bay, Cape Town, enlisted for twelve years in the Royal Navy at Chatham, Kent on 22nd June 1918 (K61053 later SS123054). He was described as 5′7″ tall, with fresh complexion, fair hair and blue eyes. Bertie was a stoker class I aboard HMS *Diligence* from 29th March, HMS *Pembroke II* from 23rd October, HMS *Dolphin* from 18th December and HM Submarine *L24* from 9th January. *L24* collided with the battleship HMS *Resolution* on 10th January 1924 and was lost with all forty-three hands.

HMS *L24* (929 tons) was built by Vickers at Barrow-in-Furness and launched on 19th February 1919. She was armed with four 21″ torpedo tubes in the bow, two 18″ tubes in broadside mounts and a 4″ deck gun. On 10th January 1924 she was involved in an exercise off Portland in the English Channel when she was struck by HMS *Resolution*. *L24* sank with all hands. There is a memorial in St Ann's Church, HMNB Portsmouth. The wreck is designated under the Protection of Military Remains Act 1986 and lies in fifty-two metres of water. Her hydroplanes are set to hard dive, indicating that she was taking evasive action at the time of the collision.

HMS *Resolution* (26,160 tons), one of five Revenge-class battleships, was completed in December 1916 but did not see any combat during the Great War. She was armed with eight 15″ Mk.I guns in four twin turrets, fourteen 6″ MK.XII guns, four 3 Pounder guns, two 3″ Mk.I anti-aircraft guns and four submerged 21″ torpedo tubes. In the 1920s and 1930s she served with the Atlantic and Mediterranean Fleets. On the outbreak of the Second World War she was assigned to the Channel Force and then to convoy escort duties in the North Atlantic. In May 1940 she participated in operations in Norway. That June she transferred to Force H and took part in the destruction of the French Fleet at Mers-el-Kebir in July. She was also involved in an attempt to neutralise the French battleship *Richelieu* during which *Resolution* was torpedoed by a French submarine. She was patched up in Freetown, Sierra Leone and then repaired at Philadelphia Naval Shipyard, USA. Thereafter she escorted convoys off the east coast of Africa until returning to Britain in September 1943 to be part of the training establishment of HMS *Imperieuse*. Her main battery guns were removed as spares. She was sold for scrap in February 1948 and was broken up at Faslane. One of *Resolution*'s 15″ guns was fitted to the monitor HMS *Roberts* and is now one of the two mounted outside the Imperial War Museum in London.

- Henry Bernard Flanagan (16th April–16th November 1915) died at 30 Harsnett Road, Colchester.
- Maire Patricia Flanagan (12th April 1921–1975) was a clerk seeking work and living with her parents in 1939. She married Frederick R Williams in 1952 at Pancras, London.

On 25th April 1923 John enlisted as an aircraftsman in the Royal Air Force (353964) for seven years regular service and five on the reserve. He was described as 5′ 5½″ tall, with dark brown hair, blue eyes and fresh complexion. He was promoted corporal next day and joined the RAF Depot, Uxbridge. He forfeited a day's pay on 4th July and was admitted to Halton Hospital 23rd May–7th June 1925. John was posted to No.5 Flying Training School, RAF Shotwick, Flintshire on 10th October. He was in arrest from 15th November and was reduced to aircraftsman 2 by District Court Martial on 3rd December for striking an airman. He was posted to No.99 Squadron in India on 16th December but this appears to have been cancelled as he was posted to the Armament & Gunnery School, RAF Leuchars in Scotland on 19th December. He re-mustered as an armourer on 5th June 1928 and this became permanent on 11th December, when he was appointed aircraftsman 1. John passed Leading Aircraftsman Education Class I on 3rd December 1928. The last entry in his service record was in January 1929, although it is believed that he served until 27th July 1939.

It is said that John served with Thomas Edward Lawrence (Lawrence of Arabia) in the RAF's Marine Branch, including aboard the aircraft carrier HMS

Thomas Edward Lawrence CB DSO (1888–1935), the archaeologist, diplomat and writer, became famous for his role in the Arab Revolt 1916–18 and the Sinai and Palestine Campaign 1915–18. He became known as Lawrence of Arabia, which was the title of a 1962 film based on his wartime activities. In 1922, Lawrence retreated from public life and served as an enlisted man mostly in the RAF, with a brief period in the Army. In the RAF he was involved in the development of rescue motorboats. He served at RAF stations at Mount Batten near Plymouth, Calshot near Southampton and Bridlington. He also served in India 1926–28. A few months after leaving the RAF on 13th May 1935 he was injured fatally in an accident while riding his motorcycle close to his cottage, Clouds Hill, near Wareham, Dorset.

Glorious. Lawrence served in the RAF August 1922–February 1923 and August 1925–March 1935 as John Hume Ross and Thomas Edward Shaw. From what is known about Lawrence's RAF career and the details in John's service record, they do not appear to have served in the same location at the same time, at least until early 1929. Thereafter, Lawrence served at various Marine Branch bases in Britain – RAF Cattewater/Mount Batten, Plymouth 1929–33 and the Marine Aircraft Experimental Establishment Felixstowe, Suffolk 1933–35, with detachments to Calshot near Southampton, Hythe in Kent, Cowes on the Isle of Wight and the Marine Unit, Bridlington, Yorkshire. It is possible that their paths crossed during this period.

HMS *Glorious* in Grand Harbour, Malta in the 1930s. She was the second of three *Courageous*-class battlecruisers built for the Royal Navy in 1916. She was involved in the Second Battle of Heligoland Bight in November 1917. *Glorious* was rebuilt as an aircraft carrier in the late 1920s and was recommissioned in 1930. She spent most of her career in the Mediterranean. In 1939 *Glorious* was involved in the hunt for *Admiral Graf Spee* in the Indian Ocean before returning to the Mediterranean. She returned to Britain in April 1940 to support the operations in Norway. While evacuating British aircraft from there in June, she was sunk by *Scharnhorst* and *Gneisenau* in the North Sea with the loss of 1,207 lives.

John went to Lourdes, France in September 1934 with a servicemen's pilgrimage, where he met his old captain, John Moran, who had become a Roman Catholic priest. Six other VCs also attended the pilgrimage – Martin Moffatt, John Ormsby, Michael O'Leary, Robert Downie, Alfred Wilkinson and John Caffrey. John attended two VC reunions – the VC Garden Party at Buckingham Palace on 26th June 1920 and the VC Dinner at the Royal Gallery of the House of Lords, London on 9th November 1929.

John was commissioned as a lieutenant in the Pioneer Corps (144348) on 1st July 1940. He was part of a poorly trained military escort to 2,542 deportees bound for Australia, sailing from Liverpool aboard HMT *Dunera* on 10th July 1940. The majority of the deportees were anti-Nazis, most of them Jewish, and some

HMT *Dunera* arriving at Sydney, Australia on 6th September 1940. SS *Dunera* entered service with the British-India Steam Navigation Co in 1937 as a passenger liner. She was taken over by the Royal Navy as a troopship and was en route to the Far East when war broke out. Following the infamous voyage to Australia with deportees in 1940, HMT *Dunera's* next notable service was during the operations in Madagascar in September 1942. She was also involved in the Sicily landings in July 1943. In September 1944 she carried the US Seventh Army HQ staff during the invasion of southern France. After the Japanese surrender in 1945, *Dunera* transported occupation forces to Japan. In 1950–51 she was refitted to bring her up to post-war troopship specifications, with a capacity of 123 first class, ninety-five second class, one hundred third class and 831 troops. Her military contract was terminated in 1960 and she was refitted as an educational cruise ship, with capacity for 187 cabin passengers and 834 children. *Dunera* was again used as a cruise ship until November 1967, when she was sold to Revalorizacion de Materiales and scrapped at Bilbao, Spain. Amongst the deportees taken to Australia aboard *Dunera* were:

- Franz Ferdinand Leopold Stampfl MBE (1913–95), who became one of the world's leading athletics coaches, pioneering interval training. In Britain he secured a job in Northern Ireland, assisted by Olympic athlete Harold Abrahams, the subject of the film *Chariots of Fire*. He married an Australian woman and moved back to London in 1946. He worked at John Fisher School as athletics coach 1950–55 and coached Roger Bannister, the first man to break the four-minute mile on 6th May 1954. Stampfl returned to Australia in 1955 as Director of Athletics at Melbourne University and trained eleven members of the Australian team in preparation for the 1956 Melbourne Olympic Games.
- Richard Wolfgang Sonnenfeldt (1923–2009), after Australia, emigrated to India and then the USA, arriving in April 1941 to be reunited with his family. After high school he was drafted into the US Army and served in Europe. After Germany's surrender, he was recruited by General William L 'Wild Bill' Donovan, head of the Office of Strategic Services, as his personal interpreter. Donovan became the first deputy of US Supreme Court Justice Robert H Jackson, US Chief of Counsel for the prosecution of Nazi war criminals at Nuremberg.

were survivors of the sinking of SS *Arandora Star* by *U-47* on 2nd July. During the journey the guards, some of whom had been released from prison to serve, mistreated their charges, bullying them in a brutal and sadistic manner, including beatings, starvation and robbery. There was an enquiry about their behaviour, which had resulted in two suicides. It is likely that John O'Neill would have been charged and tried, but he died before the case came to trial. The Company OC, Major William Patrick Scott, was severely reprimanded and three guards were tried by court martial, one of whom, RSM Charles Albert Bowles, was reduced to the ranks and sent to prison for twelve months. The deportees were later released by the Australian Government and about one thousand served in the Australian Military Forces. Most of the remainder returned to Britain and many joined the armed forces or intelligence services there.

As a lieutenant in 1/6th Argyll and Sutherland Highlanders, William Davidson Bissett was awarded the VC for his actions east of Maing, France on 25th October 1918. His story appears in the final volume of this series, *Victoria Crosses on the Western Front – The Final Advance in Picardy October–November 1918.*

On returning from Australia John served in 26th Company from 8th December 1940, 121st Company from 4th February 1941, 274th Company from 9th January 1942, 206th Company in Northern Ireland under the command of Major WD Bissett VC from 12th February, 282nd Company from 15th June and 295th Company in 17 Group Army Pioneer Corps from 16th September, based at Huyton, near Liverpool, Lancashire. His duties included dock work and fire watching during air raids. He was billeted at Hoylake and West Kirby, Cheshire.

John O'Neill died of heart disease at Hoylake, Cheshire on 16th October 1942. His funeral was held at Hoylake Trinity Church and he is buried in Hoylake (Holy Trinity) Churchyard, Trinity Road, Hoylake (Grave 8). A Commonwealth War Graves Commission headstone was erected on his grave in the 1980s. The Leinster Regiment Association dedicated a turfstone on the grave on 31st October 2004. The stone was unveiled by his niece, Mrs Betty McCaughey, and her cousin Mrs Molly Hayes. John is commemorated in a number of other places:

John O'Neill during the Second World War.

- Memorial arch in Hamilton to the sixteen Lanarkshire VCs. The others commemorated are – Frederick Aikman, William Angus, Thomas Caldwell, Donald Cameron, John Carmichael, William Clamp, William Gardner, John Hamilton, David Lauder, Graham Lyall, David MacKay, Hugh McIver, William Milne, William Reid and James Richardson.

Holy Trinity Church was consecrated on 1st November 1833. In 1860 it became the Parish Church of Hoose, Little Hoose and Great Hoose. During its lifetime, two daughter churches were built, St Hildeburgh's, which is now the parish church for Hoylake, and St John's, now the parish church for Meols. Holy Trinity was declared unsafe and closed in 1974. It was demolished in 1976 and all that remains today is the graveyard, which includes twenty-three CWGC graves. Julian, son of the Beatle, John Lennon, was christened at Holy Trinity in 1963. His mother, Cynthia, lived almost opposite the church at the time.

John O'Neill's grave in Hoylake (Holy Trinity) Churchyard. In front of the CWGC headstone is the Leinster Regiment Association turfstone (Memorials to Valour).

The memorial arch in Hamilton to the sixteen Lanarkshire VCs.

- Merseyside
  - A Department for Communities and Local Government commemorative paving stone was dedicated at Birkenhead War Memorial, Hamilton Square Gardens, Birkenhead on 11th November 2018.
  - Named on the Victoria Cross Roll of Honour, Victoria Cross Memorial Alcove, Wallasey Town Hall, Brighton Street, Wallasey.
  - Wirral Victoria Cross Memorial, Hamilton Square, Birkenhead.
- Irish Regiments VC Memorial, National Memorial Arboretum, Alrewas, Staffordshire.

The Wirral Peninsula Victoria Cross Memorial at the base of Birkenhead War Memorial.

- Memorial dedicated at Glasgow Central Station on 8th May 2022 honouring fifty-five VCs from Glasgow and the West of Scotland.
- His VC action featured in Issues 628 and 1186 of the Victor Comic entitled 'O'Neill's Revenge' dated 3rd March 1973 and 'A True Story of Men at War' dated 12th November 1983.

The Victoria Cross Roll of Honour, Victoria Cross Memorial Alcove, Wallasey Town Hall (Memorials to Valour).

Kathleen married William E Dixon in 1949 in Surrey. She was living at 37 Legion Court, Green Lane, Morden, Surrey at the time of her death there.

In addition to the VC and MM he was awarded the 1914–15 Star, British War Medal 1914–20, Victory Medal 1914–19, George VI Coronation Medal 1937, French Médaille Militaire and Knight of the Belgian Order of Leopold II. He was entitled to the War Medal 1939–45 but it was not with his other medals when offered for sale. It is likely that his family never claimed it. The VC was listed for £535 in Seaby's Coin & Medal Bulletin of February 1962. However, the medals were stolen from Seaby's, together with the medals and decorations awarded to General Sir

The Order of Leopold II, named in honour of King Leopold II of Belgium, was established on 24th August 1900 originally for the Congo Free State, but in 1908 the Order was incorporated into the Belgian honours system. The Order of Leopold II is awarded for meritorious service to the sovereign as a token of his personal goodwill and may also be awarded to foreigners as a gift of merit. The Order stands third in seniority after the Order of Leopold and the Order of the Crown. It is issued in five classes and three medals, with the Knight being the fifth level.

The French Médaille Militaire, established in 1852, is awarded for meritorious service or bravery in action and is the third highest award of the French Republic. During the First World War 230,000 medals were awarded. Foreign recipients include the black American fighter pilot Eugene Jacques Bullard, Winston Churchill, Dwight D Eisenhower, Field Marshal Bernard Montgomery, President Franklin D Roosevelt and President Josip Broz Tito (Fdutil).

Thomas Makdougall Brisbane, 1st Baronet GCH GCB (1773–1860). John's VC was never recovered and its current location is not known.

3102 PRIVATE THOMAS RICKETTS
1st Battalion, Royal Newfoundland Regiment

Thomas Ricketts, known as Tommy, was born on 15th April 1901 at Middle Arm, White Bay, Newfoundland. His father, John Francis Ricketts (born c.1840), born at Smart's Island, Bonavista, Newfoundland, was a fisherman. He married Elizabeth Langford (born c.1842, died before 1893) on 24th November 1865 at Big Island, White Bay, Newfoundland, where she was born. He married Amelia Elizabeth née Cassell (1872–20th August 1905), born at Harbour Deep, White Bay, on 6th November 1893 at Middle Arm, White Bay. After his mother died, Tommy was brought up by an aunt and his sister, Dinah. John was released from a penitentiary helpless and destitute in August 1918 after four years. He requested that the allotment made from Tommy's Army pay to his sister, Rachel, be reallocated to him and this was done on 23rd October. Tommy had four siblings from his father's two marriages:

- John Ricketts (born 12th March 1869), born at Middle Arm, White Bay.
- Dinah Ricketts (born 28th October 1885) married Azariah Applin (26th April 1885–22nd March 1937), a labourer, on 19th May 1902 at St Peter's Church, Québec. Azariah had married Elizabeth Gould (1880–97) on 6th November 1897 at Forester's Point, Newfoundland. She died due to complications with the birth of their daughter, Jane Applin (13th September 1897–7th September 1920), who died at Montréal, Ontario. Azariah and Dinah had six children all born at Québec:
    - Florence Applin (born 8th July 1902).

St John's, capital and largest city of Newfoundland, is on the eastern tip of the Avalon Peninsula and is the most easterly city on the North American mainland. It may be named after John Cabot, who sailed into the harbour on the Nativity of John the Baptist on 24th June 1497, or after a Basque fishing town named San Juan. It is shown on maps from 1519. The area was first used by fishermen setting up seasonal camps in the early 1500s. On 5th August 1583, Sir Humphrey Gilbert claimed the area as England's first overseas colony but he was lost at sea during the return voyage, which ended any immediate plans for settlement. By 1620 fishermen from the west country of England controlled most of Newfoundland's east coast and after 1630 the town was established as a permanent community. The population grew slowly in the 17th century, particularly in the summer with migratory fishermen. The town was seized temporarily by the Dutch in June 1665. A second Dutch attack in 1673 was defeated by Christopher Martin, an English merchant captain, who landed six cannons from his vessel and constructed a breastwork and battery commanding the Narrows leading into the harbour. With only twenty-three men he beat off three Dutch warships. The French captured and destroyed the town in the Avalon Peninsula Campaign of 1696. The French attacked again in the 1705 Siege of St John and captured it in 1708 at the Battle of St John. Following a surprise capture of the town by the French early in 1762, the British responded and at the Battle of Signal Hill, the French surrendered. This was the final battle of the Seven Years' War in North America. In the late 1700s Forts Amherst and Waldegrave were built to defend the harbour entrance. During the 18th century the population grew and the town became a garrison, a centre of government and a commercial hub. It was a naval base during the American Revolutionary War and the War of 1812. The town was destroyed by five major fires in 1816, 1817, 1819, 1846 and 1892. St John's was officially incorporated as a city in 1888. On 12th December 1901 Guglielmo Marconi received the first transatlantic wireless signal at St John's, transmitted from his wireless station in Poldhu, Cornwall. In June 1919 Alcock and Brown took off from Lester's Field in St John's in the first non-stop transatlantic aircraft flight, which ended at Clifden, Connemara, Ireland. During the Second World War the harbour was a base for Royal Navy and Royal Canadian Navy anti-submarine operations. It was also the site of an American air base, which transferred to Canadian control in 1960. In December 1942 a fire at the Knights of Columbus Hostel resulted in ninety-nine military and civilian deaths. St John's was severely affected in the 1990s by the collapse of the cod fishery, the driving force for the provincial economy for centuries. However, a decade later the city's proximity to various oil fields led to an economic recovery.

- Olive May Applin (born 1st January 1904) does not appear in the 1911 Census but a son named Allen (born 1904) was recorded with the family at that time. This discrepancy cannot be explained. An authority signed by a priest was granted for Olive to marry Noel Belanger on 17th November 1939, he being Roman Catholic and she Anglican. However, at the time no marriage contract was signed by the two parties.
- Julia Applin (born 5th December 1905).
- Selina Elizabeth Applin (born 20th September 1907).
- Reginald John Applin (born 1st January 1910).

- Joseph George Clifford 'Cliff' Applin (27th November 1911–19th June 1988) served in the Royal Canadian Artillery during the Second World War (E0010), enlisting at Québec on 6th September 1939, described as 5′7½″ tall, with fair complexion, blue eyes and brown hair. He was promoted to corporal and served in Britain and Europe before returning to Canada, where he was discharged on 30th January 1946 (1939–45 Star, France & Germany Star, Defence Medal and Canadian Volunteer Service Medal with clasp). He married Ellen Wood (14th May 1922–13th May 1969), born at Gateshead, Co Durham, in 1942 at Bromley, Kent. She died at St Laurent, Québec and he at Ste Anne de Bellevue, Québec. They had five children including – Julia A Applin 1942, Brian C Applin 1944, both registered at Bromley, Kent and Debbie Applin 1958.

• George Ricketts (2nd October 1896–3rd December 1917), born at Seal Cove was a fisherman when he enlisted in the Newfoundland Regiment at St John's on 14th July 1915 (1703), described as 5′10″ tall, weighing 144 lbs and his religious denomination was Church of England. He made an allotment of $0.60 per day to his sister, Miss Rachel Ricketts later Mrs Rachel Gavin, from 30th September 1915 until he cancelled it on 30th April 1917. George was transferred to Québec by train on 27th October and embarked for Britain aboard SS *Corsican* the same day. He was admitted to Bladda Infirmary, Paisley, Scotland 4th-18th February 1916 for measles and transferred to St Mary's Convalescent Hospital until 4th March. On 26th June he sailed for Rouen, France from Southampton and joined the Battalion on 12th July, one of 127 men to join the Battalion that day after the disaster at Beaumont-Hamel on 1st July. He was wounded by a gunshot to the cheek on 5th December and was admitted to 14th Corps Main Dressing Station. On 12th December he was transferred to 2/2nd London Casualty Clearing Station and to 6th General Hospital, Rouen the next day. He was evacuated to England aboard HMHS *Warilda* on 22nd December and was admitted to 3rd London General Hospital,

George Ricketts is commemorated on the Beaumont-Hamel (Newfoundland) Memorial.

Wandsworth next day. On 21st February 1917 he was granted furlough until he joined the Depot on 2nd March. George embarked for France at Folkestone on 3rd June, disembarked at Boulogne the same day and rejoined his unit on 19th June in the Ypres Salient. He was admitted to 87th Field Ambulance on 6th September with pyrexia of unknown origin and rejoined the Battalion on 29th September. George was missing in action during the Battle of Cambrai at Marcoing on 3rd December. On 1st July 1918 he was assumed to have been killed. His body was never recovered and he is commemorated on Beaumont-Hamel (Newfoundland) Memorial, Newfoundland Park, near Albert, France. The memorial is duplicated in Bowring Park, St John's, Newfoundland.

- Rachel Ricketts (May 1899–27th December 1994) married Edward Gavin (c.1898–c.1924), a fisherman, on 22nd August 1916 at Seal Cove, Newfoundland. He was born and died at Middle Arm. Rachel married Edward Purchase (6th August 1891–2nd March 1969), born at Fogo, Newfoundland, c.1930 at Botwood, Newfoundland. He had married Hilda F Payne (20th October 1891–18th January 1928) on 20th October 1914 and they had four children – see below. Edward died at Fogo. Rachel is buried at Lewisporte, Notre Dame Bay, Newfoundland. Rachel had at least seven children from her two marriages:
    - Lydia/Lyddia Gavin (born 1920), born at Hauling Point, Newfoundland.
    - George Thomas Gavin (21st December 1923–23rd April 2019). He married Margaret, who predeceased him, and they had a daughter, Janette Gavin.
    - Norman B Purchase (1933–20th April 2017) married Maisie Stryde c.1953. He died at James Peyton Memorial Hospital, Gander, Newfoundland. They had a daughter, Donna Purchase.
    - Frank Y Purchase (born c.1935), born at Fogo.
    - Harold E Purchase (born c.1936).
    - Elvie Purchase, who married as Simms.
    - Mildred Purchase, who married as Dyke.

  Edward's children from his first marriage to Hilda:
    - George Purchase (1914–31st December 1987) married Gladys Gillingham (1915–4th March 1970).
    - Beatrice Mary Purchase (24th February 1918–8th August 1996) married George P Tizzard (born 1915). They had a son and a daughter.
    - Stella Pearl Purchase (30th October 1921–9th January 2011) married Edward White (1921–98), born at Carbonear, Bay De Verde, Newfoundland. He died at Salmon Cove, Newfoundland and she at Hilltop Manor, Cambridge, Waterloo Regional Municipality, Ontario. They had four children – Lester White, Hilda White, William White and Stella White.
    - Marietta Purchase (1925–2007) married as Osmond.

Roland's paternal grandfather, James Ricketts (born c.1818), born at New Harbour, Newfoundland, married Lucy née Ford (born c.1816), born at Shoe Cove, Newfoundland, on 23rd November 1835 at Greenspond, Newfoundland. James is believed to have died at Pool's Island, Newfoundland. In addition to John they had nine other children:

- Elizabeth Ricketts (born 3rd October 1836), born at Smart's Island, Bonavista, Newfoundland.
- Mary Ricketts (born 18th August 1844).
- Anne Patience Ricketts (born 7th September 1845).
- William Ricketts (born 3rd November 1846), a fisherman born at Greenspond, married his cousin, Mary Ann Cassell (July 1869–c.1949), on 8th November 1890 at Harbour Deep. Mary had a daughter, Harriet Cassell (3rd September 1888–13th September 1958). William and Mary were living at 198 St Barbe in 1911. She died at Jackson's Arm, White Bay. They had nine children – Alfred Ricketts (13th June 1891–2nd April 1981), Louisa Ricketts (21st July 1892–5th September 1959), Thomas William Ricketts (26th September 1893–1972), Amelia Diana Ricketts (April 1896–1983), James Ricketts (1901), Edmund Ricketts (November 1903–27th December 1927), Patience Ricketts (1905–25th December 1930), Benjamin Ricketts (3rd September 1907–10th November 1973) and Naomi Ricketts (1908).
- Thomas Ricketts (17th September 1850–22nd March 1926), born at Smart's Island, was a fisherman. He married Sabiah Rogers (born 1855) on 15th December 1882 at St James Church, Pool's Island, Bonavista. He died at Valleyfield, Newfoundland. They had at least a daughter, Lucy Ellen Ricketts (born 19th September 1883).
- James Ricketts (born 13th June 1852).
- Job Pitcher Ricketts (born 9th November 1853).
- Cornelius Kenneth Ricketts (19th July 1856–27th May 1905) married Elizabeth Jane Stuckless (1869–28th April 1947), born at Purbeck Cove, on 4th September 1888 at White Bay. He died at Sop's Arm. They had seven children:
    - Nathaniel Ricketts (22nd September 1889–2nd May 1969).
    - Selina Jane Ricketts (born 24th September 1890).
    - Alexander William Ricketts (15th October 1892–14th February 1977).
    - Thomas Ricketts (1896–14th October 1918) enlisted in 1st Newfoundland (4020) at St John's on 25th October 1917, described as a fisherman, twenty-three years and one month old, 5′ 5″ tall and weighing 125 lbs. He allotted $0.60 per day from his Army pay to his brother, Alexander. Thomas embarked at St John's aboard SS *Missanabie* or *Florizel* on 11th December. He was treated at Hazeley Down Military Hospital, Twyford, Hampshire for measles 3rd-23rd March 1918. On 25th May 1918 he embarked at Folkestone, Kent with a draft of 120 other ranks from 2nd Battalion, Winchester, Hampshire and disembarked in France on 27th May. He joined 1st Battalion on 31st May and was killed on 14th October in the same action for which his cousin was

  - awarded the VC. Thomas is buried in Dadizeele New British Cemetery, Belgium (V E 26).
  - Albertha Ricketts (21st February 1897–1939).
  - Moulton Julian Ricketts (1901–28th December 1941).
  - Prudence Lucy Ricketts (26th April 1903–11th December 1974) married Stewart Ricks.

Thomas Ricketts' grave in Dadizeele New British Cemetery, Belgium.

Elizabeth married Alfred Pittman (July 1864–1945), a fisherman born at Sop's Island, on 4th December 1910 at Western Cove, Newfoundland. They were living at St Barbe, Newfoundland in 1921. Elizabeth died at Westport. They had a daughter, Marle Pittman in 1907. Alfred had married Mary Ann Thoms (1867–1903) on 3rd October 1888 at Western Cove, White Bay. She had a daughter, Caroline Pittman (21st April 1887–1962). Mary and Alfred had four children – Archibald C Pittman (1892–1987), Elias Pittman (1893–1966), Robert John Pittman (1894–1985) and Minnie Pittman (1897–1982).
- Julian Ricketts (born 24th July 1864) born at Big Island, White Bay.

His maternal grandfather, George Cassell (June 1842–2nd September 1921), born at Herring Neck, was a fisherman. His surname has also been seen as Castle. He married Diana née Bath (9th December 1842–12th March 1918) on 21st October 1862 at Herring Neck, where she was born. They were living at 199 St Barbe in 1921. She died at Cat Cove, White Bay and he at Harbour Deep, White Bay. In addition to Amelia they had eleven other children:

- Elias Cassell (c.1862–26th August 1911) born at Hooping Harbour, Northern Peninsula, Newfoundland, married Lucy Pollard (29th July 1869–before 1904), born at Grand Fers Arm, on 21st September 1889 at Harbour Deep. Newfoundland. Elias married Keziah Brenton (c.1883–c.1932), born at Williamsport, on 22nd December 1904 at Hooping Harbour. He died at Hooping Harbour. Elias had six children from his two marriages – Lucretia Cassell (11th May 1890–7th January 1988), Lydia Cassell (12th January 1892–24th May 1973), Elisha Cassell (14th January 1894–26th August 1923), Lillian 'Lily' Cassell (1906–83), Mabel Cassell (14th December 1907) and Ashton 'Eddy' Cassell (10th October 1910–19th October 1989). Keziah is believed to have married Joseph Reeves (born c.1882). She died at Hooping Harbour.
- Elizabeth Jane Cassell (born c.1866 – died before 1881).
- Mary Ann Cassell (born July 1869) had a daughter, Harriet Cassell (3rd September 1888). Mary married her cousin, William Ricketts, on 8th November 1890 – see the fourth child of the paternal grandparents above.

- Prudence Cassell (c.1873–14th January 1904), born at Harbour Deep, married George Gillingham (c.1869–c.1900), born at Big Cove, on 2nd October 1892 at Harbour Deep. He died at Sop's Island. They had four children:
    - Fanny Gillingham (August 1892–9th June 1983), born at Williamsport, White Bay, married Eli Brenton (18th August 1886–c.1949), born at Duggan's Cove, White Bay, on 26th September 1913 at Williamsport, White Bay. Fanny and Eli both died at Williamsport. They had seven children including – George Cedric Brenton (16th August 1912–2009), Charlotte Prudence Brenton (August–9th September 1914), twins Julia Brenton and Eva Brenton (born July 1915), Mary Anne Brenton (2nd July 1918–1992) and Walter Brenton (c.1923–30th May 1929).
    - Annie Gillingham (born 1893), born at Harbour Deep, White Bay.
    - Henry Gillingham (4th April 1896–23rd July 1957) enlisted in the Newfoundland Regiment (3008) on 5th August 1916, making his mark. He was described as a fisherman, 5′ 6″ tall, weighing 114 lbs, with dark hair, fair complexion and brown eyes. His next of kin was his sister, Fanny. He allotted $0.50 per day from his Army pay to his brother, Thomas, from 1st September 1916 until 31st October 1918. He embarked aboard SS *Florizel* on 31st January 1917 and disembarked at Windsor, Nova Scotia on 3rd February. He embarked aboard SS *Ausonia* at Halifax, Nova Scotia on 16th April and served with 2nd Battalion at Newton-on-Ayr, Scotland. Henry embarked at Southampton, Hampshire on 11th June and disembarked at Rouen, France next day. He joined 1st Battalion on 2nd July and was wounded in the left leg and right arm at Cambrai on 20th November. He was treated at 89th Field Ambulance and No.48 Casualty Clearing Station on 22nd November and was transferred to 16th General Hospital, Le Tréport on 23rd November and 56th General Hospital, Étaples on 29th November. On 16th December he was evacuated to Britain aboard HMHS *Essequibo* and was admitted to 3rd London General Hospital, Wandsworth on 19th December. He was transferred to Brooklands Military Hospital, Weybridge on 4th February 1918 and to Summerdown Military Convalescent Hospital, Eastbourne on 20th March. Henry was granted leave 15th-24th May, staying at Belmont Cottage, St Leonards Road, Ayr, and was then fit for light duties. He returned to France on 31st August from Folkestone and joined D Infantry Base Depot, Rouen on 2nd September. However, he was returned to Britain on 13th September, with medical class B and joined 2nd Battalion. A medical board at Hazeley Down Camp, Hampshire on 28th November recommended repatriation to Newfoundland and he embarked at Tilbury on 12th December aboard SS *Corsican*. He disembarked in Newfoundland on 21st December and a medical board on 26th December recommended discharge. Henry was demobilised on 16th January 1919 permanently physically unfit. Henry returned to Harbour Deep. He married Susannah

'Susie' Davis (June 1898–1987), born at Brown's Cove, White Bay, on 24th June 1920 at White Bay and they had seven children – Sidney Gillingham (1920), Harvey Ronald Gillingham (9th June 1923–7th April 2001), Lillian Gillingham (17th March 1925–17th November 1979), Ethel 'Hattie' Gillingham (c.1927), Emily Gillingham (c.1930), Gerald Gillingham (29th December 1934–28th May 2003) and Gordon David Gillingham (23rd June 1938–c.1993). Henry and Susie both died at Jackson's Arm, White Bay.

- ◦ Thomas Gillingham (1897–9th March 1956) enlisted in the Newfoundland Forestry Companies (8509) at St John's on 24th August 1918. He was described as a lumberman, 5′ 5½″ tall, weighing 124 lbs, with blue eyes, light hair and his religious denomination was Church of England. His next of kin was his sister, Fanny. On 1st October he stole a purse and $30 from a comrade for which he was ordered to make good the loss and was placed in detention for twenty days. Thomas was discharged on 24th January 1919 permanently unfit for service. He married Eva Jane Hellimore née Hannam (5th December 1895–1973), born at Leading Tickles, Newfoundland, on 13th January 1920 at Winter House Cove. Eva had married Victor Emmanuel Hellemore (8th October 1889–12th December 1918). Eva and Thomas had four children including – Stella Madeline Gillingham (16th October 1925–2015), Prudence Jane Gillingham (21st September 1929–19th August 1930) and Randolph Guy Gillingham (27th April 1934–2020). Thomas died at Sops' Arm and Eva at Pollard's Point, White Bay.

Prudence married William Pollard (died 3rd May 1942) on 17th March 1902 at South West Cove. They had a daughter, Clara Pollard (23rd January 1903–27th July 1990). Prudence died at Harbour Deep. William had married Miriam Cassell (c.1870–4th February 1896) c.1895 at Harbour Deep, where she was born and died. William married Virtue Ann Randell (3rd January 1886–9th January 1976) on 12th August 1906 at Big Harbour, where she was born. He died at Harbour Deep and she at Roddickton, Canada Bay. They had seven children including – Alfred Pollard (1905–85), Sylvester George Pollard (1915–85), Cecil Pollard (1916–2005) and Susanna Pollard (1920).

- Selina Cassell (c.1876–17th April 1910) married George Marsh (c.1864–18th August 1930), a fisherman born at Winter House Cove. They had three children – Willis Bennett Marsh (1900–32), David John Marsh (26th November 1903) and Elias John Marsh (28th February 1908).
- Lydia Cassell (c.1878–29th November 1915) married John James Critch (1868–21st February 1928) on 2nd September 1895 at Grand Vache, White Bay, where he was born. She died at Little Harbour Deep and he at Springdale, Newfoundland. They had eleven children – Laura Delilah Critch (2nd June 1896–c.1930), Henry Critch (1897), Francis 'Frank' Critch (18th September 1899–6th August 1934), Charles James Critch (1903–2nd September 1970), Gilbert Critch (1904), Elias John Critch (1905–27th October 1924), Robert Critch (1907), Martha Critch

(1908), Edna Critch (12th June 1909), Phoebe Ann Critch (29th December 1912–13th March 1990), Susanna Lydia Critch (29th December 1912–29th December 1926), Margaret Critch (1913) and Samuel Critch (1915–5th August 1980). Frank enlisted in the Royal Newfoundland Regiment (4939) at St John's on 6th May 1918, making his mark. He was described as a fisherman, 5′ 3″ tall, weighing 116 lbs, with light brown hair, fair complexion, brown eyes and his religious denomination was Methodist. He allotted $0.70 per day to his father from his Army pay from 1st June. He embarked for Britain at Halifax, Nova Scotia on 11th June. He embarked for France on 26th October and joined 1st Battalion on 3rd November. On 16th November he was found to be deficient iron rations for which he was admonished and paid to replace them. On 3rd December he was admitted to No.44 Casualty Clearing Station and transferred to No.32 Casualty Clearing Station on 10th December. He was transferred to 20th General Hospital, Dannes Camiers with a mild foot problem on 12th December and was discharged to a base depot on 27th December and joined D Infantry Base Depot, Rouen on 30th December. Frank rejoined his unit on 14th January 1919. On 11th March and 15th April at Rouen he was found to be deficient kit for which he paid. He returned to England from Rouen on 22nd April, disembarking at Southampton next day and joined at Hazeley Down Camp on 23rd April. He embarked aboard SS *Corsican* at Liverpool on 22nd May and disembarked in Newfoundland on 1st June. He was demobilised on 28th June and was discharged at St John's on 12th July 1919.

- George William Cassell (January 1880–c.1967), a fisherman born at Herring Neck, married Mary Ann Marsh (24th May 1873–c.1958), born at Winter House Cove, on 6th December 1904 at Leading Tickles, Twillingate. They were living at 320 Leading Tickles in 1921. He died at Deer Lake. They had five children – Prudence Dinah Cassell (5th October 1906–25th January 2003), Noah Cassell (March 1909–13th December 1935), Louisa S Cassell (21st May 1911–12th July 1986), Lydia Mary Cassell (6th March 1913–23rd January 1943) and Lewis William Cassell (29th August 1918 or 1919–8th August 1941).
- John Thomas Cassell (c.1882–c.1969), a fisherman born at Harbour Deep, married Priscilla Randell (born c.1882) on 10th June 1904 at Great Harbour Deep. They had eight children including – Ishmael Cassell (1905–16th April 1927), Emanuel Cassell (1906–9th June 1939), Rosanne Cassell (1908), Selina A Cassell (1910–95), Laura May Cassell (1912–58), Charlotte Cassell (1916) and Roland Cassell (4th October 1921–17th September 1985).
- Rachel Cassell (17th May 1885–c.1971) married Nathaniel Cassell (sic) (c.1881–14th June 1914) on 8th October 1903 at Great Harbour Deep. They had six children – Daniel Cassell (1900), Elizabeth J Cassell (1901–17th July 1971), Lydia Cassell (1906–5th April 1993), Theophilus Cassell (1st August 1908–1985), Alexander John Cassell (1911–15th April 2001) and Effie Cassell. Rachel had a son, Harvey Budgell (sic) (1920–89). She married William Budgell (c.1870–22nd

April 1951) on 18th July 1922 at Jackson's Arm. They had a son, Ford Colin Budgell (1922–8th April 2000). William and Rachel both died at Pilley's Island.
- Lucy Cassell (23rd June 1888–before 1935), born at Duggan's Cove, White Bay.
- Jessie Cassell (born c.1894) was adopted.

Tommy received little or no early education due to the remote locality in which he lived. Aged five he fell into the sea and was dragged out by the tide. Richard Baker, a deckhand on a visiting schooner, who was a non-swimmer, dived in and rescued Tommy. Both were half dead when they reached the shore. When Tommy and his brother, George, enlisted they were not able to sign their names and made a mark instead.

Tommy was a fisherman when he enlisted in the Newfoundland Regiment at St John's on 2nd September 1916, described as 5′ 5½″ tall, weighing 126½ lbs, with light brown hair, fair complexion and brown eyes. He gave his age as eighteen years and three months although he was only fifteen years and five months. He was charged with being drunk at St John's on 2nd December and was admonished. Tommy embarked aboard SS *Florizel* at St John's on 31st January 1917, as part of the Windsor draft that had been delayed for ten weeks because of an outbreak of measles and had been quarantined at Windsor, Nova Scotia. He disembarked

SS *Florizel*, a passenger liner and flagship of the Bowring Brothers Red Cross Line, was one of the first ships designed to navigate icy waters. Bowring Brothers operated the New York, Newfoundland and Halifax Steamship Co Ltd. *Florizel* was modified each spring to participate in the annual seal hunt. She participated in the rescue of sealers during the Great 1914 Newfoundland Sealing Disaster. Following modification in October 1914 she carried the first 540 men of the Newfoundland Regiment, one of thirty-three liners and six Royal Navy warships in a convoy to Europe. On 23rd February 1918 *Florizel* departed St John's for Halifax and then on to New York, with seventy-eight passengers and sixty crew aboard. Shortly after passing through the St John's Narrows the weather deteriorated. None of the lighthouses south of Bay Bulls were sighted but after eight hours steaming the captain believed that the ship had rounded Cape Race and he ordered a course change. However, *Florizel* was short of the Cape and the white froth of waves crashing onto Horn Head Point was mistaken for ice. The ship crashed into the rocks at full speed. An SOS message was picked up by the Admiralty wireless station at Mount Pearl and rescue vessels were sent. It was the evening of 24th February when the first ships arrived. Of the 138 passengers and crew, forty-four survived the initial crash and were rescued. Bravery medals were awarded to several crew members of HMS *Briton* and *Prospero* and these were presented by the Prince of Wales when he visited St John's in 1919. Captain Martin was held responsible, because of the lack of soundings during the voyage. However, he was later found not to have been at fault. The Chief Engineer had reduced speed as soon as she left port, bypassing the captain's orders to proceed at full speed. As a result the ship made less distance than the captain believed.

The French Croix de Guerre was first awarded in 1915 to individuals or units distinguishing themselves by acts of heroism. Some notable recipients include:

- Josephine Baker – American born French dancer, singer and actress for her work in the Resistance.
- Jacques Cousteau – pioneer diver and underwater filmmaker.
- General Dwight D Eisenhower – Supreme Allied Commander during Operation Overlord.
- Noor Inayat Khan and Violette Szabo – British SOE agents awarded the George Cross and executed by the Nazis.
- Audie Murphy – actor and the most decorated US soldier of WW2, including the Medal of Honor.
- General George S Patton – commander of US Third Army in the Second World War.
- Theodore Roosevelt – son of President Theodore Roosevelt, awarded the Medal of Honor for 6th June 1944 on Utah Beach.
- James Stewart – actor, for his role in the liberation of France as a USAAF Colonel.
- Major Richard D Winters – Easy Company, 506th Parachute Infantry Regiment, made famous by the TV series and book *Band of Brothers*.
- Sergeant Alvin C York – American First World War Medal of Honor winner and subject of a film in 1941 starring Gary Cooper.

at Ayr, Scotland on 3rd February. He made an allotment of $0.60 per day from his army pay to his sister, Rachel, on 1st February 1917 until it was reallocated to his father in October 1918. He went to Rouen, France from Southampton, Hampshire on 11th June and joined the Newfoundland Battalion on 2nd July in the Ypres Salient. He took part in the Battle of Langemarck on 16th August and the Battle of Poelcapelle on 9th October. On 20th November he received a gunshot wound to the right thigh at Marcoing during the Battle of Cambrai. He was treated at 89th Field Ambulance and was transferred to No.48 Casualty Clearing Station and 1st Canadian General Hospital, Étaples next day. On 28th November he was evacuated to England and admitted to 1st London General Hospital, Camberwell, London. He was granted Command Depot furlough 10th–19th December and then reported to No.24 Company Depot, Ayr, Scotland. He transferred to No.7 Command Depot, Ripon, Yorkshire on

Field Marshal Sir Claud William Jacob GCB GCSI KCMG (1863–1948). During the Great War he commanded the Dehra Dun Brigade, 21st Division and II Corps. After the war he commanded a corps of the British Army of the Rhine before returning to India as Chief of the General Staff, later GOC Northern Command, temporarily C-in-C India and then Military Secretary to the India Office.

10th January 1918. Having been classified medically fit A3, he was ordered to report to the 2nd Battalion at Winchester, Hampshire on 4th February.

Tommy returned to France, embarking on 3rd April, disembarking on 6th April and rejoining his unit on 30th April. **Awarded the VC for his actions at Ledeghem, Belgium on 14th October 1918, LG 6th January 1919.** He was the youngest Army VC of the war and the only member of the Royal Newfoundland Regiment to be awarded the VC. The Battalion was part of the British Army of the Rhine in Germany, based at Hilden southeast of Düsseldorf. The award of the VC was announced at a Battalion parade on 23rd December. The Battalion was granted the whole of 24th December as a holiday. **Awarded the French Croix de Guerre 1914–18, LG 19th June 1919.** It was presented by Lieutenant General Sir Claud Jacob KCB, GOC II Corps on or about 28th December 1918.

Tommy was granted leave and then joined 2nd Battalion at Winchester on 19th January 1919. Earlier that day he was presented with the VC by the King at a private ceremony at York Cottage, Sandringham, Norfolk. The investiture was arranged hastily ahead of Tommy's return to Canada. Whilst at Sandringham he was introduced to Sir Dighton Probyn VC, at that time the second oldest surviving VC. The Royal family had lost their youngest son, Prince John (12th July 1905–18th January 1919), the day before.

Tommy was promoted sergeant on 29th January and sailed from Liverpool, Lancashire aboard SS *Corsican* next day. He disembarked at Furness-Withy Pier, St John's on 8th February 1919 and was placed in a carriage drawn by young men and joined a procession to be cheered by thousands of people. Tommy was interviewed by a reporter for *The Evening Telegram* named Joseph 'Joey' Roberts Smallwood (1900–91), who became Premier of the Province 1949–72. Tommy was sent to Bell Island (home of Matthew Brazil, who was awarded the DCM for the part he played in Tommy Ricketts VC action) for another parade on 19th February. Tommy was presented with an illuminated address and a purse of gold, then visited various schools and was feted by a number of organisations, including being taken through the mines. He was billeted in a boarding house at 53 Colonial Street, St John's when he reported sick with tonsilitis on 25th February and was treated until

York Cottage, Sandringham, Norfolk where Thomas Ricketts received his VC from the King.

SS *Corsican* (11,419 tons) was built for the Allan Line by Barclay, Curle & Co Ltd in Glasgow. Her maiden voyage on 31st October 1907 was from Liverpool to St John, New Brunswick. She was chartered by Canadian Pacific Line in 1908 and on 12th August 1912 suffered slight damage in a collision with an iceberg near Belle Isle. In August 1914 she became a troopship and in 1917 was taken over by Canadian Pacific Line. On 24th August 1918 she commenced her first voyage on the London – Québec – Montréal route. However, on 30th January 1919 she resumed the Liverpool – St John's service, later switching to the Glasgow, London, Liverpool or Antwerp to Canada service. In November 1922 she was renamed *Marvale* and her accommodation was altered to cabin and third class only. On 21st May 1923, she was wrecked in thick fog when she ran into Freel´s Rock, off Pine Point, Newfoundland. All 437 persons aboard were saved.

Joseph Roberts 'Joey' Smallwood (1900–91) was the driving force who brought Newfoundland into the Canadian Confederation in 1949. He became the first Premier and held the post until 1972. He promoted economic development, the welfare state and the modernisation of education and transport (Yousuf Karsh).

A Newfoundland Regiment contingent leaving Furness-Withy Pier, St John's on 5th February 1915.

8th March. Tommy was demobilised in St John's on 1st July 1919 to live c/o George House on Robinson's Hill. House was a teacher at Bishop Feild College, St John's and may have helped to prepare Tommy to enter school in 1920. Tommy attended dinners in his honour, toured schools in uniform and was a special guest at remembrance events and unveilings during the 1920s, despite not relishing the limelight. On 3rd June 1920 he was presented with $500 donated by Mr GWB Ayre to the most highly decorated Newfoundlander. The presentation was made by the Governor at Government House.

Tommy wanted to further his limited schooling. Even before he returned to Newfoundland two fundraising campaigns had been started. The *RT Ricketts VC*

Bishop Feild College was founded in 1844 as the Church of England Academy. It was renamed in 1892 the Church of England College and before 1894 the name changed again to Bishop Feild College after Bishop Edward Feild, a school inspector and second Bishop of Newfoundland. Originally for Anglican-affiliated boys of Newfoundland Cathedral, it later admitted girls. It was an independent private school until the 1960s, when it joined the school board. It is now Bishop Feild School.

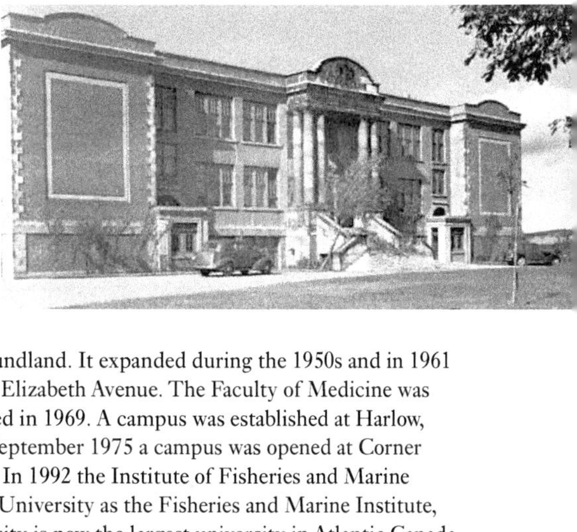

Memorial University College was founded in September 1925 on Parade Street, St John's as a memorial to Newfoundlanders and Labradorians who died in the Great War. It was partly funded by the Carnegie Corporation of New York. It was later rededicated to include the Province's war dead of the Second World War. The initial enrolment was fifty-seven students. In 1933 the College merged with the adjacent Normal School. When Newfoundland joined the Canadian Confederation, the government elevated the status of the College to a university in August 1949, renaming it the Memorial University of Newfoundland. It expanded during the 1950s and in 1961 it moved from Parade Street to its present location on Elizabeth Avenue. The Faculty of Medicine was established in 1967 and the first students were admitted in 1969. A campus was established at Harlow, England in 1969 for approximately fifty students. In September 1975 a campus was opened at Corner Brook which by 2010 was known as Grenfell Campus. In 1992 the Institute of Fisheries and Marine Technology in St John's was affiliated with Memorial University as the Fisheries and Marine Institute, later renamed the Marine Institute. Memorial University is now the largest university in Atlantic Canada and Newfoundland and Labrador's only university. In 2018 there were 3,800 faculty and staff and 18,000 students from almost one hundred countries.

Monument, commenced by WW Blackall, Church of England Superintendant of Education, in January was intended to build a school and provide a teacher at Middle Arm. However, it was decided to move it to Seal Cove because there were insufficient children at Middle Arm. By March it had grown to $1,466. A second fund was set up to cover the education of former soldiers, with the aim of raising $10,000 in ten days. By the ninth day $5,872.01 had been donated. The local *Daily Star* newspaper also collected money for him. Tommy enrolled at Bishop Feild College, St John's in September 1919 with fourteen other former soldiers. He went on to join the first class at Memorial University College, St John's in 1925. A year later he commenced a pharmaceutical apprenticeship at T McMurdo & Co Drugstore. Tommy began running his own pharmacy on the corner of Job and Water Streets, St John's in 1934 and trained a number of apprentices.

He greeted Field Marshal Earl Haig when he disembarked at King's Beach on 29th June 1924 and stood with dignitaries when the Newfoundland National War

Field Marshal Earl Douglas Haig (19th June 1861 – 29th January 1928) commanded the BEF on the Western Front from late 1915 until the end of the war. The costly offensives on the Somme in 1916 and during Third Ypres in 1917 earned him the title of 'Butcher Haig'. However, he weathered the battering of the German spring offensives in early 1918 and led the BEF during the final Hundred Days campaign that ended the war. It was probably the greatest victory ever achieved by a British-led army.

The dedication of the Newfoundland National War Memorial on 1st July 1924.

Memorial was unveiled by Haig on 1st July. On 24th February 1930 Tommy took part in the play *Journey's End* at the Casino Theatre, St John's. All the parts were played by ex-servicemen and the play ran for a week.

Tommy Ricketts married Edna May Edwards (27th March 1913–20th May 2010) in 1933 at St Thomas' Church, St John's, where she was born. They met when he took lodgings with her parents at 131 Penneywell Road, St John's in the early 1930s. They lived above the pharmacy at 100 Water Street West, which was later renumbered 516 Water Street. By 1945 they were living at 4 Craigmillar Avenue. They had two children:

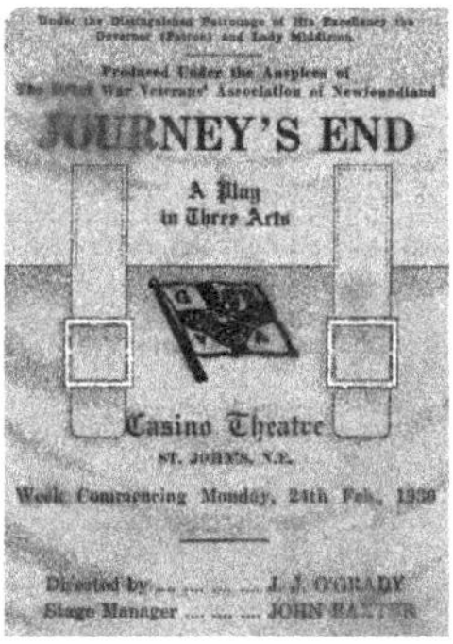

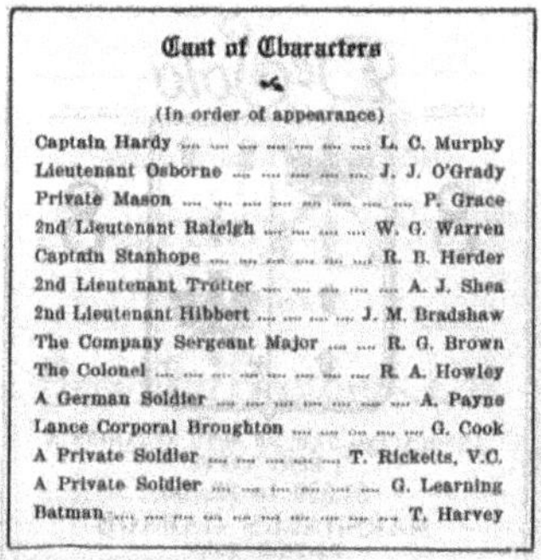

Cast of Characters

(In order of appearance)

Captain Hardy	L. C. Murphy
Lieutenant Osborne	J. J. O'Grady
Private Mason	P. Grace
2nd Lieutenant Raleigh	W. G. Warren
Captain Stanhope	R. B. Herder
2nd Lieutenant Trotter	A. J. Shea
2nd Lieutenant Hibbert	J. M. Bradshaw
The Company Sergeant Major	R. G. Brown
The Colonel	R. A. Howley
A German Soldier	A. Payne
Lance Corporal Broughton	G. Cook
A Private Soldier	T. Ricketts, V.C.
A Private Soldier	G. Learning
Batman	T. Harvey

Journey's End, a 1928 play by RC Sherriff, is set in the trenches near St Quentin 18th-21st March 1918. It was first performed at the Apollo Theatre, London on 9th December 1928 and starred Laurence Olivier. The play gained in popularity, including internationally. There was a film version in 1930 and a German remake, *The Other Side*, the following year. A one-hour version was televised by the BBC live from Alexandra Palace on 11th November 1937. A radio adaptation was produced for BBC Radio 4 in November 1970. The play was the basis for the film *Aces High* in 1976, although that film was based on the Royal Flying Corps rather than the infantry. In 1988 it was again broadcast on television. A second feature film was released in 2017. Pictured here are the cover of the programme for *Journey's End* at the Casino Theatre in February 1930 and the cast list.

- Dolda Lorraine Ricketts (30th March 1934–17th June 2019) was not with the family at the time of the 1935 Census. She also became a pharmacist and worked with her father for about two years before moving to Nova Scotia. She married Leonard ET Clarke (10th October 1934–14th March 1991). He was a principal in 1974, when they were living at 12 James Street, Dartmouth, Halifax Co, Nova Scotia. They both died at Dartmouth. They had two children:
    - Beverley 'Bev' Susan Clarke (1962–4th September 2007), born at Halifax, Nova Scotia, married Pierre Beaulieu. They were living at 48 Lakefront Road, Dartmouth, Halifax in 1996, on Harvard Drive in 2001 and at Lawrencetown at the time of her death at Queen Elizabeth II Health Sciences Centre, 1276 South Park Street, Halifax.
    - Barry Clarke.

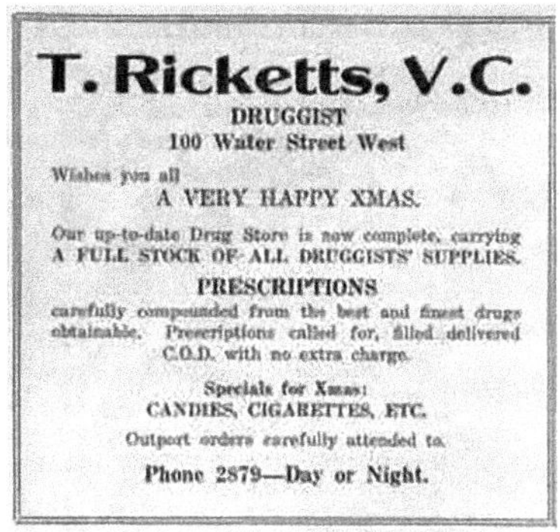

An advertisement for Tommy's dug store from Christmas 1936.

- Thomas 'Tommy' G Ricketts MD FRCP(C) (22nd May 1935–15th September 2020) was educated at Bishop Feild College, St John's and Dalhousie University,

St Thomas' Church was built in 1835–36, when there was a need for a second Anglican church in St John's to service the growing population. The church escaped the great fire in 1846 but a violent storm the same year led to the construction of wings to stabilise the structure five years later. The bell was imported from England and was installed in 1847. Until 1870, St Thomas' was also the garrison church. In 1874 the church was lengthened by almost ten metres to accommodate more people and the east gallery and side galleries were removed. The church was enlarged again in 1883 by extending the chancel and adding a vestry and additional space for the organ. Canon Wood Hall was built next to the church in the late 1800s for meetings and other church activities. It was destroyed by fire in 1966. The last major alteration was in 1903, when the chancel was again lengthened. About the same time space under the church was excavated for a choir room which was restored in 2004 and an extension room added. The church then had seating for over 1,300 people. In 1910 a pipe organ was installed. A set of tubular chimes was installed in the tower as a memorial after the Great War and an electronic chime system after the Second World War. The oak doors and panelling at the west end of the church are a Second World War memorial. In 1922, a space was dug out for a small chapel for the Brotherhood of St Andrew, a men's service group, and this was restored and rededicated in 1982. The old tower bell was restored in 1965. In 1976 St Thomas' School, which had opened in 1927, closed and it was converted into the parish hall. St Thomas' Anglican Church became a Registered Heritage Structure in June 1986.

Government House, the official residence of the Governor of Newfoundland and later the Lieutenant Governor of Newfoundland and Labrador. The first governors were naval officers and lived aboard their flagship anchored in St John's harbour until Admiral Richard Edwards moved into Fort Townshend, where the first Government House was completed in 1781. The current building was completed in 1831.

Halifax, where he studied medicine, graduating in 1958. He met Janice Juanita Hunter (born 5th August 1936) at the University and they married in 1959. He worked at Bonne Bay Cottage Hospital, Norris Point, Newfoundland and later ran a family practice at Grand Falls, Windsor, Newfoundland. He specialised in radiology in 1970 and moved to Toronto, Ontario, where they lived at Guildwood Village. He worked at Scarborough General Hospital, Toronto 1974- 2003. They had five children – Catherine E Ricketts, Thomas Y Ricketts, George A Ricketts, John D Ricketts and Carolyn V Ricketts.

Edna's parents were John E Edwards (23rd September 1886–23rd April 1963), born in London, England, and Kate née Vatcher (4th January 1889–16th November 1982). He emigrated to Newfoundland. They both died at St John's.

Tommy attended two VC reunions – the VC Dinner at the Royal Gallery of the House of Lords, London on 9th November 1929 and the 3rd VC & GC Association Reunion at the Café Royal, London on 18th July 1962. While in London in 1929 he visited General Sir Reginald Hart VC GCB KCVO at his home in Putney. On his return to St John's he received a hero's welcome and was met at the station by Mayor Tasker Cook. This was followed by a parade to a reception at Government House and a dinner at the Church Lads' Brigade Armoury at which guest speakers included Prime Minister Sir Richard Squires, future Prime Minister FC Alderdice and Lieutenant General Sir Hugh Tudor.

The CLB Armoury on Harvey Road, St John's is the headquarters of the Brigade in Newfoundland. The original Armoury was designed by a former Brigade member and was built in 1910. On 21st December 1992 it was destroyed in the Harvey Road Fire. The Marching Home campaign was launched and over two years sufficient funds were raised to build a new CLB Armoury on the same site.

Lieutenant General Sir Henry Hugh Tudor KCB CMG (1871–1965) was commanding 9th (Scottish) Division at the time of Tommy's VC action. However, he is mainly remembered for his roles in the Irish War of Independence 1919–21 and the Palestine Police. He was commissioned in the Royal Horse Artillery on 25th July 1890 and was in India 1890–97. He served in South Africa during the Second Boer War and was badly wounded at Magersfontein in December 1899. He was again in India 1905–10, then Egypt and was there when the Great War broke out. On the Western Front he rose from a captain commanding an artillery battery to a major general commanding a division. Tudor was a professional and forward-looking officer, who has been described as an expert tactician. He spent a lot of time in the front lines and was almost killed at Ypres in October 1917, when a shell fragment smashed his helmet. He was the first British general to use smoke shells and an early advocate of predicted artillery fire. In May 1920 he was appointed Police Adviser in Ireland and was promoted to Lieutenant General. At the time the morale of the Royal Irish Constabulary and its effective strength were declining. Tudor realised that he had to raise police morale, punish crime and restore law and order. Controversially he created the Auxiliary Division, the notorious Black and Tans. In February 1922, Churchill appointed Tudor to a new post, General Officer Commanding and Inspector-General of Police and Prisons in Palestine. However, he failed to properly manage his dual civil and military responsibilities and was dismissed in March 1924. He emigrated to Newfoundland and lived there for the rest of his life.

Tommy was always a shy and modest man who disliked having his photograph taken. After the attention he received in the 1920s, he withdrew from public engagements. However, in June 1939 he was part of an honour guard for the visit of King George VI to Newfoundland. Tommy would walk to Remembrance parades with his medals in his pocket, put them on for the ceremony and immediate afterwards place them back in his pocket. He was invited to functions when Princess Elizabeth (later Queen Elizabeth II) went to St John's in 1951 but politely declined. The same thing happened when Princess Mary, the Princess Royal, Colonel-in-Chief of the Royal Newfoundland Regiment, visited in 1964 to present new colours to the Regiment on the fiftieth anniversary of its formation. He failed to collect the annual gratuity awarded to all VC recipients for many years. After his death arrangements were made for his widow to be paid the arrears in a lump sum.

Tommy, on the right, with five other members of the Church Lads' Brigade, four of whom are also wearing war medals.

Tommy suffered from poor health following a heart attack in the late 1940s. He died of a heart attack while working in his pharmacy on

Tommy's and Edna's grave in the Anglican Cemetery, St John's (Memorials to Valour).

Tommy's funeral cortège.

10th February 1967. His state funeral with full military honours took place at St Thomas' Anglican Church, St John's on 13th February. He lay in state before the funeral, with a guard of honour from the Royal Newfoundland Regiment and Royal Canadian Legion. In addition to family members, the funeral was attended by Lieutenant Governor Fabian O'Dea, Premier Joey Smallwood and representatives from the Royal Canadian Mounted Police, Newfoundland Constabulary, Royal Canadian Legion and Royal Newfoundland Regiment. He is buried in the Anglican Cemetery, Forest Road, St John's. Tommy is commemorated in a number of other places:

- Newfoundland
  - Lewisporte branch of the Royal Canadian Legion was named after him. On 10th November 1967 his son opened a new lounge there.
  - Tommy Ricketts Memorial Peace Park, Conception Bay South, Newfoundland.
  - Memorial at the site of his shop in St John's unveiled on 10th June 1972.
  - Display at the Royal Newfoundland Regiment Room, Canadian Forces Station, St John's.
  - The Thomas (Tommy) Ricketts Award, School of Pharmacy, Memorial University of Newfoundland provides financial assistance for experiential learning for pharmacy students. The inaugural presentation took place on 17th January 2019.
- Canada
  - Ricketts Trophy – donated to the Canadian Forces by the Royal Newfoundland Regiment in 1981, is awarded annually to the team of the Canadian Regular Forces that attains the highest aggregate score in the Light Machine Gun

team matches in the Canadian Forces Small Arms Competition. The trophy is a replica Lewis gun mounted on a wooden base.

- A wooden plaque bearing fifty-six maple leaves each inscribed with the name of a Canadian-born VC holder was dedicated at the Canadian Forces College, Toronto, Ontario on Remembrance Day 1999.
- Victoria Cross obelisk to all Canadian VCs at Military Heritage Park, Barrie dedicated by The Princess Royal on 22nd October 2013.
- Named on one of eleven plaques honouring 175 men from overseas awarded the VC for the Great War. The plaques were unveiled by the Senior Minister of State at the Foreign & Commonwealth Office and Minister for Faith and Communities, Baroness Warsi, at a reception at Lancaster House, London on 26th June 2014 attended by The Duke of Kent and relatives of the VC recipients. The Canadian plaque was unveiled outside the British High Commission in Elgin Street, Ottawa on 10th November 2014 by The Princess Royal in the presence of British High Commissioner Howard Drake, Canadian Minister of Veterans Affairs Julian Fantino and Canadian Chief of the Defence Staff General Thomas James Lawson.

The Victoria Cross obelisk in Military Heritage Park, Barrie, Ontario (Memorials to Valour).

The Canadian VC memorial plaque (back right) outside the British High Commission in Ottawa (Memorials to Valour).

The York Cemetery VC Memorial.

The 49 Cent postage stamps issued by Canada Post on 21st October 2004.

- ◦ Plaque No.24 on the York Cemetery VC Memorial, West Don River Valley, Toronto, dedicated on 25th June 2017.
- ◦ Two 49 cents postage stamps in honour of the ninety-four Canadian VC winners were issued by Canada Post on 21st October 2004 on the 150th Anniversary of the first Canadian VC's action, Alexander Roberts Dunn VC.

Issue No.351 of the Victor Comic (Victor Comic).

- Twenty-two Berberis shrubs representing the twenty-two members of the Church Lads' Brigade who were awarded the VC were planted in the Church Lads & Church Girls Brigade Memorial Plot at the National Memorial Arboretum, Alrewas, Staffordshire.
- Communities and Local Government commemorative paving stones for the 145 VCs born in Australia, Belgium, Canada, China, Denmark, Egypt, France, Germany, India, Iraq, Japan, Nepal, Netherlands, New Zealand, Newfoundland, Pakistan, South Africa, Sri Lanka, Ukraine and United States of America were unveiled at the National Memorial Arboretum, Alrewas, Staffordshire by Prime Minister David Cameron MP and Sergeant Johnson Beharry VC on 5th March 2015.
- His VC action was featured in Issue No.351 of the Victor Comic entitled 'Running the Gauntlet' dated 11th November 1967.

The memorial at Tree (De Beurt) Farm (Memorials to Valour).

The Canadian War Museum in Ottawa.

The King George VI Coronation Medal was awarded to the Royal Family, selected officers of state, officials, servants of the Royal Household, ministers, government and local government officials, mayors, public servants, members of the armed forces and police in Britain, the colonies and Dominions. A total of 90,279 medals were awarded.

- Memorial at the Newfoundland Memorial, Courtrai, Belgium, erected by the Newfoundland government to commemorate the Royal Newfoundland Regiment's actions during the Great War.
- Memorial stone at Tree Farm (De Beurt Farm), at the junction of Beurtemolenstraat with Driemastenstraat, off Gullegemestraat, Sint-Eloois-Winkel, Ledegem, Belgium.

In addition to the VC he was awarded the British War Medal 1914–20, Victory Medal 1914–19, George VI Coronation Medal 1937, Elizabeth II Coronation Medal 1953 and French Croix de Guerre 1914–18. He insisted that his medals should not be sold for profit. After his death his family allowed the group to be displayed at the Newfoundland Naval and Military Museum, Confederation Building, St John's and later at the Railway Coastal Museum, St John's. On 22nd October 2003 his widow donated the medals to the Canadian War Museum in the presence of their two children. Some surprise was expressed that the medals did not remain in Newfoundland, which was not part of Canada when Tommy was awarded the VC. The VC is held by the Canadian War Museum, 1 Vimy Place, Ottawa, Ontario, Canada. However, the two Coronation medals are not part of the group.

42364 LANCE CORPORAL ERNEST SEAMAN
2nd Battalion, The Royal Inniskilling Fusiliers

Ernest Seaman was born on 16th August 1893 at 9 Derby Street, Heigham, Norwich, Norfolk. His father is not known. His mother, Sarah Elizabeth Seaman née March (27th May 1855–1933), born at Horsford, Norfolk, married Henry William Seaman (1851–89), a miller born at Litcham, Norfolk, at St Faith's, Norfolk in 1874. They were living at Derby Street, Heigham, Norwich in 1881. Sarah was a laundress in 1891 and 1901 and was still living at 9 Derby Street, Heigham. She married Edward Augustus Palmer (1854–1934), born at Erpingham, Norfolk, in 1904 at Norwich. Edward was landlord of the King's Head Inn, Bungay Road, Scole, Norfolk and also ran a pony-and-trap service for passengers from Diss Station. Both their deaths were registered at Depwade, Norfolk.

Edward had married Anna Sophia Elizabeth Stimpson (1849–26th February 1894) on 14th May 1888 at St John's Church, Lowestoft, Suffolk. He was a carpenter in 1891, when they were boarding at the home of his parents at Holt Road, Briston, Norfolk. He was boarding at the home of Frederick and Rose Clapham at Carpenter's Shop, Briston, Norfolk in 1901. Edward and Anna had a son:

Horsford, ten kilometres north of Norwich, is surrounded by Horsford Forest, a County Wildlife Site. The remains of Horsford Castle are to the east of the village.

- Cyril Augustus Palmer (25th April 1889–15th March 1973) was living with his maternal grandmother at 271 London

Litcham is close to the three market towns of Dereham, Fakenham and Swaffham. The area was well populated during the Roman period and there are some Bronze Age remains. Litcham is mentioned in the Domesday Book, including a church of which nothing now remains above ground but probably stood on the site of the current Church of All Saints, which dates from c.1300. It was rebuilt in 1412 and the red brick tower was added in 1669. Edward I granted Litcham the right to hold a weekly market and that continued until 1836. In the past most inhabitants were involved in agriculture but the tanning industry was also important. Parts of The Bull, a coaching inn, date back to the 14th century. A Methodist Chapel was built in 1909. The Priory, which dates from the 14th century, was probably a chapel or hermitage. In 1977 Litcham was designated a conservation village and has eleven listed buildings.

Horsham St Faith is eight kilometres north of Norwich. There are the remains of a motte and bailey castle and there was a Benedictine priory, dedicated to St Faith, until the Dissolution of the Monasteries. From the early 12th century until 1872 the village hosted one of the country's largest cattle fairs every 17th October. The church, which is shared with the Methodists, dates back to the 13th century and has undergone many changes, including a major restoration in 1873. Nearby is Norwich International Airport, the former RAF Horsham St Faith. In August 1941, a Blenheim of No.18 Squadron took off from Horsham St Faith and dropped a box by parachute over the airfield at Saint-Omer-Longuenesse in France. It contained a pair of artificial legs for Wing Commander Douglas Bader. From September 1942 the airfield was used by the US Eighth Air Force for bomber and fighter groups. The RAF airfield closed in August 1963.The village is the birthplace of Saint Robert Southwell c.1561, a Roman Catholic Jesuit priest, poet and hymnodist. He was arrested and imprisoned in 1592, and eventually tried and convicted of high treason for his links to the Holy See. He was hanged at Tyburn on 21st February 1595 and was canonised by Pope Paul VI in 1970 as one of the Forty Martyrs of England and Wales.

Road, Kirkley, Suffolk in 1901. He was living with his father by 1911, by when he was a grocer. Cyril married May Rose Riley (8th May 1886–16th December 1980), born at Darlaston, Staffordshire, in 1916 at Edmonton, Middlesex. She was living with her parents at 43 Government Row, Enfield, Middlesex in 1891. By 1911 she was a cashier in a grocery store, living with her mother at Blanly, Holmwood Road, Waltham Cross, Middlesex. Cyril was the branch manager of a grocer's cooperative in 1939, when they were living at 4 Cleveland Road, Lowestoft. They were living at 130 Stradbroke Road, Pakefield, Lowestoft at the time of their deaths there. May and Cyril had a daughter, Molly E Palmer in 1925.

In addition to Ernest, Sarah had nine other children including:

- William Henry Seaman (4th September 1875–1949), a driver born at Norwich, married Mary Ann Rich (4th March 1869–1958), a domestic servant, on 14th February 1900 at St Mary's and St Saviour's, Surlingham, Norfolk, where she was born. He was living at Caledonian Road, London at the time. William was a coachman in 1901, when they were living at 124 Hemingford Road, Islington, London. By 1911 he was described as an assistant superintendent assurance for the Salvation Army. They were living at 106 Canonbury Road, Islington at the time. By 1939 both William and Mary were Salvation Army officers, living at 171 Ivydale Road, Camberwell, London. They had five children including:
    - Mary Alice Seaman (13th April 1901–1988), born at Islington, was a clerk bookkeeper in 1939, living with her parents. She married Arthur J Smith on 5th June 1961 at Samford, Suffolk.
    - Ethel Lucy Seaman (19th September 1902–16th March 1991) married Herbert Stanley Moorhouse (30th March 1907–1st March 1971), born at Dewsbury, Yorkshire, in 1935 in Surrey. He was living with his parents at 19 Upper Cross Street, off Bradford Road, Dewsbury, Yorkshire in 1911. Herbert and Ethel were living at 1 Narford Road, Hackney, London in 1939. He died at Enfield, London and she at Wallingford, Berkshire. They had a daughter, Sheila E Moorhouse, in 1941.
    - William James Henry Seaman (31st October 1907–4th January 1998), born at Hampstead, London, married Stella Underwood Bennett (16th May 1906–1986), born at Newcastle-upon-Tyne, Northumberland, in 1932 at Southampton, Hampshire. Her father, Henry Bennett, was a Salvation Army staff officer. William was a bank clerk in 1939, when they were living at 31 Waltham Avenue, Wembley, Middlesex. He later became a bank manager and Stella was involved with the Salvation Army. Their deaths were registered at Truro, Cornwall. They had a daughter, Brenda Seaman, in 1933.
    - Helen Ivy Maud Seaman (30th November 1910–13th February 2003), born at Islington, married Thomas Albert Bradley (1st July 1913–19th March 2006), born at Hartlepool, Co Durham, in 1935 at Lancaster, Lancashire. He was an assurance agent in 1939, when they were living at 23 Allerton Road, Stoke Newington, London. He was also a volunteer with the Auxiliary Fire Service at the time of the 1939 Register. They both died at Ipswich, Suffolk. They had two children – Beryl I Bradley 1937 and Norman T Bradley 1940.
- Charles March Seaman (21st March 1877–December 1943) was a box maker in 1891. He married Caroline Theresa Jones Berry (c.19th November 1873–2nd March 1967) on 15th June 1898 at Yarmouth, where she was born. She was known as Theresa. Charles was a barman in 1899, when they were living at 8 Lady Haven Road, Cobholm, Yarmouth. By 1901 he was a labourer in a sawmill and they were living at the home of his widowed mother-in-law, Matilda Berry,

at 34 Alderson Road, Yarmouth. By 1902 he was a publican, living with his family at 127 Middlegate Street, Yarmouth. By 1911 he was a general labourer, living with his family at 1 George's Place, Manby Road, Yarmouth. He was a timber porter in July 1920 and a tram conductor in 1923, when they were living at 6 Clintock Place, Great Yarmouth. At the time of the 1939 Register he was an incapacitated quayside labourer in the Infirmary, 150A Caister Road, Great Yarmouth. Theresa was living with her daughters, Ivy and Doris, at 6 Clintock Place. He died at Kettering, Northamptonshire and she at 6 Clintock Place. They had seven children:

- Frederick Edwin Evelyn Seaman (15th January 1899–10th March 1969), born at 8 Lady Haven Road, married Clara Eva W Brunson (24th December 1899–1976), born at Runham, Norfolk, in 1925 at Yarmouth. She was known as Eva. Frederick was a brewer's labourer in 1939, when they were living at 94 Admiralty Road, Great Yarmouth. He died there and Eva at Waveney, Suffolk. They had a son, Donald F Seaman, in 1927.
- Charles Baden Seaman (9th August 1900–12th February 1959) served in the Royal Naval Reserve (SBC 830) and the Royal Engineers (301183), from which he was demobilised on 22nd November 1919. He enlisted in 4th Norfolk at Great Yarmouth on 13th July 1920 (5765621). He was described as a motor driver, 5′8″ tall, weighing 148 lbs, with fresh complexion, blue eyes, brown hair and his religious denomination was Church of England. He was discharged on 12th July 1921. Charles was a chauffeur when he married Winifred Mary Pearce (13th December 1899–13th June 1983) on 29th December 1923 at Great Yarmouth Parish Church. She was born there and lived with her parents at 15 Stanley Terrace. Charles was a corporation transport ticket inspector in 1939, when they were living at 25 Raleigh Avenue, Great Yarmouth. They had seven children – Joan Winifred Seaman 1924, Brian Charles Pearce Seaman 1926, Norman J Seaman 1928, Russell Frank Seaman 1931, twins David G and Derek E Seaman 1937 and Patrick R Seaman 1943. Winifred married Jack Edward Potter (30th January 1901–19th May 1969), born at Shepherd's Bush, London, in 1959 at Great Yarmouth. He was living with his parents at 113 Nightingale Lane, Hornsey, London in 1911. Winifred and Jack were living at 91 Mill Lane, Bradwell, Great Yarmouth at the time of his death. Jack had married Rosina Pryke (1896–1953) in 1928 at Islington, London, where she was born. She was living with her parents at 40 Cornwallis Road, Islington in 1901. Her death was registered at Harrow, Middlesex. Jack and Rosina had a son, Alan J Potter, in 1930. Winifred married her brother-in-law, Richard George Thetford (12th November 1903–1984), born at Norwich, in 1978 at Great Yarmouth. She was living at 9 Charles Avenue, Thorpe St Andrew, Norwich at the time of her death there. Richard had married Lily Adeline Pearce (14th February 1908–1976) in 1931 at Great Yarmouth, where she

was born, the sister of Winifred Mary Pearce. She lived with her parents at 15 Stanley Terrace, Great Yarmouth. Richard was a watchmaker employed as an instrument and time switch mechanic in 1939, when they were living at 26 Russell Avenue, Great Yarmouth. They had two children – Charmian Thetford 1935 and Valerie Thetford 1940.

- Narcissus Nell Seaman (19th November 1902–October 1980), born at 127 Middlegate Street, Yarmouth, was a barmaid at Nelson Tavern, South Denes, Great Yarmouth in 1939. She married Robert Stephen Skoyles (9th November 1884–1957) in 1941 at Great Yarmouth, where he was born. He was a grocer's assistant in 1901, when he was living with his parents at 1 Jireh Place, Great Yarmouth and at 1 Black's Buildings, Russell Road, Great Yarmouth in 1905. He was a warehouseman employed by Clowes Hall Quarry when he enlisted in The Prince of Wales's Own Royal Norfolk Artillery (Militia) on 21st March 1905 (3356). He was serving in 1st Norfolk Rifle Volunteers at the time. He was described as 5′8″ tall, weighing 125 lbs, with fresh complexion, hazel eyes, light hair and his religious denomination was Church of England. Robert transferred to the Special Reserve on 25th April 1908. His father, Robert Skoyles (1862–1920) was an illiterate unemployed labourer when he enlisted in The Prince of Wales's Own Royal Norfolk Artillery (Militia) c.1880. He was discharged on 30th April 1894 permanently unfit for service. Robert junior was a wharf labourer in 1939, when he was living at 29 South Market Road, Great Yarmouth. She died at St Nicholas Hospital, Great Yarmouth.
- Gladys Seaman (born and died 1905).
- Ivy Agnes Seaman (20th August 1908–1969) married Henry William Mower (1908–7th December 1957), a motor engineer, in 1934. He was living with his parents at Norwich Loke, North Walsham, Norfolk in 1911. Ivy was living with her mother in 1939 and it is not known where Henry was. They were living at 9 Micawber Avenue, Great Yarmouth at the time of his death at Gorleston Hospital, Great Yarmouth. Her death was registered at Acle, Norfolk. They had a son, Geoffrey W Mower, in 1940.
- Matilda Theresa Seaman (28th March 1912–January 1974) married William Albert B Cooper (15th September 1912–August 1991) in 1939. He was an invoice clerk in 1939, when they were living at 2 Fisher Avenue, Great Yarmouth. She died at St Nicholas Hospital, Great Yarmouth. They had two sons, including Rodney HW Cooper 1940.
- Doris EE Seaman (born 20th November 1914) was totally incapacitated in 1939, living with her mother.

- Mary Ann 'Polly' Seaman (5th February 1879–7th August 1947) married Walter Daniel Green (4th April 1874–1961), a tailor, at Norwich in 1899, where he was born. They were living at 61 Napier Street, Norwich in 1939. They both died at Norwich. They had eight children, all born at Norwich:

- Harold Walter Green (20th May 1900–October 1969) served in the Army during the Great War. He married Nora Johnson (born 1891), born at Malton, Yorkshire, on 23rd October 1918 at St Peter's Church, Hunslet, Yorkshire. She was living at 17 Bismarck Terrace, Hunslet at the time of the marriage and he was based at Richmond, Yorkshire. He was a general labourer in 1939, living at 65 Woodcock Close, Norwich. Nora was not with him, but he was recorded as married. What became of Nora is not known. They had a son, Harold P Green, in 1919.
- Elsie Maud Green (28th July 1901–21st March 1973) married Arthur John Robinson (21st April 1899–15th July 1937), born at Barford, Norfolk, on 6th June 1927 at Norwich. They had two sons – Ernest Arthur Robinson 1927 and Kenneth George Robinson 1928. Elsie was a school cleaner in 1939, living with her sons at 22 Union Street, Norwich. She married William Webster (9th January 1898–October 1975), a general labourer living at 1 Lanchester Court, Norwich, in 1939. William had married Beatrice Constance Aldous (16th January 1899–1937) in October 1919 at Norwich. She was living with her parents at 143 King Street, Norwich in 1911. William and Beatrice had a son, William Charles Arthur Webster, in 1921.
- Sidney Victor Green (29th November 1907–6th May 1973) married Winifred Mary Wilder (born 30th June 1910), born at George Green, Slough, Buckinghamshire, in July 1930 at Norwich. She was living with her parents at 1 Wood Cottage, St George's Green, Norwich in 1911. Sidney was a tailor coat hand and Winifred was a silk draper in 1939, when they were living at 18 Salford Street, Norwich. In 1957 twins Brian T Green and Bridget S Green were born to a Green/Wilder marriage at Norwich. Despite the time lag between the marriage in 1930, no other marriage appears to account for the births. Winifred married Leonard Edmund Ayres (26th February 1912–November 1986), born at Bethnal Green, London, on 20th March 1984 at Norwich. Leonard had married Bridget Carew (16th September 1914–October 1982), born at Cuckfield, Sussex, in 1936 at Edmonton, Middlesex. Leonard was a quantity surveyor in 1939, when they were living at 141 St John's Road, Wembley, Middlesex.
- Reginald 'Reggie' Green (19th March 1909–April 1991) married Emily Maud Kerrison (30th October 1909–December 1998) in July 1933 at Norwich, where she was born. She was living with her parents at 15 Chapel Street, Norwich in 1911. Reggie was a fish fryer in 1939, when they were living at 24 Salford Street, Norwich. They had three children – Ronald F Green 1934, June D Green 1936 and Joyce I Green 1938.
- Frank William Green (5th July 1910–October 1998) married Lily Edith Horton (26th June 1913–22nd January 1999) in July 1936 at Norwich, where she was born. He was a fishmonger and she was a shoe trade heel painter in

1939, when they were living at 38 Sherbourne Place, Norwich. They had a son, Terry K Green, in 1936.

    - Leslie Noel Green (19th February 1913–March 1987) was a general labourer in 1939, living with his parents. He married Ruby Ethel Goff (18th August 1911–April 1985) in April 1942 at Norwich, where she was born. She was living with her parents at 49 Half Mile Road, Norwich in 1939, when she was a chocolate worker. They had at least one child, Leslie DG Green, in 1950.
    - George E Green (April–July 1915).
    - Ernest George (14th May 1918–November 1993) was a general labourer in 1939, living with his parents. He married Irene Millicent Long (20th April 1917–April 1996) in 1942 at Norwich, where she was born. She was a clerk receptionist, living with her parents at 200 Coleman Road, Norwich in 1939. They had two children – Robert E Green 1943 and Josephine A Green 1947.
- Harry Seaman (9th September 1880–1940) was a grocer's porter in 1901, living with his mother. He was assisting his stepfather in his public house in 1911. Harry married Sarah Pearman (27th March 1889–December 1980), born at Lavenham, Suffolk, in 1912 at Woodbridge, Suffolk. She was living with her parents at Prentice Street Lavenham in 1891. Harry was a stoker in 1939, when they were living at 4 Kathleen Cottages, Deben, Suffolk. He died at Trimley St Mary, Suffolk and she at Ipswich. They had nine children, all registered at Woodbridge:
    - Ida Ellen Seaman (born 1913).
    - Reginald Seaman (13th July 1915–August 1986) was a professional gardener in 1939 in private service, living with his future wife and her mother at Oak Villas, Deben. He married Muriel Eva Churchyard (8th February 1918–April 2006) there in 1940. They both died at Ipswich. They had four children – Gweneth M Seaman 1943, twins Lesley R and Shirley R Seaman 1947 and Monica A Seaman 1954.
    - Dorothy Vera Seaman (30th January 1917–July 2001) was a general servant for Alfred E and Doris Knowlson at their home on Cockfosters Road, Enfield, Middlesex in 1939. She married Sydney Bullocke (26th March 1897–18th December 1969) in 1966 at Samford, Suffolk. They were living at 37 Cornwall Road, Felixstowe, Suffolk at the time of his death there. She died at Ipswich. Sydney had married Elsie Florence Bloomfield (3rd January 1896–1964), born at Ufford, Suffolk, in 1927 at Plomesgate, Suffolk. Sydney was a male nurse at St Audry's Hospital, Woodbridge and an Air Raid Precautions warden in 1939, when they were living at 16 Chapel Lane, Deben, next door to her parents. There were no children.
    - Ernest James T Seaman (13th February 1919–February 1999) was a farm labourer in 1939, living with his parents. His death was registered at Chelmsford, Essex.

- ◦ Ronald Seaman (23rd April 1920–8th March 1988) was a paper roundsman in 1939, living with his parents. He was living at 75 High Road, Trimley St Mary, Ipswich at the time of his death there.
- ◦ Lionel Edward Seaman (25th March 1924–25th February 1992) was a milk roundsman in 1939, living with his parents. He was living at 16 St Mary's Close, Trimley St Mary at the time of his death there.
- ◦ Marie JS Seaman (born October 1926).
- ◦ Donald J Seaman (born 30th September 1930).
- ◦ Peter Bryan Seaman (1932–17th July 2010) married Brenda Dorothy Lovelock (born 1934), born at Guildford, Surrey, in 1954 in Surrey. She was living with her parents at Crossways, Bagshot, Surrey in 1939. Peter was living at 7 Philip Avenue, Felixstowe, Suffolk at the time of his death there. They had four children – Lynn Seaman 1955, John Seaman 1957, Jeanette Seaman 1960 and David Seaman 1964.

- Sidney March Seaman (1882–89).
- Ethel Maria Seaman (8th July 1889–23rd August 1974) was assisting her stepfather in his public house in 1911. She married George Hector Goodrick (born 28th May 1884), a carpenter born at Scole, Norfolk, in 1914 at Depwade, Norfolk. George was appointed licensee of the Castle public house, Mileham, Norfolk on 4th July 1919, which closed in 1920, and of the Royal Oak public house, Mileham on 19th November 1920. It is not known what became of George, but Maria was appointed the licensee of the Royal Oak on 8th April 1921. Ethel married Arthur George Rye (2nd March 1890–19th May 1965) on 21st June 1926 at Mileham. He was an agricultural labourer in 1939, when they were living at The Drift, Mitford and Launditch, Norfolk. He died at Mileham and she at Dereham, Norfolk. Ethel had three children from her two marriages:
  - ◦ Edward Ernest Goodrick (27th July 1914–20th April 1972), born at Depwade, was an agricultural threshing machine operator in 1939, living with his mother and stepfather. He married Rosalind Noel Mackley (24th December 1911–30th June 1984), born at West Ham, London, at Norwich in 1940. Her father, George Henry Mackley (1879–30th November 1917), was serving in 1/13th London (493452) when he was killed in action (Cambrai Memorial, Louverval, France). Rosalind was a clerk in a boot and shoe factory in 1939, living with Annie Maria Ludkin (1882–

The Royal Oak public house, Mileham was run by Ernest's aunt and uncle from November 1920 until August 1926. It closed in 1983 and is now a private dwelling.

1959), a widow, at 342 Unthank Road, Norwich. Rosalind and Edward had a son, Martin G Goodrick, in 1947. They were living at 6 Burghwood Close, Mileham, Kings Lynn, Norfolk at the time of his death there.

  - Ivy Ethel Goodrick (1916–2004) married Victor Frederick Turner (26th June 1902–12th October 1973), born at Diss, Norfolk, at Depwade in 1934. They had a son, Frederick V Turner, in 1945. Victor was a smallholder in 1939, when they were living at Mousehole Farm, Diss. They had two children – Sybil I Turner 1936 and Frederick V Turner 1945.
  - Hilda M Rye (1926–18th July 1967), born at Mitford, married Felix Mendelsohn Garner (23rd January 1909–1983), a farmer born at Saham Toney, Norfolk, in 1946 at East Dereham. Hilda died at Chelmsford, Essex. They had two children – Angela Garner 1947 and Peter Anthony Garner 1953. Felix had married Elsie M Howe (born 1st August 1914), in 1935 at Wayland, Norfolk. They were living at The Hall, Longham, Mitford and Launditch in 1939. The marriage ended in divorce. Elsie married Walter Dyball at Fakenham in 1951 and they had two children – Richard C Dyball 1952 and Anne L Dyball 1954. Hilda and Felix had five children – William E Garner 1936, Michael E Garner 1939, Ethel M Garner 1940, Pauline A Garner 1941 and Mary J Garner 1944. Felix married Sophia Mary Frances Cox-Rogers née Lee (31st October 1901–11th April 1984), born at Gosport, Hampshire, in 1967 at Epping Forest, Essex. She was a stenographer at the time of the 1939 Register, living at 2 Kenilworth Road, Luton, Bedfordshire. Sophia was living at 5 Glynde Court, Westfield Close, Polegate, East Sussex at the time of her death there.

- Reginald 'Reggie' Harold Edward Seaman (27th June 1898–1st February 1975) had changed his surname to Palmer by 1911. He is believed to have married

Ernest's maternal grandparents were married at All Saints' Church, Horsford in 1847. The church contains a Norman font. The west tower was built in the late 1440s but many details of the tower and the church were replaced and restored in 1869 when the north aisle was built. The 13th century north nave door and chancel windows are rare survivors from an earlier building. The screen, which dates from before 1503, has been heavily restored since. There is a cluster of 15th century glass in the north aisle window. The date 1703 is picked out with red tiles on the gable. This may refer to the year of one of two great storms of that century and may commemorate repairs to damage to the chancel or that it survived undamaged. There is an outstanding example of a 19th century window produced by the Royal Bavarian Institute for Stained Glass in Munich, which commemorates three sisters, Edith, Dorothea and Nona Day, who died of consumption in 1891, 1892 and 1893 in Davos and Cairo (Simon Knott).

Florence Maud Lister (6th June 1898–1972) at Rochford, Essex in 1931. They had a daughter, Peggy J Palmer, at Norwich in 1931. He was living at Northfield House, Lovelace Road, Norwich at the time of his death.

Nothing is known about Ernest's paternal grandparents. His maternal grandfather, William March (1820–April 1907), born at Horsford, Norfolk, married Maria née Armes (1815–January 1907), also born at Horsford, on 12th April 1847 at All Saints' Church, Horsford. William was not with the family at Horsford at the time of the 1851 Census. He was a brickmaker's labourer in 1861, when they were living at Turnpike Road, Horsford. By 1871 he was a farmer of ten acres, when they were living at Heath, Horsford. They had moved to 127 Holt Road, Horsford by 1881. He was a brickmaker by 1901, again living at The Heath, Horsford. William died at Thorpe St Andrew, Norwich. In addition to Sarah, Maria had four other children, the first before her marriage to William:

- John Armes (1845–1910), born at Horsford, whose surname appears as March in the 1851 Census, was a brickmaker's labourer in 1861. He married Elizabeth (c.1846–1913), born at Offord Cluny, Huntingdonshire, who has not been identified further. John was the publican of The George and Dragon, St Peter Mancroft, Norwich in 1891 and The White Horse Inn, Trowse with Newton, Norfolk in 1901. Their deaths were registered at Henstead, Suffolk.
- Pamela Ellen March (1850–January 1931) was not with the family at the time of the 1861 Census. She married Christopher Hawes Hardingham (21st April 1847–1940), born at Booton, Norfolk, on 16th October 1873 at St

The Grade II listed former George and Dragon public house, where John Armes was the publican from 29th September 1890 until 29th March 1892. It closed in 1988 and was used by a building society for offices until becoming a burger restaurant.

The White Horse Inn, Trowse with Newton, where John Armes was the publican until 15th October 1909.

Agnes Church, Cawston, Norfolk. He was a horse dealer in 1911, when they were living at The Heath, Horsford. Her death was registered at St Faith's. He was living at 125 Queens Road, Norwich in 1939 and died there next year. They had six children and adopted another:

- James William Hardingham (1874–27th May 1888).
- John Henry Hardingham (12th May 1877–1951) married Bessie Holman (15th March 1891–1972) at Erpingham in 1915. They had three children – William J Hardingham 1916, Edna D Hardingham 1921 and Peggy Hardingham 1925.
- Alice Maria Hardingham (1879–1962) married Samuel George Sheppard at St Faith's in 1903.
- Elizabeth Mary Hardingham (8th January 1883–1958).
- Mary Ann Frances Hardingham (born 1885).
- William March Hardingham (1887–11th June 1917) was serving in 1st Royal Fusiliers (37361) when he died of wounds (Mendinghem Military Cemetery, Belgium – I E 6). The CWGC records his wife as Ada Hardingham, 35 Connaught Road, Suffield Park, Cromer, Norfolk. However, it is understood that she was Alice MM Covell (1889–1952) and they married at Erpingham in 1913, where she was born. They had a daughter, Hilda E Hardingham, in 1916. Alice/Ada married Lewis A Roberts at Norwich in 1923.
- Herbert Jack Newton (30th October 1901–1978), born at Queensborough, Kent, was adopted.

• Mary Ann March (1853–17th March 1897) married William Mackley (16th July 1853–22nd November 1885), a gamekeeper born at Norwich, on 14th December 1876 at St Andrew's Church, Trowse, Norwich. He was the publican of the Queen Adelaide, 57 Pitt Street, Norwich from 14th October 1879. He was also a bird merchant in 1881. Mary took over the licence on 9th February 1886 and was still living there at the time of her death. They had two children:
  - Maud Mary Mackley (born 1878) married Charles Christopher Durrant at Norwich in 1898.
  - Sydney William Mackley (1880–1912).

• Frances Maria March (born 1860) was a barmaid at her brother-in-law's public house in 1881.

William March Hardingham's grave in Mendinghem Military Cemetery, Belgium.

Ernest was educated at Scole Council School (later Scole Primary School), Norwich Road, Thelverton, Diss, Norfolk. He was known as

The Grand Hotel, Felixstowe, at the bottom of Bent Hill on Undercliffe Road, where Ernest worked after leaving school. The hotel was formerly the Bent Hill Restaurant, which was extended by acquiring several houses on Undercliff Road. By 1910 it had fifty bedrooms and was fitted with electric light. It ceased to be residential in the early 1950s, since when it has been converted into a number of bars.

By the late 17th century, London's St James's area had numerous elite chocolate houses, including White's, The Cocoa Tree and Ozinda's, which were the forerunners of later gentlemen's clubs. In 1746 The Cocoa Tree was the headquarters of the Jacobite party in Parliament. The Cocoa Tree Chocolate House, later Club, was at 46 Piccadilly from 1757 until sometime between 1787 and 1793, then moved to 64 Piccadilly. In 1799 it moved to 64 St James's Street, seen here, probably merging with an existing club on the site. The shop seen below the club was owned by James Woodward, a famous gun maker. The business was bought by Purdey in 1949. The Cocoa Tree became renowned as a Tory stronghold and for heavy drinking and high stakes gambling. The focal point in one of the main rooms was a large golden, ornamental tree. It was patronised by the Prince Regent, Lord Byron, Richard Brinsley Butler Sheridan (1751–1816) the Irish politician, playwright, poet and owner of the Theatre Royal, Drury Lane and Edward Gibbon (1737–94), the historian and MP. Although political affiliations declined in the 19th century, the Club's notoriety for heavy drinking did not. The building was badly damaged by fire in 1926 and the club closed in 1932. The building has since been replaced.

'Peddler Palmer' at school. He worked as a page boy at the Grand Hotel, Felixstowe, Suffolk and was later employed aboard a trans-Atlantic P&O liner and as a billiard marker at the Cocoa Tree Club in London. He is reported to have emigrated to Canada in 1912 but returned to enlist in 1915.

Ernest tried to enlist in the Army in December 1915 but was not considered strong enough for field service and was assigned to the Expeditionary Force Canteens in the Army Service Corps (EFC/A/367702). He went to France on 28th December 1915. Fitness standards were lowered with the increasing number of casualties and he was drafted into the Royal Inniskilling Fusiliers in late 1917. He was regarded as a good soldier, who consistently volunteered for any extra work, regardless of danger or difficulty. His constant devotion to duty and gallantry in attending to his wounded comrades under heavy fire was recognised by a recommendation for the MM by Captain VES Mattocks, commanding A Company, 2nd Royal Inniskilling

When the BEF departed for France in August 1914 the Army was unable to provide adequate canteen facilities. The Canteen and Mess Society was the only contractor that was more concerned with soldiers' welfare than with profit. The Society and Richard Dickenson & Co, the most experienced canteen contractors, were invited by the War Office to establish a special department that subsequently became the Expeditionary Force Canteens, whose personnel served in the Army Service Corps. The new organisation struggled to match the huge expansion of the Army and other contractors found loopholes to exploit the situation. In January 1915 a Board of Control was formed and two years later the Army Canteen Committee was registered at the Board of Trade as a company trading not for profit. It absorbed the Canteen and Mess Society, took over the contracts of Dickenson's and all the other firms supplying the Army in Britain. Three months later it took over canteens abroad where British troops were stationed in peacetime. The Expeditionary Force Canteens were left in charge in the main theatres of war. In June 1917 the Royal Navy joined and the Army Canteen Committee became the Navy and Army Canteen Board. After the Great War the Expeditionary Force Canteens and Navy and Army Canteen Board had made large profits and opinion was divided on what to do with the money. Churchill, as Secretary of State for War set up a committee in March 1920 to advise on a future organisation for the Armed Forces. The findings were unanimous, that there should be one organisation for all three services. As a result, the Navy, Army & Air Force Institutes (NAAFI) was established on 6th December 1920 (Australian War Memorial).

Fusiliers. However, the award was not approved. Promoted lance corporal on 15th September 1918. **Awarded the VC for his actions at Terhand, Belgium on 29 September 1918, LG 15 November 1918.**

Ernest was killed during his VC action on 29th September 1918. He has no known grave and is commemorated on the Tyne Cot Memorial, Belgium (Panel 70). The posthumous VC was presented to his mother by the King in the ballroom at

Ernest Seaman's name on the Tyne Cot Memorial.

St Andrew's Church, Scole probably dates from the late Saxon period but the majority of the current building is 14th century, with heavy Victorian restoration in 1874. The church was the target of an arson attack in 1963 and was restored in 1964, including a stained-glass east window by Patrick Reyntiens, who created the famous baptistry window at Coventry Cathedral.

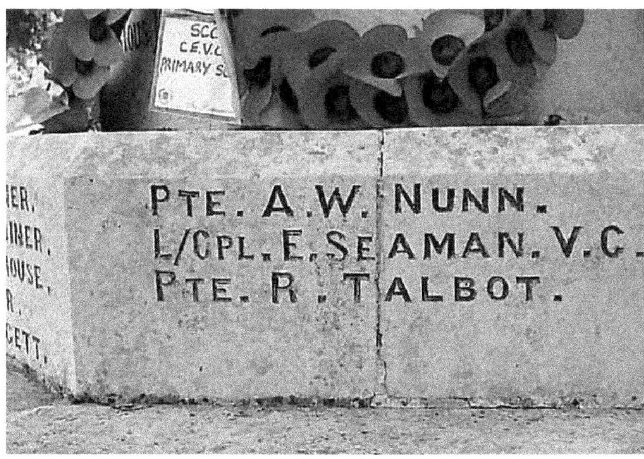

Ernest is commemorated on the Scole War Memorial (Memorials to Valour).

Buckingham Palace on 13th February 1919. Ernest is commemorated in a number of other places:

- Norfolk
  - Ernest Seaman Close, Scole.
  - St Andrew's Church, Scole Roll of Honour and framed citation.
  - Scole War Memorial.
  - Department for Communities and Local Government commemorative paving stones were dedicated at Norwich War Memorial, City Hall, Norwich on 29th September 2018 and Scole War Memorial, Bungay Road, Scole.
- Felixstowe War Memorial, Suffolk.

The Department for Communities and Local Government commemorative paving stone at Scole War Memorial (Memorials to Valour).

Felixstowe War Memorial (Memorials to Valour).

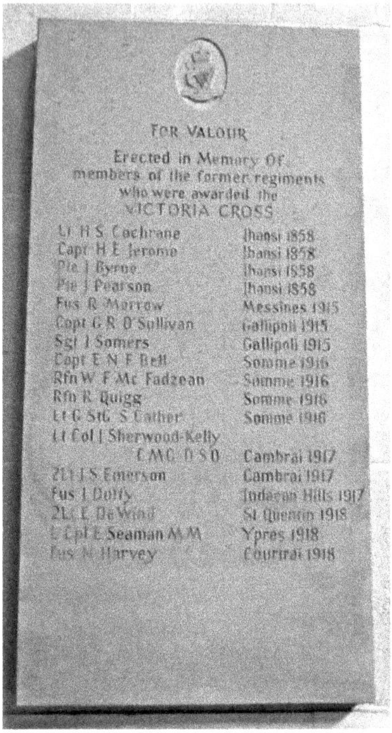

The memorial to VCs of former Irish regiments in St Anne's Cathedral, Belfast (Memorials to Valour).

The memorial to Ernest Seaman in Terhand, Belgium.

- Irish Regiment VC Winners Memorial, National Memorial Arboretum, Alrewas, Staffordshire.
- Northern Ireland
    - St Anne's Cathedral, Belfast, memorial to the VCs of former Irish regiments.
    - Wall Painting, Carrick Rangers Club, Carrickfergus, Co Antrim, Northern Ireland.

The memorial to the VCs of 36th (Ulster) Division at Ulster Tower, Thiepval (Memorials to Valour).

The British War Medal was instituted on 26th July 1919 for all ranks who served for twenty-eight days in an operational theatre between 5th August 1914 and 11th November 1918, or who died on active service before completing twenty-eight days. Eligibility was extended to 1919–20 for mine-clearing at sea and operations in North and South Russia, eastern Baltic, Siberia, Black Sea and Caspian Sea. Many veterans were awarded the 1914–15 Star, British War Medal and Victory Medal. They became known as Pip, Squeak and Wilfred after a strip cartoon published in the *Daily Mirror* from 1919 to 1956.

The Royal Logistic Corps Museum at Worthy Down, Winchester.

  - 36th Ulster Division VC Memorial Garden, Lower Newtownards Road, Belfast, Co Antrim, Northern Ireland.
- Memorial at the junction of Magerheidstraat and Oude Ieperstraat, Terhand, Belgium.
- A memorial stone at Ulster Tower, Thiepval, France, naming all the VCs of 36th (Ulster) Division, was dedicated on 1st July 1991 by the Royal Irish Rangers.

In addition to the VC he was awarded the 1914–15 Star, British War Medal 1914–20 and Victory Medal 1914–19. The VC is held by the Royal Army Service Corps/Royal Corps of Transport Institution and is displayed in the Royal Logistic Corps Museum, Worthy Down, Winchester, Hampshire.

30245 PRIVATE JAMES TOWERS
2nd Battalion, The Cameronians (Scottish Rifles)

James Towers was born on 8th September 1897 at 8 Wildman Street, Preston, Lancashire. His father, also James Towers (1871–22nd April 1930), was a cotton weaver/loomer born at Preston. He married Betty 'Betsy' née Dixon (20th August 1870–16th January 1945), a cotton weaver born at 95 Haydock Street, Preston, on 3rd August 1889 at St Peter's Parish Church, Preston. She was living at 23 Victoria Street and he at 104 Brook Street at the time. They were living with her mother at 23 Victoria Street in 1891, at 8 Wildman Street in 1894, at 25 Bloomfield Street in 1901 and by 1911 had moved to a rented farm, The Filberts, Mill Lane. They later moved to Church Farm, D'Urton Lane, Broughton and to Iris, Lightfoot Lane, Woodplumpton, near Preston, where they both subsequently died. James junior had four siblings:

- John William Towers (10th October 1889–6th July 1947) was a railway labourer in 1911, living with his parents. He married Mary Elizabeth Coupe (28th May 1891–1962), a ring spinner, in 1915. In 1911 she was living with her widowed mother and siblings at 38 Great George Street, Preston. John was a horse carter for the London, Midland and Scottish Railway in 1939, when they were living at 38 Great George Street. They were still living there at the time of his death at the Royal Infirmary, Preston. They had a son, James Towers (born and died 1918).
- Thomas Towers (18th December 1890–1st July 1944) was a fruit dealer in 1911, living with his parents. He served as a private in 1/7th King's (405731) during the Great War. He married Mary Sharples (17th March 1894–1976) on 24th May 1915 at Fulwood, Lancashire. They were living at 17 Victoria Road, Fulwood in 1939, by when he was a volunteer auxiliary ambulance driver. They were living at 12 Victoria Road at

St Peter's Church was built in 1822–25 and the steeple was added in 1851–52. In 1973 it became part of Preston Polytechnic, later the University of Central Lancashire. The building is Grade II* listed.

the time of his death at the Royal Infirmary, Preston. They had at least twelve children, all born at Preston:

- James Towers (29th December 1915–May 1988) married Mary Lily Tattersall (12th January 1911–July 1955) in 1938. She was living with her parents at 11 Aughton Street, Preston in 1911. He was a house and ship painter and decorator and she was a cotton weaver in 1939, when they were living at 169 Tulketh Brow, Preston. They had twins, James and Richard Towers, in 1946.
- Mary Towers (born and died 1917).
- Thomas John Towers (1st April 1919–February 2002) married Winifred Emily Mary Dyer (2nd June 1920–30th December 1985) on 16th July 1938 at St Colmcille's Church, Holywood, Co Down, Northern Ireland. She was born in Ireland and was living with her parents at 46 Malabar Street, Millwall, London in 1911. She died at Liverpool, Lancashire and his death was registered at Knowsley, Lancashire. They are understood to have had seven children.
- Hannah Towers (22nd December 1920–6th March 2003) was an auxiliary nurse in 1939, living with her parents. She married George Henry Hunter (2nd November 1913–12th March 1977), born at Great Yarmouth, Norfolk, on 7th February 1945, at Amounderness, Lancashire. They both died at Preston. They had two children – David G Hunter 1945 and Sheila M Hunter 1949.
- Elizabeth 'Bessie' Ann Towers (23rd April 1923–23rd January 2005) was a dressmaker in 1939, living with her parents. She married Arthur George Odams (1921–15th April 2010), born at Kettering, Northamptonshire, on 8th May 1947. He was living with his parents at 30 Cowper Street, Kettering in 1939. They both subsequently died at Kettering. They had three children – Patricia A Odams 1949, Christine M Odams 1952 and Martin Arthur Odams 1966.
- Thomas (sic) Towers (18th August 1924–January 1980) was a brick setter in 1939, living with his parents. His death was registered at Spalding, Lincolnshire.
- Benjamin Towers (1926–27).
- William Towers (14th May 1927–July 1975). He married Dorothy Lakeland (10th January 1932- 1st August 2011) in 1949. They had four children – Stephanie A Towers 1949, Stephen W Towers 1951, Nigel R Towers 1961 and Alison J Towers 1964. Dorothy married Maurice Huddleston (born 1936) in 1979. They lived at Bamber Bridge, Preston. Maurice had previously married Sadie J Walton (1936–2017) in 1958 and she married Colin Roskell in 1987, who had also been married previously.
- Frank Towers (born July 1929) married Lily Kidd (born 1931) in 1951. She was living with her parents at 1 Rugby Street South, Preston in 1939. Frank

and Lily were living at Warrington, Cheshire in 2007. They had two sons – Ian M Towers 1955 and Peter L Towers 1960.
  - Harold Towers (19th August 1932–January 1987) married Kathleen Norris (29th April 1936–24th September 1991) in 1955. She was living with her parents at 23 Shakespeare Road, Preston in 1939. They had two children – Paul A Towers 1957 and Karen M Towers 1960.
  - David Towers (24th March 1934–2016) married Eileen Bernadette Mary Navis in 1959. They emigrated to Australia. He was a clerk and she was a machine operator in 1977, living at 4/4 Elizabeth Street, St Albans, Lalor, Victoria. He died at 94 Exford Road, Melton South, Victoria. They are believed to have had a daughter.
  - Dorothy Towers (born 1937).
- Hannah Towers (1st February 1894–1954) was a cotton weaver in 1911. She married John Taylor in 1917. She was a sweets confectioner in 1939, living on her own at 76 Plungington Road, Preston. Hannah married Thomas Wilding on 24th February 1948.
- Benjamin Towers (1903–24th May 1968) married Helen Badger (11th August 1899–1st April 1984) born at the Calf's Head Public House, Worston, Lancashire, at Preston in 1925. Benjamin was James's best man at his wedding in 1926. He was a poultry farmer and market-gardener and she was a jam maker in 1939, when they were living at Lagonda, Lightfoot Lane, Woodplumpton, near Preston. They were living at 96 Todd Lane, Walton-le-Dale, Lancashire at the time of his death there. She was living at 143 Hoyle's Lane, Cottam, near Preston at the time of her death there. They had a daughter:
  - Irene Towers (21st April 1926–28th January 2013) married Clifford Salt (13th June 1924–26th May 2007), born at Colne, Lancashire, in 1946. He was an apprentice electrical engineer in 1939, living with his parents at 202 Every Street, Nelson, Lancashire. They had two children – Michael C Salt 1949 and Jacqueline Salt 1951.

James' paternal grandfather, Cuthbert John Towers (26th July 1851–October 1896), a cotton loomer born at 16 Harrington Street, Preston, was living with his parents at 9 Allan Street, Preston in 1861. He married Elizabeth Ann née Coward (1850–86) on 30th July 1870 at St John's Church, Preston. Elizabeth was living at 12 Edward Street, Preston in 1851. Cuthbert and Elizabeth were living at 49 Back Court, Gordon Street, Preston in 1881. She died due to complications with the birth of her daughter, Elizabeth. Cuthbert was boarding at 72 Senior Street, Preston with his son, William, in 1891. In addition to James they had four other children:

- Margaret Jane Towers (16th August 1875–1951), a cotton rover, married James Woodruff (9th February 1866–1952), a cotton spinner, on 28th May 1898 at Emmanuel Parish Church, Preston. He was living at 9 Hawkins Street and she at 9 Wildman Street, Preston at the time. They were living at 9 Hawkins Street, Preston with Margaret's aunt, Ann Wood, a widowed cotton rover, in 1901. They had moved to 88 Brook Street by 1911 and to 19 Greenbank Avenue by 1939. They had three children:

- Mary Elizabeth Ann Woodruff (14th May 1899–April 1976) married John Innerdale (1st November 1900–1971) in 1949.
- Thomas Woodruff (1902–possibly 1929).
- Hilda Woodruff (born 11th November 1904).

- William Towers (21st November 1879–21st February 1950) was a cart driver on a farm in 1901, living with his brother, James, at 25 Bloomfield Street, Preston. He married Berthena 'Bertha' Sharples (1878–21st February 1938) on 11th April 1903 at St Thomas's Church, Preston. She was a cotton weaver living with her parents at 100 Old Lancaster Lane, Preston in 1901. William was a potato dealer in 1911, when they were living at 21 Cardigan Street. They were living at 26 Plungington Road, Preston when he enlisted at Preston on 29th November 1915 and transferred to the Reserve next day. He was mobilised for service in the Royal Artillery on 15th January 1917 (190036 & 166549), joining No.2 Depot RFA and 7th Reserve Battery next day. William was described as a publican and carter, 5′7″ tall and weighing 147 lbs. On 1st June he transferred to the Royal Garrison Artillery and went to France the same day. He was admitted to 39th General Hospital, Le Havre next day and joined 331st Siege Battery on 12th August. He transferred to 12th Siege Battery on 26th November. On 24th January 1919 he was posted to Prees Heath and transferred to the Class Z Army Reserve on demobilisation on 23rd February, by when his address was 5 Alsop Street, Preston. They were living at 201 Emmanuel Street at the time of Bertha's death at Preston Royal Infirmary. William was still living there in 1939 with his son, William, next door to his son, Harold. William was a malt beer motor delivery driver. William and Bertha had three children:
  - Harold Towers (5th January 1906–24th October 1965) is believed to have married Elsie Dickinson (12th January 1906–1967) in 1927. He was a painter and decorator in 1939, when they were living at 203 Emmanuel Street. They had four children – Bertheana Towers 1928, Harold Towers 1930, William Towers 1934 and Shirley Towers 1937.
  - Fred Towers (20th October 1908–1994) is believed to have married Ruth Rigby in 1932. They had two children – Fred Towers 1932 and Sheila Towers 1939.
  - William Towers (3rd April 1916–1992) was a painter and decorator in 1939.
- Mary Jane Towers (1882–83).
- Elizabeth Ann Towers (11th March 1886–25th January 1959) was living with her sister, Margaret and family, in 1901, 1911 and 1939. She never married and was living at 19 Greenbank Avenue, Preston at the time of her death there.

His maternal grandfather, Thomas Dixon (1843–81), a cotton spinner, married Hannah née Whittingham (1842–1914) in 1866. They were living at 95 Haydock Street, Preston in 1870 and had moved to 94 Murray Street by 1881. Hannah was living at 23 Victoria Street in 1891 and at 12 Wildman Street in 1911. In addition to Betty they had six other children, all born at Preston:

- John Dixon (1868–96) married Ruth Jane Thorne (15th May 1864–1943), born at Stoke Wake, Sturminster, Dorset, on 22nd June 1890 at St Peter's Parish Church, Preston. They were both living with his parents at 23 Victoria Street at the time. He was a cart driver and she was a cotton winder in 1891, living with his mother. Ruth was living with her children at 95 Murray Street in 1901. By 1911 she had moved to 67 Lincoln Street and was living alone at 75 Trafford Street in 1939. They had three children, including Bertha Dixon 1892 and Thomas Dixon 1893.
- William Dixon (born c.1869) was a cotton weaver in 1891 and a cotton overlooker in 1911, living with his mother.
- Ellen Dixon (1872–1914) was a cotton weaver in 1891 living with her mother. She married John Joseph Southworth (9th January 1871–1953), a weaver, on 30th July 1892 at Emmanuel Parish Church, Preston. She was living at 12 Wildman Street and he at 34 West View, off Ribbleton Lane, at the time. He was living with his parents at 151 Ribbleton Lane, Preston in 1881. Ellen and John were living at 5 Surrey Street in 1901 and at 91 Senior Street in 1911. John married Elizabeth Escrick (2nd November 1877–1955), born at Hutton Cranswick, Yorkshire, at Preston in 1917. She was living with her mother and siblings at 26 Langton Street South, Preston in 1911. John was living in retirement at 3 Lockhart Road in 1939, while Elizabeth was living at 3 Pollard Street. John had at least fourteen children from his first marriage:
    - Stephen Southworth (5th March 1893–10th October 1948) was a railway servant in 1911, living with his parents. He is believed to have married Sarah A Coupe (31st March 1890–1970) in 1914. They had four children – Ellen Southworth 1916, Evelyn Southworth 1917, Bessie Southworth 1920 and Irene Southworth 1928.
    - Elizabeth Ann Southworth (19th August 1894–1960) was a cotton weaver in 1911, living with her parents.
    - Hannah Southworth (1st December 1896–3rd April 1957) was a cotton weaver in 1911, living with her parents. She married Albert FCG Booth (1890–1960) registered at Fylde in 1918. They had five children – Leonard F Booth 1919, Constance M Booth 1920, Bessie Booth 1921, Frank Booth 1923 and Noreen Booth 1929.
    - Thomas Southworth (18th January 1898–1899).
    - Ellen Southworth (July 1899–March 1900).
    - Caroline Southworth (6th November 1901–1957) married Henry Wells in 1921.

  - William Southworth (born and died 1903).
  - Bessie Southworth (13th May 1905–16th April 1976) married Thomas Herd (6th March 1905–1972) in 1929 and they had a daughter, Eileen Herd in 1920.
  - Leah Southworth (7th April 1907–1967), a twin with Ruth, married William Bell in 1927. They had six children – Stephen Bell 1927, Joyce S Bell 1929, Kathleen S Bell 1930, Marjorie Bell 1934, Evelyn A Bell 1936 and Vincent B Bell 1938. Leah married William Whittaker in 1967.
  - Ruth Southworth (7th April 1907–6th November 1971), a twin with Leah, married Richard Crook in 1929. They had two sons – Richard Crook 1936 and Colin Crook 1942.
  - Rachel Southworth (25th July 1908–October 1909).
  - Alexandra Southworth (25th July 1908–29th October 1978) married Joseph Wilkinson in 1930. They had four children – Ellen J Wilkinson 1930, Leonard Wilkinson 1932, Alexandra Wilkinson 1938 and Peter Wilkinson 1946. Her death was registered at Camden, London.
  - John Southworth (1910–11).
  - Thomas Southworth (born and died 1913).
- Thomas Dixon (1874–1935) was a cotton weaver in 1891, living with his mother. He married Leah Wilson (12th July 1875–1952), a cotton weaver, on 14th June 1900 at St Thomas's, Preston. He was living at 103 Lancaster Road North and she at 44 Sizer Street North at the time. She was living with her parents at 61 Bootle Street in 1881 and with her mother at 7 Emmett Street in 1891. Thomas and Leah were living with his mother in 1911, by when he was a weaver overlooker. Leah was living with her children at 106 Plungington Road in 1939. They had three children:
  - Hannah Dixon (5th January 1901) was an assurance agent in 1939.
  - Thomas Dixon (14th December 1904) was a watchmaker and jeweller in 1939.
  - Margaret Dixon (23rd February 1911) was a draper and dressmaker in 1939.
- James Dixon (1875–1933) was a cotton weaver in 1891, living with his mother. He was a weaver overlooker by 1911, still living with his mother.
- Benjamin Dixon (1877–82).

James was educated at Emmanuel Church of England School, Plungington, Preston and then worked on his father's farm in D'Urton Lane, Broughton. He enlisted as a driver in 3/9th Lancashire Battery, 3/2nd West Lancashire Brigade, Royal Field Artillery, at Preston on 23rd August 1915 (2915). He was described as 5′ 3″ tall and gave his age as nineteen years and eleven months. He was discharged from Weeton Camp, near Blackpool, Lancashire on 21st September, when his true age was discovered. James is reputed to have enlisted in 5th Dragoon Guards in August 1916 but no trace of this service record has been found. According to one newspaper

Emmanuel Church of England School.

Weeton Camp was established during the Great War. It was used by the RAF, along with RAF Squires Gate and the Army camp at Kirkham, for training during the Second World War and until 1965. The Barracks were improved in the 1960s and became the home of 1st Lancashire Fusiliers. It continues to house an infantry battalion.

report he was wounded at Third Ypres and by September 1918 he was serving with 2nd Cameronians. **Awarded the VC for his actions at Méricourt, France on 6th October 1918, LG 6th January 1919.**

James was discharged in January 1919. He arrived at Preston by train on 18th January and avoided the waiting press, walking quietly out of the station with a comrade. He was disinclined to talk about his exploits and said that he had had enough fuss. James visited his old school on 7th March 1919 and was presented with War Bonds by the headmaster. The VC was presented by the King in the quadrangle at Buckingham Palace on 8th May 1919.

He attended the Broughton Peace Day march from Church Farm to Broughton House, Preston in July 1919, presided over by Mr R Hardiman, Chairman of the Council. He was presented with a gold watch, a wallet containing National Savings certificates valued at £150, £15 cash and a framed illuminated address. James was one of the VC Honour Guard at the burial of the Unknown Warrior at Westminster Abbey on 11th November 1920.

James returned to work on his father's dairy farm and delivered milk by horse and cart. He took over running the farm when his father retired and set up his own poultry farm and milk distribution business. James Towers married Ethel Birchall (8th February 1905–2nd September 1988) on 5th April 1926 at St John the Baptist Church, Broughton. They were living in Lightfoot Lane, Woodplumpton, Lancashire in 1929 and had moved to Méricourt, Lightfoot Green, Bartle, Preston by 1939, when Ethel was a confectioner cake maker. They had a daughter:

- Marion Towers (born 22nd February 1927). She married Ronald Llewellyn Castle (born 6th July 1926), known as Llewellyn, on 2nd October 1948. He was living at Pineway, Fulwood, Preston at the time. He was living with his parents at 45 Moss Nook, Ormskirk, Lancashire in 1939. They had two children:

St Paul's Church was built 1823–25 and a chancel was added in 1881. The church was declared redundant in January 1979. In 1981 it was bought by Red Rose Radio and converted for use by two radio stations – Rock FM and Greatest Hits Lancashire – until 2020. The building is Grade II listed.

83 Windermere Road, Lancaster, where James Towers' wife lived with her parents (The Move Market).

- ◦ Glynis Castle (born 1949) married Alan Tomlinson (born 1944) in 1972 at Preston. They had two children.
- ◦ David L Castle (born 1954) married Wendy Fazackerley (born 1956) in 1976. They had at least two children.

Ethel's father, Joseph Birchall (7th January 1881–1946), born at Garstang, Lancashire, married Sarah Ann née Shuttleworth (12th December 1878–1970), a weaver, on 25th December 1902 at St Paul's Church, Preston. She was living at 23 Euston Street and he at 15 St Paul's Square at the time. Joseph was a clerk with the London and North Western Railway Company in 1911, when they were living at 83 Windermere Road, Lancaster. They had moved to Primrose Cottage, 78 Black Bull Lane, Fulwood, Lancashire by 1939. In addition to Ethel they had a son:

- Frank Birchall (16th September 1903–8th December 1981) was a cattle farmer in 1939, living with his parents. He died at 78 Black Bull Lane, Fulwood.

James with his VC in later life.

James was initiated as a member of the Independent Order of Oddfellows at Pleasant Retreat Lodge, Preston on 9th December 1929. He attended a number of VC reunions:

Preston Royal Infirmary originated as a House of Recovery constructed in 1829–33. It was extended in 1866–70 to create the Preston and County of Lancaster Royal Infirmary. This became the Preston and County of Lancaster Queen Victoria Royal Infirmary in 1929. Two storeys were added to the main block in 1936. The hospital joined the National Health Service as Preston Royal Infirmary in 1948. Its services transferred to the Royal Preston Hospital and it closed in 1990. Two buildings gained Grade II listing status in April 1988 and were converted into student halls of residence.

James Towers Way (Memorials to Valour).

- VC Garden Party at Buckingham Palace on 26th June 1920.
- VC Dinner at the Royal Gallery of the House of Lords, London on 9th November 1929.
- Victory Day Celebration Dinner & Reception at The Dorchester, London on 8th June 1946.
- VC Centenary Celebrations at Hyde Park, London on 26th June 1956.
- The 1st, 2nd and 4th to 10th VC Association Reunions on 24th July 1958, 7th July 1960, 16th July 1964, 14th July 1966, 19th July 1968, 18th June 1970, 14th July 1972, 23rd May 1974 and 22nd April 1976 held at the Café Royal, London, except for 1970, which was at the Connaught Rooms, Covent Garden, London.

The commemorative paving stone at the Cenotaph, Market Square, Preston.

Broughton-in-Amounderness War Memorial, with the James Towers plaque on the right.

James Towers died at Preston Royal Infirmary on 24th January 1977. He was cremated at Preston Crematorium on 28th January and his ashes were scattered there. He is commemorated in a number of other places:

- James Towers VC Close, Lonsdale Estate, Preston.
- James Towers Way, Broughton-in-Amounderness, Lancashire.
- A Department for Communities and Local Government commemorative paving stone was dedicated at the Cenotaph, Market Square, Preston on 6th October 2018.
- Plaque at Broughton-in-Amounderness War Memorial, Garstang Road, Broughton, Lancashire.

Ethel was living at 15 Ashtree Court, 240 Tag Lane, Preston at the time of her death there.

In addition to the VC he was awarded the British War Medal 1914–20, Victory Medal 1914–19, George VI Coronation Medal 1937 and Elizabeth II Coronation Medal 1953. The VC group was sold at a Sotheby's auction on 30th June 1983 for £7,500 and became part of the James J Atkinson Collection. The VC group was sold to a private collector on 7th April 2005 by Noble Numismatics Pty, Sydney, New South Wales, Australia, at the Hotel Intercontinental, Sydney for A$220,000. The group was sold by Dix Noonan Webb on 25th March 2015 to an unknown buyer for £144,000. The group was sold again at a Dix Noonan Webb auction on 14th April 2021 to Lord Ashcroft for £200,000.

The Queen Elizabeth II Coronation Medal 1953 was awarded immediately after the coronation on 2nd June 1953 as a personal souvenir from the Queen to members of the Royal Family, selected officers of state, members of the Royal Household, government and local government officials, mayors, public servants, members of the armed forces and police in Britain, the colonies and Dominions. It was also awarded to members of the Mount Everest expedition, two of whom reached the summit for the first time four days before the coronation. A total of 129,051 medals were awarded.

Sources

Regimental Museum.
The following Museums and Regimental Headquarters kindly provided information:

The Cameronians Regimental Museum, Hamilton; RHQ King's Own Scottish Borderers, Berwick-upon-Tweed; Royal Inniskilling Fusiliers Regimental Association, Enniskillen, Co Fermanagh, Northern Ireland; Canadian War Museum, Ottawa; Royal Artillery Historical Trust.

Individuals
The following individuals provided information and assistance:

Doug and Richard Arman, Rob Gorle, David Harvey, Alastair Jack, Anne C Johnston, Alan Jordan, David Harvey, Mary A Kelly, Eddie McGuffie, Sue Overton, Charles Snape, Vic Tambling.

Divisional Histories
Listed in numerical order:

The History of the 9th (Scottish) Division 1914-19. J Ewing. Murray 1921.
The History of the 20th (Light) Division. Capt VE Inglefield. Nisbet 1921.
The Story of the 29th Division – A Record of Gallant Deeds. Capt S Gillon. Nelson 1925.
The Thirty-Fourth Division 1915-19 – The Story of its Career from Ripon to the Rhine. Lt Col J Shakespear. Witherby 1921.
The History of the 36th (Ulster) Division. C Falls. Linenhall Press 1922.

Regimental/Unit Histories
Works appear by Regiment in precedence order:

<ins>Royal Artillery</ins>

The Royal Artillery War Commemoration Book. Anon. G Bell 1970.
History of the Royal Regiment of Artillery, Western Front, 1914-18. Gen Sir Martin Farndale. Dorset Press 1986.
ARTYVICS – The Victoria Cross and the Royal Regiment of Artillery. Marc J Sherriff. Witherbys, Aylesbury St, London.

The Royal Scots

The Royal Scots 1914-19. Maj J Ewing. Oliver & Boyd 1925. Two volumes.

Royal Scots Fusiliers

The History of The Royal Scots Fusiliers (1678-1918). John Buchan.

The King's Own Scottish Borderers

The King's Own Scottish Borderers in the Great War. Capt Stair Gillon. Nelson 1930.

The Cameronians (Scottish Rifles)

A Short History of the Cameronians (Scottish Rifles). Col HC Wylly. Gale & Polden 1924.

History of the Cameronians (Scottish Rifles), Volume II 1910-22. Col HH Story. Published 1961.

The Royal Inniskilling Fusiliers

The Royal Inniskilling Fusiliers in the Great War. Sir F Fox. Constable 1928.

Machine Gun Corps

Machine Guns, Their History and Tactical Employment (Being also a History of the Machine Gun Corps 1916-22). Lt Col GS Hutchinson. MacMillan 1938.

Canadian Expeditionary Force

Official History of the Canadian Army in the First World War - Canadian Expeditionary Force 1914-19. Col GWL Nicholson 1962.

Newfoundland

The Fighting Newfoundlander. A History of the Royal Newfoundland Regiment. Colonel GWL Nicholson CD.

General Works

A Bibliography of Regimental Histories of the British Army. Compiler A S White. Society for Army Historical Research 1965.

A Military Atlas of the First World War. A Banks & A Palmer. Purnell 1975.

Topography of Armageddon, A British Trench Map Atlas of the Western Front 1914-18. P Chasseaud. Mapbooks 1991.

Before Endeavours Fade. R E B Coombs. Battle of Britain Prints 1976.

British Regiments 1914-18. Brig E A James. Samson 1978.

Orange, Green and Khaki, The Story of the Irish Regiments in the Great War 1914-18. T Johnstone. 1992.

Biographical/Autobiographical

The Dictionary of National Biography 1901-85. Various volumes. Oxford University Press.

The Cross of Sacrifice, Officers Who Died in the Service of the British, Indian and East African Regiments and Corps 1914-19. S D and D B Jarvis. Roberts Medals 1993.

Australian Dictionary of Biography.
Dictionary of Canadian Biography.
Valiant Hearts. Atlantic Canada and the Victoria Cross. John Boileau. Nimbus Publishing, Halifax, Nova Scotia 2005.

Specific Works on the Victoria Cross

The Register of the Victoria Cross. This England 1981 and 1988.
The Story of the Victoria Cross 1856 - 1963. Brig Sir J Smyth. Frederick Muller 1963.
The Evolution of the Victoria Cross, A Study in Administrative History. M J Crook. Midas 1975.
The Victoria Cross and the George Cross. IWM 1970.
The Victoria Cross, The Empire's Roll of Valour. Lt Col R Stewart. Hutchinson 1928.
The Victoria Cross 1856 - 1920. Sir O'Moore Creagh and E M Humphris. Standard Art Book Company, London 1920.
Victoria Cross – Awards to Irish Servicemen. B Clark. Published in The Irish Sword summer 1986.
For Valour, The Victoria Cross, Courage in Action. J Percival. Thames Methuen 1985.
VC Locator. D Pillinger & A Staunton. Highland Press, Queanbeyan, New South Wales, Australia 1991.
Black Country VCs. Barry Harris. Black Country Society 1985.
The VC Roll of Honour. J W Bancroft. Aim High 1989.
A Bibliography of the Victoria Cross. W James McDonald. W J Mcdonald, Nova Scotia 1994.
Canon Lummis VC Files held in the National Army Museum, Chelsea.
Recipients of the Victoria Cross in the Care of the Commonwealth War Graves Commission. CWGC 1997.
Victoria Cross Heroes. Michael Ashcroft. Headline Review 2006
Monuments to Courage. David Harvey. 1999.
Irish Winners of the Victoria Cross. Richard Doherty & David Truesdale. Four Courts Press, Dublin, Ireland 2000.
The Victoria Crosses and George Crosses of the Honourable East India Company & Indian Army 1856-1945. National Army Museum 1962.

Works on Other Honours and Awards

Distinguished Conduct Medal 1914-18, Citations of Recipients. London Stamp Exchange 1983.
The Distinguished Service Order 1886-1923 (in 2 volumes). Sir O'Moore Creagh and E M Humphris. J B Hayward 1978 (originally published 1924).
Orders and Medals Society Journal (various articles).
South African War – Honours and Awards 1899-1902. Lionel Leventhal Ltd.

Official Publications and Sources

History of the Great War, Order of Battle of Divisions. Compiler Maj A F Becke. HMSO.
History of the Great War, Military Operations, France and Belgium. Compiler Brig Gen Sir J E Edmonds. HMSO. Published in 14 volumes of text, with 7 map volumes and 2 separate Appendices between 1923 and 1948.

Unit War Diaries in the National Archives under WO 95
Military maps in the National Archives under WO 297.
Medal Cards and Medal Rolls in the National Archives under WO 329 and ADM 171.
Soldiers' Service Records in the National Archives under WO 97, 363 and 364.
Officers' Records in the National Archives under WO 25, 76, 339 and 374.
Army Lists
Location of Hospitals and Casualty Clearing Stations, BEF 1914-19. Ministry of Pensions 1923.
London Gazettes
Census returns, particularly for 1881, 1891 and 1901.
Births, Marriages and Deaths records in the Family Records Centre, Islington, London.
Service records from the Library and Archives of Canada.
Officers and Soldiers Died in the Great War.

Reference Publications
Who's Who and Who Was Who.
The Times 1914 onwards.
The Daily Telegraph 1914 onwards.
Kelly's Handbook to the Titled, Landed and Official Classes.
Burke's Peerage.
Debrett's.
The Landed Gentry of Ireland 1958.

Internet Websites
History of the Victoria Cross - www.victoriacross.org.uk - Iain Stewart.
Commonwealth War Graves Commission - www.cwgc.org
Free Births, Marriages and Deaths – www.freebmd.org.uk
Memorials to Valour - http://www.memorialstovalour.co.uk
Scotland's People - www.scotlandspeople.gov.uk
Irish Births, Marriages and Deaths - https://civilrecords.irishgenealogy.ie/churchrecords/civil-search.jsp

Periodicals
This England magazine – various editions.
Coin and Medal News – various editions.
Journal of The Victoria Cross Society - no longer published
Stand To – journal of the Western Front Association.

Useful Information

(Some details may be affected by Brexit)

Accommodation – there is a wide variety of accommodation available in France and Belgium. Search online for your requirements. There are also numerous campsites, but many close for the winter from late September.

Clothing and Kit – consider taking:

Waterproofs.
Headwear and gloves.
Walking shoes/boots.
Shades and sunscreen.
Binoculars and camera.
Snacks and drinks.

Customs/Behaviour – local people are generally tolerant of battlefield visitors but please respect their property and address them respectfully. The French are less inclined to switch to English than other Europeans. If you try some basic French, it will be appreciated.

Driving – rules of the road are similar to UK, apart from having to drive on the right. If in doubt about priorities at junctions, always be prepared to give way to the right, particularly in France. In many areas, particularly rural, you usually have to give way to vehicles coming in from the right, even from apparently minor roads onto major routes. Obey laws and road signs – police impose harsh on-the-spot fines. Penalties for drinking and driving are heavy and the legal limit is lower than UK (50mg rather than 80mg). Most Autoroutes in France are toll roads. In rural areas the speed limit is 80kph but in many places the old 90kph signs remain. The red-framed name board at the entrance to a village or town automatically imposes a 50kph speed limit.

Fuel – petrol stations are only open 24 hours on major routes and larger supermarkets. Payment by credit/debit card in automatic tellers is increasingly becoming the norm. The cheapest fuel is generally at hypermarkets.

Mandatory Requirements – if taking your own car you need:

Full driving licence.
Vehicle registration document.
Comprehensive motor insurance valid in Europe (Green Card).
European breakdown and recovery cover.
Letter of authorisation from the owner if the vehicle is not yours.
Spare set of bulbs, headlight beam adjusters, warning triangle, GB sticker, high visibility vest and breathalyzer. Requirements do vary, so check before departing.
An emission quality sticker (Crit'Air) is required if driving in Paris or certain other cities/areas.

Emergency – keep details required in an emergency separate from your wallet or handbag:

Photocopy passport, insurance documents and EHIC/GHIC (see Health below).
Mobile phone details.
Credit/debit card numbers and cancellation telephone contacts.
Travel insurance company contact number.
Who to contact in an emergency.

Ferries – the closest ports are Boulogne, Calais and Dunkirk. The Shuttle is quicker, but usually more expensive.

Health

European Health Insurance Card – entitles the holder to medical treatment at local rates. Apply online at www.ehic.org.uk/Internet/startApplication.do. It is issued free and is valid for five years. You are only covered if you have the EHIC with you when you go for treatment. Since Brexit, EHIC is being gradually replaced by a Global Health Insurance Card (GHIC).

Travel Insurance – you are also strongly advised to have travel insurance. If you receive treatment get a statement by the doctor (*feuille de soins*) and a receipt to make a claim on return.

Personal Medical Kit – treating minor ailments saves time and money. Pack sufficient prescription medicine for the trip.

Chemist (*Pharmacie*) – look for the green cross. They provide some treatment and if unable to help will direct you to a doctor. Most open 0900–1900 except Sundays. Out of hours services (*pharmacie de garde*) are advertised in Pharmacie windows.

Doctor and Dentist – hotel receptions have details of local practices. Beware private doctors/hospitals, as extra charges cannot be reclaimed – the French national health service is known as *conventionné*.

Rabies – contact with infected animals is very rare, but if bitten by any animal, get the wound examined professionally immediately.

Money

ATMs – at most banks and post offices with instructions in English. Check your card can be used in France and what charges apply. Some banks limit how much can be withdrawn. Let your bank know you will be away, as some block cards if transactions take place unexpectedly.

Credit/Debit Cards – major cards are usually accepted, but some have different names – Visa is Carte Bleue and Mastercard is Eurocard.

Exchange – beware 0% commission, as the rate may be poor. The Post Office takes back unused currency at the same rate, which may or may not be advantageous. Since the Euro, currency exchange facilities are scarce.

Local Taxes – if you buy high value items you can reclaim tax. Get the forms completed by the shop, have them stamped by Customs, post them to the shop and they will refund about 12%. Brexit may change this.

Passport – a valid passport is required.

Post – postcard stamps are often available from vendors, newsagents and tabacs.

Public Holidays – just about everything closes and banks can close early the day before. Transport may be affected, but tourist attractions in high season are unlikely to be. The following dates/days are public holidays:

1 January
Easter Monday
1 May
8 May
Ascension Day
Whit Monday
14 July
15 August
1 & 11 November

25 December

In France many businesses and restaurants close for the majority of August.

Radio – if you want to pick up the news from home, try BBC Radio 4 on 198 kHz long wave. BBC Five Live on 909 kHz medium wave can sometimes be received. There are numerous internet options for keeping up with the news.

Shops – in large towns and tourist areas they tend to open all day. In more remote places they may close for lunch. Some bakers open Sunday a.m. and during the week take later lunch breaks. In general shops do not open on Sundays and those that do have limited hours.

Telephone

To UK – 0044, then delete the initial 0 and dial the rest of the number.

Local Calls – dial the full number even if within the same zone.

Mobiles – check yours will work in France and the charges.

Emergencies – dial 112 for medical, fire and police anywhere in Europe from any landline, pay phone or mobile. Calls are free.

British Embassy (Paris) – 01 44 51 31 00.

Time Zone – one hour ahead of UK.

Tipping – a small tip is expected by cloakroom and lavatory attendants and porters. Not required in restaurants when a service charge is included.

Toilets – the best are in museums and the main tourist attractions. Towns usually have public toilets where markets are held; some are coin operated. Otherwise on the battlefields facilities are sparse. Finding a local café may be the best option, although they are closing as rapidly as British pubs.

Index

Notes:
1. Not every person or location is included. Most family members named in the Biographies are not.
2. Armed forces units, establishments, etc are grouped under the respective country, except for Britain's, which appear under the three services – British Army, Royal Air Force and Royal Navy. Royal Naval Division units appear under British Army for convenience.
3. Newfoundland appears under Canada although not part of it at the time.
4. Cemeteries/Crematoria, Cathedrals, Churches, Hospitals, Museums, Schools, Ships, Trenches, Universities and Commonwealth War Graves Commission appear under those group headings.
5. All orders, medals and decorations appear under Orders.
6. Belgium, Britain, France and Germany are not indexed in the accounts of the VC actions, as there are too many mentions. Similarly, England, Britain and United Kingdom are not indexed in the biographies.